PAIN GENERATION

Pain Generation

*Social Media, Feminist Activism,
and the Neoliberal Selfie*

L. Ayu Saraswati

NEW YORK UNIVERSITY PRESS
New York

NEW YORK UNIVERSITY PRESS
New York
www.nyupress.org

References to Internet websites (URLs) were accurate at the time of writing. Neither the author nor New York University Press is responsible for URLs that may have expired or changed since the manuscript was prepared.

Library of Congress Cataloging-in-Publication Data
Names: Saraswati, L. Ayu, author.
Title: Pain generation : social media, feminist activism, and the neoliberal selfie / L. Ayu Saraswati.
Description: New York : New York University Press, [2021] | Includes bibliographical references and index.
Identifiers: LCCN 2020039538 (print) | LCCN 2020039539 (ebook) | ISBN 9781479808342 (hardback) | ISBN 9781479808335 (paperback) | ISBN 9781479808328 (ebook) | ISBN 9781479808359 (ebook other)
Subjects: LCSH: Sexual harassment. | Social media. | Social justice. | Feminism.
Classification: LCC HF5549.5.S45 S485 2021 (print) | LCC HF5549.5.S45 (ebook) | DDC 302.23082—dc23
LC record available at https://lccn.loc.gov/2020039538
LC ebook record available at https://lccn.loc.gov/2020039539

New York University Press books are printed on acid-free paper, and their binding materials are chosen for strength and durability. We strive to use environmentally responsible suppliers and materials to the greatest extent possible in publishing our books.

Manufactured in the United States of America

10 9 8 7 6 5 4 3 2 1

Also available as an ebook

CONTENTS

The Neoliberal Self(ie)

Fuck your race. Your[1] from a race of sick fuck, genocidal, child rapping, perverts. You are an ugly mother fucking person. What pervert jerking kitty porn web search did your chink father sticks his faggot dick into to get you out?!?!

Read on its own, this online message is violent and aims to evoke emotional pain in the Asian American woman to whom it is addressed. When it is screenshot, reposted on Instagram, and read against a caption provided by the woman being harassed that says, "Japan is so well known for all their talented child rappers, I can see how this guy got a little jealous, but jeez. ☹ #pervmagnet #childrappers," the violent message loses its sting. The harasser is not only recast as powerless but also ridiculed for his spelling errors, lack of intelligence, and racism. The harassed emerges as an empowered, witty, and strong woman, who not only takes back her power but also, as I will explicate throughout this book, projects what I call the "neoliberal self(ie)" gaze.[2]

The neoliberal self(ie) gaze is a mode of seeing and storifying the self on social media as a good neoliberal subject who is appealing, inspiring, and entertaining. It is a way of looking at the self (or other objects that represent the "self" or things that the self enjoys, etc.) from a camera angle that can best capture the self (using a selfie stick or a camera drone if one must), from a filtered vantage point (most smartphones come with built-in filter apps to enhance the user's image), and from a wittily expressed narrative perspective (the caption that provides an image with an appealing story). It is thus a propped-up, prosthetic extension and performance of the self. In the specific posting above, for instance, the neoliberal self(ie) is articulated by way of the harassed woman not cowering in the face of sexual harassment, but powerfully and strategically crafting entertaining comments about it on social media.

This book thus makes visible, names, and troubles this phenomenon of feminists turning to social media to respond to and enact the political potential of pain inflicted by acts of sexual harassment, sexual violence, and sexual abuse. It exposes the problematic neoliberal logic governing this digital space and how this logic limits the conditions of possibility of how one might use social media for feminist activism. As this book will make clear, the feminists discussed here (from Japanese American Mia Matsumiya—whose Instagram account, perv_magnet, is quoted above—to Sikh Punjabi Canadian poet rupi kaur to Korean American Margaret Cho) do *not* overtly champion neoliberalism and should thus not be conflated with the neoliberal feminists that theorist Catherine Rottenberg examines in her book *The Rise of Neoliberal Feminism*—those who espouse the "lean in" kind of feminism, for instance. In some ways, this is what makes the cases studied in this book intriguing and important to analyze: they exemplify and are often celebrated as decolonial, consciously antiracist, and progressive feminists, with seemingly no explicit indebtedness to neoliberal feminism. Nonetheless, I argue, the *underlying structure* of their social media campaigns is governed by, and therefore projects and perpetuates, neoliberal values such as "self-improvement/investment in the self/entrepreneurship," "personal responsibility," and the "sharing economy"—hence the term "neoliberal self(ie) gaze."

This argument, rather than meant to suggest that all online activism will inevitably be neoliberalized, points to the plasticity and porosity of neoliberalism and feminism. As I discuss at the end of the book, by way of turning to Muslim[3] Pakistani American Sahar Pirzada's Twitter activism, it is possible to evade and subvert the neoliberal self(ie) gaze.

By anchoring my analysis in theories and criticisms of neoliberal feminism, this book illustrates the complexity of how in using a technological apparatus and digital platforms that are governed by neoliberal logic, these feminists take on a "neoliberal self(ie) gaze" in their social media activism—and therein lies its dangers. To put forward such an argument is to claim that the stakes here are high: if feminists do not recognize and seriously challenge how neoliberalism structures our activism on social media, thereby altering our online activism practices, it may undercut our work toward social justice. Those forms of feminist activism that project a neoliberal self(ie) gaze may go viral and become social media sensations, or even succeed in sending some harassers or abusers (the few "bad apples") to prison, yet the white heteropatriarchy capitalist structures and corporations remain standing. In some cases, these corporations even co-opt the feminist activists' ideas to improve their corporate branding, further weakening our feminist movements.

↳ But do they really support them?

Understanding the Neoliberal Self(ie)

The neoliberal self(ie) emerges as a specific technology of the digital self in this historical moment when competing (and at times, cooperating) political ideologies (neoliberalism and feminism), technological apparatuses (e.g., smartphones with reversible camera lenses), and digital platforms (social media such as Instagram) collude and collide. Because the neoliberal self(ie) as a thinkable concept arises out of these contexts, it is necessary that I first traverse each layer of its production to provide readers with some groundings to better understand these key concepts that will be deployed throughout this book. Although the discussion of these concepts may read as a definition (and to a certain extent, it is), it should serve instead as a point of orientation, without which readers may feel lost. It should be incorporated as a tool in navigating the book, rather than considered as a fixed object that stubbornly defies any possibility of remaking the shape of its meanings, as readers may (and are encouraged to) venture out on their own trails of thinking.

Neoliberalism and Feminism

Neoliberalism is framed in this book as a governing logic in social media. To begin, a definition is necessary: neoliberalism is "a political-economic ideology and practice that promotes individualism, consumerism, deregulation, and transferring state power and responsibility to the individual" (Leve 279). This maximization of individualism and the retreat (or the "remaking") of the state—the neoliberal regime—began to be formalized in the 1970s, during the economic crisis and stagflation that contributed to an increase in the part-time and flexible workforce (mostly women) (Čakardić 42). Neoliberalism depends on individualism to distract from and justify the loss of state resources and the growing inequality that is a product of deregulation. In the process of shifting the responsibility from the state to the individual, neoliberalism "normatively construct[s] and interpellat[es] individuals as entrepreneurial and capital-enhancing actors," forever "ready for personal metamorphoses, improvement and innovation"; under neoliberalism, individuals are thus no longer seen as "coherent," as was the case in liberalism (Čakardić 37; Rottenberg 57). Ironically, therefore, because they have to keep performing their entrepreneurial subjectivity in all aspects of their lives (from workplace to personal relationships) and continually make calculated choices to manifest a better version of themselves, neoliberal subjects are "controlled through their freedom": the freedom to choose how to best invest in themselves (Brown, "Neo-liberalism").

It is this neoliberal language of freedom and choice that seems to be compatible with feminism. "Choice feminism," which later transmuted into neoliberal feminism, sees women as no longer victims of the system since they can now allegedly exercise their agency to choose based on "rational, economic calculation" (Budgeon 306; Oksala 114). Here, choice is prioritized over equity and equated with feminism (Budgeon 306; Čakardić 38).

In this way, neoliberalism can be seen as benefiting (some) feminists *as individuals* (who make choices to invest in themselves and fulfill their own needs), but shortchanging feminism *as a movement* advocating justice and equality. Thus, to fully understand feminist movements, we need to consider neoliberal feminism[4] as another category within existing classifications of feminism (alongside liberal feminism, radical feminism, etc.) and how neoliberalism has become an important, yet dangerous, ideology in the trajectory of feminist movements (Ferguson 229)—in particular, as it takes place on social media. This is what this book addresses.

This book, in providing a thorough examination of how neoliberalism structures feminist activism on social media, uses the three core concepts of neoliberal feminism formulated by political scientist Michaele Ferguson as its organizational basis. Each of the three analytical chapters in this book focuses on one of these three core concepts:

(1) "*liberation through capitalism*" (Ferguson 230, emphasis original). Women—as entrepreneurs—are seen as liberated when they can participate equally and successfully in the capitalist marketplace (230). To rise above their problems by being inspiring entrepreneurs who successfully sell products such as poems printed as canvas art is to practice a neoliberal way of being, for example (chapter 2);

(2) "*privatization of political responses*" (Ferguson 230, emphasis original). Rather than demanding that the state respond to their pressing political issues, feminists turn to themselves or other private means to address such problems. For example, when feminists take matters into their own virtual hands in regard to sexual harassment/abuse/violence by sharing their *personal* stories on social media, without explicating the nuanced complexity of the *systemic* oppression that creates the conditions of possibility for such abuse to happen, and by online shaming or attacking the harassers *as individuals*, they become complicit in addressing sexual violence as an individual rather than a structural issue (chapter 3); and

(3) "*individualization of persistent gender inequality*" (Ferguson 230, emphasis original). Through the lens of neoliberal feminism, gender inequality is seen as a result of bad individual choices. The neoliberal logic is that if the problem arises from bad individual choices, then the solution must be addressed at the individual level. Here, the notion of personal responsibility is key. As philosopher Johanna Oksala points out, "because the neoliberal subject is a free atom of self-interest fully

responsible for navigating the social realm by using cost-benefit calculation, those who fail to succeed can only blame themselves" (117). This means that, seen through the lens of neoliberal ideology, when women do not heal after sexual abuse, for instance, they are at fault for failing to heal (chapter 4).

Another core element of neoliberal feminism, theorized by Rottenberg and used to construct the neoliberal self(ie) concept throughout this book, is the management and performance of "positive affect." Rottenberg points out that neoliberal subjects are constructed as happy subjects. Happiness here is "either linked to the balancing [of life and work] act itself . . . or held out as a promise for the future" (18). Neoliberal feminists focus on "affect, behavior modification, and well-roundedness" rather than "socioeconomic and cultural structures shaping our lives" (15, 42). The disciplining of subjects through affect, or the "affective and psychic life of neoliberalism," is central to the neoliberal feminist subject formation (Gill and Kanai 324). This pressure to project a happy self on social media is what drives neoliberal self(ie)s to represent themselves as happy, entertaining, or successful, no matter what happens to them (even sexual harassment, violence, and abuse). To post how horrible one's life is, without framing it as something that one can (or will) overcome, or as something that can entertain and uplift other's spirit, would simply betray the core makeup of what it means to perform a good neoliberal self(ie). A neoliberal self(ie) gaze therefore always projects a "positive affect."

I conceptualize the neoliberal self(ie) gaze to build on Michelangelo Magasic's notion of the "selfie gaze." Magasic constructs the notion of the "selfie gaze" within the context of the individual traveler/tourist and defines it thus: the "traveller's selfie gaze searches for sites that will improve the traveller's esteem in the eyes of their social networks" (177). Note here that, under neoliberalism, taking selfies is no longer considered an embarrassing or narcissistic endeavor, but rather as necessary to build one's esteem/brand as an entrepreneur/innovator. The "selfie gaze" is seen as a form of "micro-celebrity" practice in which the audience becomes the "fan-base" (177). The selfie gaze adopts an "omnivorous voice" that "mixes elements of high and low culture and appeals to a wide audience" (177).

The neoliberal self(ie) gaze departs from Magasic's articulation of the selfie gaze—beyond the obvious fact that the neoliberal self(ie) gaze is not limited to travels—in that when an image is said to be taken from a "neoliberal self(ie) gaze" vantage point, the image does not have to be an "actual selfie," or, at least, the common understanding of selfie, which is when "the camera is turned upon the taker as a mode of self-presentation" (Magasic 176). An image can be taken by someone else and still embody a neoliberal self(ie) gaze. The image does not even have to be of a person. It can be of food or some object propped up in a certain way to highlight the neoliberal self(ie).

Moreover, the neoliberal self(ie) gaze speaks to the desire/obsession to see the self in a success story, our own or others', and often has a tone of celebrating the self. For instance, neoliberal self(ie) postings often suggest, "Look at me, I am doing so well," and invite others to be like the successful self: "I can help you to be successful like me if you purchase what I sell." In social media, the neoliberal self(ie) becomes a brand that can be turned into gold. The neoliberal self(ie) gaze and the self-centered culture on social media can thus be understood within a neoliberal culture that places excessive value on the individual as an entrepreneurial self, a self that can be capitalized on. The term that the social media world uses, "influencer," captures perfectly the neoliberal self(ie) whose work is to present oneself as a successful neoliberal person (traveler, beauty expert, health expert) who can "influence" others. As such, a "neoliberal self(ie)" must always be presented as appealing and entertaining for it to acquire any currency and be marketable.

Thus, the neoliberal self(ie) is a self(ie) that is shaped not only by the self's ability to see their own reflection in the camera,[5] and therefore to edit the image or text to fit what the self prefers to represent, but also by the perceived audience's desire (i.e., who will "like" a post or make a posting go viral and therefore provide currency on social media) for what the self should be. Although presented as appealing, the neoliberal self(ie) gaze cannot simply be equated with narcissism or unhealthy obsession with the self. This is because the neoliberal self(ie) gaze is constructed to fit the perceived audience's desire. It is about the (audience) other as much as the self. It is an internalized externalized-for-the-audience-to-see gaze. As such, the neoliberal self(ie) gaze is an "interactive" gaze.

In proposing the term neoliberal self(ie), I name and make visible the dominant gaze on social media. Indeed, what is shared on social media has mostly focused on the "self" (i.e., what the self is interested in, what the self is doing or eating; even the prompt on social media such as Facebook is "What's on *your* mind?" and the "your/you" here is often hailed as a neoliberal subject). In this sense, social media gives permission and even encourages people to focus on themselves. The neoliberal self(ie) gaze is driven by how social media creates an urge to tell the world what happens to us, and to know what happens to others/the world (J. Sandoval 108). It is a form of policing the self and other (neoliberal) subjects.

The neoliberal self(ie) should thus be understood *not as a person, but as a practice; not as a figure, but as figurative; not as a subjectivity, but as a performativity*. In this way, my articulation of the neoliberal self(ie) is also influenced, in part, by digital culture scholars Edgar Gómez Cruz and Helen Thornham's work on the selfie in which they argue that we need to think of the selfie beyond its "traditional semiotics," where we read the selfie as "narcissistic" or as part of "self-branding," and rather see "the practices and contexts of selfies that are articulated" as a form of "mediated communication" (2–3). Thus, they argue, we need to "move from focusing on the narratives *about* the visual or the narratives *of* the users to focus on the socio-technical practices that constitute—if not condition—those narratives" and to "locate the selfie within a wider practice of identity performativity" (7, 8, emphasis original). My conceptualization of the neoliberal self(ie) indeed goes beyond reading the image or the person—it is *not* a critique of these individuals/feminists per se. Rather, I focus on the operating neoliberal ideology that governs, structures, and limits these feminist social media activism practices. In my analysis, I also pay careful attention to the technological apparatus and digital platforms that make the circulation and production of this form of neoliberal self(ie) possible.

Technological Apparatus and Digital Platforms: Framing Social Media as Phantasmagoria

The neoliberal self(ie) is made possible by specific technological inventions. The selfie (in its original meaning of an image of the self) is enabled by a smartphone feature—a camera lens that can be turned toward the user—as well as technology that makes it easy for the user to upload the image onto social media apps that are already integrated into mobile phones (Sturken, "Advertising"). These technological innovations magnify people's need to constantly connect, often through telling stories of their lives (hence the notion of "selfies," in Cruz and Thornham's sense of the word, as "visual chats"), and create what is perceived to be an Internet addiction.

Although social psychologist Sherry Turkle reminds us not to get attached to the "language of Internet addiction" (21) because it can restrict our thinking and ability to be critical toward this practice, I find it to be both an appropriate concept that explains my own relationship with social media (the constant clicking and scrolling at all hours of the day and night) and a good analytical place to start. In other words, I insist that there needs to be a language, a concept, to understand why social media captivates us, so that we can demystify the magical power of social media. Indeed, finding a fitting metaphor matters because metaphors are "constitutive" of how we understand and imagine the Internet's use and impact on our lives (Sturken and Thomas 7).

In this book, I use the metaphor "phantasmagoria" to grasp the addictive and affective hold of social media. "Phantasmagoria" comes from the Greek words *phantasma* (phantom) and *agoreuein* (allegory, or, for Walter Benjamin, "profane illumination") (Andreotti and Lahiji 29). It was used in 1797 by the Belgian physicist Étienne-Gaspard Robert (stage name Robertson) for his "ghostly performances" (Cohen 95). The phantasmagoria became popular in the early nineteenth century as "a visual spectacle created by a 'magic lantern,' or a lens with images that were back lit by candle, and projected onto a wall" often featuring horror or ghost stories complete with sound effects (Tremblay 21). At its core, the phantasmagoria highlights "an appearance of reality that tricks the senses through technical manipulation" (Buck-Morss 22).

When philosopher Walter Benjamin used the term "phantasmagoria" in his book *The Arcades Project*, he used it to describe the phenomenon of the nineteenth-century Paris shopping arcades. As Benjamin points out, the new behavior, economy, commodity, and technology displayed at the Paris shopping arcades created a phantasmagoria linked to the entertainment industry (14). Working with Benjamin's notion of phantasmagoria to observe the phenomenon of social media, Mark Tremblay, in his master's thesis, *Flânerie: From the Streets to the Screen*, astutely observes that social media feeds can be likened to a Paris street scene— they both can be perused by flâneurs and reveal the commodification and consumerism of their corresponding societies (34).

Building on Tremblay's framing of social media as phantasmagoria, I, too, find phantasmagoria useful as a metaphor for social media. However, I find phantasmagoria's capacity to evoke affect, in particular, the way it floods our senses and anaesthetizes us, as well as its function as a sensory distraction and ability to produce affect alienation, most helpful in explicating our addiction to social media. Philosopher and historian Susan Buck-Morss defines phantasmagoria as "technoaesthetics":

> The perceptions they provide are "real" enough—their impact upon the senses and nerves is still "natural" from a neurophysical point of view. . . . The goal is manipulation of the synaesthetic system by *control of environmental stimuli*. It has the effect of anaesthetizing the organism, not through numbing, but through *flooding the senses*. These simulated sensoria alter consciousness, much like a drug, but they do so through *sensory*

distraction rather than chemical alteration, and—most significantly—their effects are experienced collectively rather than individually. . . . As a result, unlike with drugs, the phantasmagoria assumes the position of objective fact. Whereas drug addicts confront a society that challenges the reality of their altered perception, *the intoxication of phantasmagoria itself becomes the social norm.* (22–23, emphasis mine)

In this sense, people go to social media the way people went to phantasmagoric/ghostly performances in the early nineteenth century, to be entertained and emotionally affected by the projected image. Phantasmagoria is thus useful here to understand social media as providing us with controlled "environmental stimuli" that have an entertaining quality, where people go knowing that what they see is only a projection of characters, yet want to *feel* the emotions nonetheless. It is these entertaining environmental stimuli that have the ability to flood our senses and have an anesthetizing effect, like a drug, that eventually turn us into social media addicts.

The metaphor of phantasmagoria is also helpful in our understanding the relationship between social media and its content providers and followers. In the nineteenth-century phantasmagoria, a key technology used in creating the image for the ghostly performance was the "magic lantern." The person using the lantern became the "trickster" who tricked the audience's senses. In the digital space, social media becomes the magic lantern that the "tricksters" (or content providers) use to create the visual spectacle. That is, the nineteenth-century magic lantern and twenty-first-century social media as magic lantern are both constructed to be technologies of manipulation. However, if in the nineteenth-century phantasmagoria the magic lantern is controlled by the trickster, in the twenty-first-century digital phantasmagoria, the magic lantern (social media) has its own goals and becomes another trickster, alongside the person using social media who *also* functions as a trickster (in the sense that they both are manipulating the senses of the viewers). In other words, the agency of the trickster in the digital phantasmagoria is being usurped and absorbed by the magic lantern. The digital trickster does not have the same control over the magic lantern as the nineteenth-century trickster did. The magic lantern of the digital world is even more magical because it has control (quite literally, and even legally) over the image that the trickster produces. Thus, another one of the differences between the nineteenth-century magic lantern and the twenty-first-century magic lantern is that the production in the twenty-first century is more obfuscated. Whereas in the nineteenth-century phantasmagoria, the audience is aware that they are being tricked by the magic lantern (the technology that produces the ghostly performance), in the twenty-first-century digital phantasmagoria, the audience/users may not be aware that they are being tricked by the magic lantern because social media companies tend to represent that their platforms are neutral, or without their own agendas, while tricking the users and content producers into believing that they are using the technology of the magic lantern for their own benefit—taking advantage of the fact that, as good neoliberal subjects, they are taught to think in terms of producing profits for themselves. In some cases, the users may be aware of the trickery of the magic lantern but continue to participate regardless.[6]

It is within this digital phantasmagoria world of affective atmosphere and spectacle production that the neoliberal self(ie) emerges. If the magic lantern in the nineteenth-century phantasmagoria created the figure of the "ghost," in the twenty-first-century digital phantasmagoria, the magic lantern (social media) produces the "neoliberal self(ie)." Similar to the ghost in the nineteenth-century phantasmagoria, the neoliberal self(ie) of the twenty-first-century digital phantasmagoria is neither real nor unreal—it is an effect, a shadowy projection, of the magic lantern.

Asian American and Racial Oscillation

As signaled by my opening this book with a post from the Instagram account of a Japanese American woman who, unlike the #MeToo movement, emphasizes the racialized, specifically Asian American women's experiences of sexual harassment, I intend to layer my analysis with a critical conversation on how gendered racialization of Asian (North) American women operates on social media. It is important to note that although Matsumiya's campaign caught mainstream media attention and has made her social media famous, it did not have a wide reach compared to, say, when Alyssa Milano, a white celebrity, tweeted on October 15, 2017, "If you've been sexually harassed or assaulted write 'me too' as a reply to this tweet." Milano's tweet and the overwhelming global response that followed even clouded the presence of Tarana Burke, the Black woman who launched the #MeToo movement in 2006. I contend that this is related to the ways in which race (as it intersects with gender, sexuality, nationality, disability, class, and celebrity status) matters in how people respond to others' articulation of pain. In an American cultural context that has framed Asians as "impervious to pain" or "superhuman figure[s] with the capacity of 'indifference' to suffering," for someone of Asian identity to point out that they're in pain may not have the same impact as when a white woman articulates the same form of pain stemming, for instance, from sexual harassment (Nakamura 143; R. Lee, *The Exquisite* 220). In other words, since Asian bodies have been constructed by/in American culture as being able to endure pain, when others witness them experiencing pain (in response to sexual harassment on social media, for example), they may not feel compelled to respond to their pain in the same way they would if their bodies had been white.

I need to make clear that nowhere in this book is "Asian" or "Asian American" ever treated as an essentialized or homogenized identity. We need to remember that "Asian" and "Asia" are signs produced under the Western colonial gaze and are a product of white supremacy (Fung 125; Lo 27). This book is thus interested in querying: at which *points of interaction* do Asians *become signified* as Asians on social media, and why? I am also intrigued here by how Asian American women operate as "a placeholder of ideology" (Shimizu 97). Thus, although I point to the specificity of how Asian American women launch social media campaigns that revolve around racialized sexual harassment/abuse/violence, I do *not* argue that these experiences are specific to Asian American women because they are Asian American women—it is not about essentialism. Rather, if this book demonstrates experiences that are specific to Asian American women, it is because gender, racial, (hetero)sexual ideologies help shape who gets to be wounded, how, and why, and how this experience of wounding is gendered, racialized, and sexualized as such.

This book thus aims to answer theorist Lisa Lowe's call to open up a conversation about the Asian American as an "epistemological object" (41). This is a mode of critically engaging with the subject of the Asian American through various forms of knowing and inter/disciplinary locations (in my case, women's studies, race and racial formation studies, and new media studies), while simultaneously revising and creating a perpetual rupture in our narrations about these subjects (and) in these various disciplines. Simultaneously, this book also hopes to respond to English professor Kandice Chuh's invitation to conceive "Asian American studies as *subjectless discourse*" (9, emphasis original). It does so by locating scattered moments of "strategic *anti*-essentialism" in these feminists' social media campaigns that resist the crafting of an Asian American identity under the legible framework of what it means to be Asian American (10, emphasis original).

To this end, this book offers the term "racial oscillation" to highlight how performing an "Asian American" subjectivity functions as a strategy rather than an identity, and to enrich various theorizations of Asian Americans' racial positioning that disrupts the Black and white binary. For instance, political scientist Claire J. Kim observes how Asian Americans have been "racially triangulated vis-à-vis Blacks and Whites, or located in the field of racial positions with reference to these two other points" (107). Literary scholar Leslie Bow also offers the concept of "interstitiality" to refer to the ways in which "subjects are made" (in her case, Asian Americans in the context of the US South) "within the space between [Black] abjection and [white] normative invisibility" (5, 9).

These thought-provoking works function to carve a theoretical pathway for thinking about Asian Americans within the complexity of racial hierarchy that goes beyond the Black and white binary. My work follows in their footsteps in that it attempts to theorize the flexibility of Asian American as a racial category that moves and slides across this racial positioning and to unrest the fixity of racial construction. However, my conceptualization of racial oscillation departs from their theories in that my interest is not in charting Asian American as a racial category that exists interstitially or triangulated between the white and Black racial categories, but rather, as a way of naming the phenomenon in which Asian Americans have the ability to oscillate between making their race invisible or visible on social media. Thus, the notion of racial oscillation functions to theorize the process/strategy of racialization *at points of interaction* on social media.

In particular, this book argues, Asian as a racial/ized category in digital spaces exists in a slippage, in the oscillating space between having the ability to pass as something that is nonthreatening to the dominant white culture—that is, to be in proximity to or even a proxy for whiteness—yet, at the same time, to remain as the Other. Angelo Ancheta has coined the term "white by analogy" to describe Asian Americans' proximity to whiteness due to their being "near the 'white' end of the color scale" within the "hierarchy of pigmentation" (quoted in Yamamoto 63–64).

Asian Americans have indeed historically occupied a paradoxical space, between the positions of "model minority"/"honorary white" and "yellow peril," between being seen as the "mundane" race and an "extraordinary corpse," and between being a "delight and repugnance" (Cheng 23; J. Kim; R. Lee; Yamamoto 3, 65). Literary scholar Tina Chen uses the term "double agents" to refer to Asian Americans' "performative possibilities" to "perform themselves into being as persons recognized by their communities and their country" in maintaining multiple allegiances "in order to construct themselves as agents capable of self-articulation and -determination" (xviii, xx). It is this capacity to construct oneself as someone who can "perform different speaking and acting subjects" (G. Chen 39) that is at the core of racial oscillation.

Racial oscillation is theorized in this book as specific to the neoliberal logic of social media within which it operates. That is, neoliberalism structures how race is narrated as an individual and individualized, rather than systematic, experience. Neoliberalism and its digital media apparatus shape the conditions of possibility for how notions of the self may be constructed in this space. On social media, for a person's race to appear appealing and for the person to project a neoliberal self(ie), meanings of race and processes of racialization are translated through a language of the individual as spectacular spectacle. As such, race is encoded into a system of entertainment whereby the self functions as an entertainer/entrepreneur. In this book, racial oscillation is conceptualized as a technology of the neoliberal self(ie) on social media (a longer conversation on this takes place across chapters 2 and 3). Race becomes something that a digital media user can deploy to fit their social media or social/economic/cultural/human capital needs. As such, racial oscillation as a process of racialization is *not limited to Asian Americans*; however, "Asian American" as a racial category has a particular (one might even argue, especially fluid) relationship to performing racial oscillation online because of the group's historicity (specific historical relationship with) and relationality to whiteness.

If I deem developing a new concept, "racial oscillation," necessary, it is because race and racialization are considered "a salient factor in various engagements with digital technology" (Noble 30). Yet racial formation theory fails to address how in online spaces race and racism are intricately intertwined with globalization as well as technoculture (Daniels 710). The old framework of racial formation considers "racism online as a matter of individual, dispersed, erratic behavior" (Tynes et al. 25). By offering the concept of "racial oscillation," I hope to name the specific ways in which digital media users' racialization or nonracialization of themselves or others is reflective and revealing of the broader and longer history of race and racism, as well as of the neoliberal logic operating on social media. In other words, racial oscillation helps us understand how race is employed by individuals in social media interactions and how it reveals systemic racism and the political ideologies of neoliberalism governing this space.

Neoliberal logic governs, for instance, how social media users deploy a self-conception of "Asian" as a "brand" to mark/market themselves online. As communication scholar Aymar Jean Christian points out, "in the new media landscape, historically marginalized voices rely on difference, that is, the Othered body and voice, along with discourses of the 'self,' to present themselves to mass audiences on networked television" (96). In other words, it is in hyping one's racial difference that a digital media user may find a niche market for oneself. In her analysis of Asian super bloggers, social media scholar Minh-Ha T. Pham argues, "under racial neoliberalism, race and racialized markers of difference are tied to market logics of consumer sovereignty, personal branding, and freedom of expression through a free market of endless consumer choices" (97). In this way, if a subject decides to racially oscillate and mark themselves as "Asian," it may be because they use it as a strategy to embolden and mark their "brand" and social media presence. Moreover, Pham argues, "Asian accommodation makes the racial category of Asianness particularly flexible and so uniquely suited to postracial definition and rearticulation" (96). Indeed, it is this flexible articulation that I refer to when I propose the term "racial oscillation," which speaks directly to contentious issues of not only flexibility and fluidity but also fixity of race, racial stereotypes, and racial articulation on digital media.

Beyond considering the flexibility of racial positioning as a form of neoliberal branding of the self, I also would like to propose the possibility of a reading that considers how when the feminists examined in this book racially oscillate, they may do so as a "methodology of the oppressed." Chicana studies scholar Chela Sandoval points out how "the differential mode of consciousness functions like the clutch of an automobile, the mechanism that permits the driver to select, engage, and disengage gears in a system for the transmission of power" (57). When subjects choose to shift gears into racially marking themselves, and then in other interactions unmarking themselves, they do so while recognizing the power relations embedded in such interactions. They may also enact the performative differential of racial oscillation to "secure influence" (57). Sandoval clarifies:

> the citizen-subject is understood to exist, just as it is understood as always capable of dissipating, but both in quotients measured in order to bring about forms of being that will be capable of *intervening in power*. This articulation between *the self and its absence* is a shifting place of mobile codes and significations, which invokes that place of possibility and creativity where language and meaning itself are constituted. (33, emphasis mine)

Thus, when the women analyzed in this book racially oscillate by marking "the self and its absence" to project the most optimum representation or anticipate the most affective interaction on social media and secure influence, they may do so as a form of "intervening in power," even if such power derives from being a neoliberal self(ie). That is, when they racially oscillate and use what Black feminist writer and activist Audre Lorde calls "the master's tools" of social media, they do so while simultaneously (re)occupying and imbuing their usage with new, at times subversive, meanings that allow them to intervene in power (see chapter 3).

More than simply understood as a flexible articulation of race, racial oscillation also allows us to comprehend the Asian American position in digital technology/social media as *being marginalized, without being at the margin*. That is, Asians and Asian Americans do indeed dominate the technology field—their domination has been called "Yellow peril 2.0" (Washington 63). Asian women have even emerged as the most desirable group on online dating sites, further evidence that Asians are not situated at the margin in the world of digital media (Chow and Hu). However, Asians remain *marginalized* in the power hierarchy. As media and communication professor André Brock points out, the combination of whiteness and maleness still functions as the norm or "default Internet identity" ("Critical Technocultural" 1016). Whiteness and maleness continue to define the Internet as they are "reproduced through digital technologies," "software designs," and "prioritization of resources and content" (Noble 91). Thus, despite the fact that Asians have power in the technology field, white male supremacy continues to be the dominant ideology in this digital space.

Turning to Social Media

By the time this book reaches readers, the social media campaigns discussed may be long gone and the hashtags no longer trending. Such is the ephemeral nature of the digital world. For the purpose of this book, however, it truly does not matter whether or not they are still circulating. What does matter is how the social media campaigns and hashtags that I chose as my case studies allow us to understand the collusion and collision between neoliberalism and feminism on social media, and the dangers and limitations of this collusion. As such, this book aims to address the big question in the field: "how technologies will affect society, democracy, and the environment" (Sturken and Thomas 10).

But why turn to social media at all? First and foremost, this book is interested in tracing how power operates in digital spaces. As digital media scholars Safiya Umoja Noble and Brendesha Tynes contend, "the Internet [i]s a system that *reflects*, and a site that *structures*, power and values" (2, emphasis original). Noble points out that "algorithmic oppression" exists in this space and is "fundamental to the operating system of the web" (10). Search engines are not only "fueled by neoliberal technology policy" but also filled with racial and gender biases (32). I am thus interested in analyzing how neoliberal ideology structures social media to understand the workings of power, racism, and sexism in this space.

This book's interest in social media is also motivated by the need to better comprehend how feminists use these digital platforms for activism. Studies have shown that social networks are considered "innovative tools of feminist activism" in that they amplify women's voices and promote events for social change (Tynes et al. 22; Flores et al. 3). Social media can indeed increase the likelihood of people's engagement with protests (Bivens and Cole 6). It can also be used to fight sexual harassment. Relatively recent examples include #MeToo and websites such as www.ihollaback.org, where women are encouraged to document their experiences of street harassment in ways that help link experiences and uncover underlying causes. Unlike these previous studies that focus on the potentials and capacities of social media for feminist activism, in this book, I meditate on social media practices to comprehend the *limits* of feminist activism on social media: how feminist activism is structured and shaped by the neoliberal logic of this space and becomes neoliberalized and used for neoliberal purposes.

My interest in social media is not solely or squarely located in explicating its relationships with feminist activism, however. I am also fascinated by social media's capacity to allow us to process emotions (particularly, of pain) differently and shift the ways in which we experience that emotion. For example, with digital technology, a person who has just ended a romantic relationship can choose to go on a social media platform and share the news to receive instant emotional support, find online support groups to help ameliorate their feelings, or go on an online dating website and browse through an "endless supply" of possible matches to make themselves feel better immediately. Thus, if social media alters how we experience and process our emotions, then this book, by way of carefully illustrating the working of the "sharing economy of emotions" (in chapter 3) and the ramifications of "affect alienation" (in chapter 2), among other things, explains *how* this happens.

As such, this book is concerned not only with "what [pain] does" (Ahmed, "The Contingency" 22), but also with what we do with pain on social media, and what social media allows pain to do and generate. In this sense, then, rather than perceiving pain as something that is negative, I am more interested in theorizing pain as conjuring up a space of creativity, connection, and conversation—pain as generative. Pain, for instance, as a "potent means of communication" can generate crucial conversations and mobilize people to do activist work (Juschka 714). It is the specificity of pain that calls for "an ethics of responding to pain," allowing it to become a site where people can create and connect with others, that I find most useful as a tool of analysis in this book (Ahmed, "The Contingency" 24).

Lastly, I turn to social media because I aim to "stud[y] culture and society *with the Internet*" (Richard Rogers quoted in Puschmann et al. 427, emphasis original). This does not mean that I consider the Internet as merely a mirror in which we can see ourselves functioning as a society or that the Internet is a neutral tool; social media companies through their practice of "content moderation" do have the power to determine which racist, sexist, and hateful content they allow on their platforms (Gillespie). Rather, in this book, the Internet is seen as "the amalgam of an artifact, the associated practices, and the beliefs of its users," which can reveal the culture within which it is designed, created, and consumed (Arnold Pacey quoted in Noble and Tynes 9; Puschmann et al. 427). I am thus particularly intrigued here by how *discourses* and *ideologies*, such as neoliberalism and feminism that may be in tension and in collusion with each other, govern the interactions on social media and how they produce new (albeit limited and problematic) ways of seeing, performing, and projecting the self in the (digital) world—the neoliberal self(ie).

Critically Reading Social Media: A Brief Note on Method

To best answer the questions raised in this book of how *discourses* of feminism and neoliberalism collude and collide on social media, that is, how feminist discourses and digital technologies have both limited and liberated us, and how the neoliberal logic that governs social media shapes and translates how feminist activism is performed in this space, a feminist discourse analysis is employed as the most productive method. Discourse analysis examines images, texts, and languages to understand "recurrent linguistic patterns revealing meaning regimes that structure knowledge" and how they function as "complex structures and hierarchies of interaction and social practice" in "context, society and culture" (Teun A. van Dijk quoted in Steele 77; Gredel 105). In employing discourse analysis, researchers are therefore interested in finding "transtextually common patterns, such as metaphors . . . , topoi . . . or epoche-specific vocabulary" (Gredel 103). In this book, I chart the patterns and metaphors structuring discourses that shape the various conversations posted on the specific social media accounts and with the hashtags that I analyze.

Moreover, an analysis of online exchanges where data was available/stored/archived allows us to see how certain texts are quoted or referenced and provides ways to understand the collaborative process of content creation in digital media (Gredel 104). My analysis is indeed mindful of the interactive and collaborative features of the Internet, such as comments, captions, and hashtags, that provide us with ways to better comprehend the texts as they circulate (Sorapure 501–505). I analyze the texts as objects of circulation and decode their meanings as they are being circulated and produced as things *intended* for circulation. I need to make a note here that all of the data included in this book is available for public viewing at the time of this research. Although in this book I do use the usernames of the feminists whose social media campaigns I examine, such as Margaret Cho's and rupi kaur's, I still maintain the privacy of their followers by erasing their usernames (my redactions are indicated by sets of three hyphens).[7]

Critical discourse analysis is similar to close reading, a primary strategy in the humanities, in that it is interested in the question of how power works and in texts' relationship with ideology; and it relies on a small number of data (Norman Fairclough quoted in Marwick 118). However, digital media is an overwhelming site of study. It is a vast, endless, and continuously changing space. In the interest of keeping my study focused and my data robust, I concentrate on specific sites of analysis in each chapter. For instance, in chapter 2, I focus specifically on rupi kaur's Instagram account and analyze all of her postings that were available up to May 3, 2019. In chapter 3, I analyze all postings on Mia Matsumiya's Instagram account, also up to May 3, 2019.

Although Instagram (Instamatic + telegram = Instagram) is now a common app, it may be useful to provide some brief context here. Originally created as a smartphone app by Kevin Systrom and Mike Krieger, the popular social media platform was launched on October 6, 2010 (Peng et al. 1074; Borges-Rey 571; Ridgway and Clayton 2). Systrom and Krieger pioneered the creation of a "shoot-and-share" mobile-only app, allowing its users to take pictures (and later, videos), add built-in filters to create visual effects for their images, and post them directly and instantly on their Instagram accounts via their mobile phones (Wallis 182). This app paved the way for a thriving and lively "phonetography" culture (Newman 223). When Instagram was acquired by Facebook in 2012, the number of the site's active users increased from 130 million to 270 million (Newman 223). Today, Instagram is one of the largest social media networks, with more than 400 million unique visitors per month and over 70 million images posted on the app every day (Ridgway and Clayton 2; Newman 223). As of 2019, the number of monthly active Instagram users, 1 billion, was still less than that of Facebook users, 2.3 billion, but Instagram users visit the site more frequently and consistently than do users of Facebook.

In chapters 2 and 3, I focus on Instagram; in chapters 4 and 5, I shift my analysis to focus on feminist activism on Twitter. In the humanities, researchers who analyze Twitter often use a small sample of tweets, which can be collected by following a specific hashtag or examining all tweets from a particular user (Marwick 118). In this book, I employ the former method (following the specific hashtag #12daysofrage that Margaret Cho created specifically to raise awareness about sexual abuse) for chapter 4, and the latter method (following the postings of a particular

Twitter user, Pakistani American Muslim feminist activist Sahar Pirzada, up to May 3, 2019) for chapter 5.

Twitter was founded in 2006 in San Francisco by Jack Dorsey, Evan Williams, and Biz Stone. The social media platform was designed based on dispatch communications and short text messaging services, setting a limit of, originally, 140, and now, 280 characters per tweet. This character limit and the simplicity it promotes is what sets Twitter apart from other social network services (SNS). Twitter also allows people to engage with and reappropriate tweets by retweeting them, thereby blurring the lines of authorship and readership. The retweet feature enables Twitter to function as a "broadcaster-like network" (Park et al. 247). Even "ordinary people" can now broadcast their thoughts through Twitter.

Another of Twitter's conversational features is the hashtag (#), introduced in mid-2007.[8] A hashtag can function as an "indexing system" that allows people to quickly search for a particular topic and to highlight the semiotic significance of a particular conversation (Bonilla and Rosa 5). Hashtags can also be seen as a digital trail, a digital archive, and "a rhizomatic form that connects diverse texts, images, and videos" (Akyel 1102; see also Rightler-McDaniels and Hendrickson 176). In other cases, hashtags have worked as "an easily personalized storytelling prompt" (Clark 796). Hashtags are therefore useful in this book as they allow me to illuminate the ways in which neoliberal and feminist discourses structure the interactions and shape the conversations surrounding sexual violence and feminist activism on social media.

Structure of the Book

This book argues that feminist activism in online spaces is governed by, and at times has been used to further, neoliberal ideology. The neoliberal logic that structures social media seeps into and shapes feminist activism in this space, even when these feminists do *not* explicitly advocate neoliberal values. Through its chapters, this book reveals the multiple layers of the phantasmagoria production that takes place within feminist social media campaigns and the ways in which the neoliberal technology shapeshifts these feminists into neoliberal self(ies).

The first three analytical chapters of this book, chapters 2 through 4, uncover how the neoliberal logic structures social media and limits feminist activism in this space. As mentioned previously, each chapter works with one of Ferguson's three core concepts of neoliberal feminism: "liberation through capitalism" in chapter 2; the "privatization of political responses" in chapter 3; and the "individualization of persistent gender inequality" in chapter 4. Although Ferguson's concepts help me organize the chapters, they do not become the focal point. Rather, these concepts function as a theoretical launchpad, a thinking *from*, rather than thinking *about*. In chapter 5, I shift my focus to reimagine what else might be possible in the realm of feminist activism on social media that could subvert the limitations of these digital platforms.

More specifically, in chapter 2, "'Making Gold Out of It': rupi kaur's Poem, Pain, and Phantasmagoria," I examine rupi kaur's Instagram account and explicate the production of the neoliberal self(ie) in her phantasmagoric world. I argue that neoliberalism, which governs the workings of the digital platform that kaur uses, functions as an alchemy that turns pain into gold—which in this capitalistic society means capital, currency, money—and turns her, a decolonial feminist, into an entrepreneur who projects a neoliberal self(ie) gaze. In this way, her feminist campaign exemplifies Ferguson's concept of "liberation through capitalism" in that in the very process of sharing poems ("content") and selling products on social media, kaur's poems and "brand" become neoliberalized, and she becomes "liberated," as she now, too, has access to capital accumulation.

This chapter thus functions, first, to detail the layers of production that kaur performs as a neoliberal self(ie) in turning pain into phantasmagoria, and second, to discuss the concept of racial oscillation as an integral part of phantasmagoria. That is, when the neoliberal self(ie) has to be projected as entertaining, appealing, and inspiring, their race must *also* be represented and positioned as such. Racial oscillation therefore explains the process whereby race can be turned into a spectacle that fits a specific audience's taste and transformed into another spectacle for a different audience. Lastly, this chapter serves to illustrate the problem with phantasmagoria and the ways in which it reproduces "affect alienation"—how people are alienated from their own feelings—because of phantasmagoria's ability to produce sensory distraction. As such, in providing a thorough examination of the book's key concepts (i.e., neoliberal self(ie), phantasmagoria, and racial oscillation), this chapter establishes a foundation for the subsequent ones.

In chapter 3, "Masking Pain, Unmasking Race: Sexual Harassment, Shaming, and the Sharing Economy of Emotions," I shift my focus to a different Instagram account: that of Mia Matsumiya's, called perv_magnet, which aims to raise awareness of online sexual harassment of Asian American women. In this chapter, I think from Ferguson's concept of "the privatization of political responses" and examine how Matsumiya takes the issue of sexual harassment into her own hands.

This examination allows me to illustrate the three modes of neoliberal self(ie) production in her social media campaign. First, I introduce a concept that I call "the sharing economy of emotions" to point out how the neoliberal economy provides technology for people to share access not only to their cars (via Uber or Lyft) and living spaces (via Airbnb) but also to their emotions, such as the feeling of pain related to online sexual harassment. Second, I demonstrate how racial oscillation operates in Matsumiya's phantasmagoria by evoking the trope of masking. I show how Matsumiya redeploys *kawaii* aesthetics to mask and unmask race during her social media interactions as a witty way to strike back at the harassers and projects her bold and bodacious neoliberal self(ie). Lastly, I reveal how Matsumiya uses sarcasm as a strategy of resistance to mask her emotion/pain and thereby preserve the impenetrability not only of her Japanese American feminist agency but also her neoliberal self(ie) on social media.

In chapter 4, "Silence as Testimony in Margaret Cho's #12daysofrage," I analyze Margaret Cho's feminist Twitter campaign, #12daysofrage, where she narrates her sexual abuse stories and asks others to share theirs, using the hashtag. As in the previous chapters, I examine how neoliberal discourse—particularly Ferguson's "individualization of persistent gender inequality"—in tension and in conjunction with feminism, shapes and limits Cho's feminist social media activism. This chapter's analysis is unique in that I focus not only on tweets that *do* share sexual abuse stories but also on tweets that respond to Cho's invitation by *not* doing so. I therefore explore the theoretical possibilities not only of speech but also of the spaces of silence surrounding the #12daysofrage hashtag.

This chapter thus lays out the multiple layers of silence operating in this campaign: first, the ideological silence of neoliberal discourse that informs Cho's online feminist activism and phantasmagoria; second, the silence that is performed through the tweets and their ideological work (i.e., functioning as testimonies). This chapter offers the concept of "silence as testimony" to elucidate the ways in which silence can function as a *collective testimony* when a group of people tweet that they cannot share their stories on a digital platform, thereby performing "silence." In this specific context, their "silence" functions as a witness, that is, a testimony, to the structure of violence that allows the abuse to happen in the first place and that produces a toxic digital culture where it is unsafe for people to share their stories in this virtual corner of the world.

The third silence is the performative silence or silence as a form of feminist agency. This chapter offers a fresh way of rethinking feminist agency and what it means to perform agency through silence, rather than "voice" or "breaking the silence." I tinker with the possibility that collective and performative silence can be a feminist option—that is, registered as a vocabulary within the repertoire of feminist agency—for responding to others' invitations to tell stories of sexual violence in digital spaces or to participate in online campaigns. It challenges the hierarchy of voice as having more value than staying silent and thus illustrates the currency of silence in the sharing economy of emotions.

I hope to shed light on how the pressure and imperative to speak, to have a voice, to tweet or share something on social media can itself be a form of violence.

In chapter 5, "What Else Might Be Possible?: Imagining Vigilant Eco-Love Practice," I shift the discussion from uncovering the limits of feminist activism on social media that is governed by the logic of neoliberalism to exploring the terrain of subversive possibility that could override the imperative and pervasive neoliberal self(ie) gaze on social media. To this end, I theorize a practice that I call "vigilant eco-love," which can function as an alternative to the neoliberal self(ie) gaze and as a promising and subversive mode of living and loving in a neoliberal, patriarchal, digital, racist, and capitalist age. I focus on Sahar Pirzada and her Twitter activism as a site to think with in theorizing what else might be possible.

In "Coda," I conclude by sharing how this book came into being and pointing out its theoretical ramifications and chief contribution: that we be mindful about how dominant ideologies and discourses inform our feminist activism and social media practices, so that we may find new ways to challenge rather than be complicit in these limiting ideologies and practices.

As these chapters will demonstrate, this book offers a fresh perspective on feminist activism on social media by making visible the neoliberal self(ie) gaze that is pervasive on social media, even and especially in progressive and decolonial spaces that have not commonly been considered as belonging to neoliberal feminists, thereby demonstrating how it limits feminist activism in this space; by pointing out the practice of racial oscillation that functions as a technology of the neoliberal self(ie) and that deepens our understanding of racial formation at points of interaction on social media; by proposing the term "the sharing economy of emotions" to highlight the importance of emotion in the sharing economy, an issue that has been overlooked in previous scholarships; by claiming the significance of "silence as testimony" in articulating feminist agency in online spaces; and by imagining a new practice on social media, one that can potentially subvert the neoliberal self(ie) gaze, that I call vigilant eco-love.

As a whole, this book purports to be a cautionary tale for feminists and activists alike, a warning not to fall into the neoliberal trap of social media that can alchemize anyone—including ourselves—into "neoliberal self(ies)" (or use us as a technology for the maintenance of neoliberalism). It is my hope that this book serves as an invitation to imagine a more subversive way to use the master's tools to "dismantle the master's house."

2

"Making Gold Out of It"

rupi kaur's Poem, Pain, and Phantasmagoria

> the world
> gives you
> so much pain
> and here you are
> making gold out of it
> *there is nothing purer than that*, rupi kaur

On October 1, 2016, after a show in Southern California, rupi kaur[1] (who self-identifies as a "Punjabi-Sikh immigrant woman") posted the poem I use for the epigraph, "there is nothing purer than that," on her Instagram account rupikaur, garnering over ninety-four thousand likes. Born in India in 1992, she moved to Canada with her family when she was four years old (her father was a political refugee). kaur is a celebrated feminist poet with over 3.6 million followers[2] on Instagram and two best-selling poetry books. (She indeed uses the word "feminist" to label herself, claiming, "I've identified myself as a feminist for as long as I can remember" [E. Smith].) Her first book, *Milk and Honey*, was self-published in 2014 and republished in 2015 by Andrews McMeel Publishing. It stayed on the *New York Times* best-seller list for over a year (seventy-seven weeks), sold more than two million copies, and was translated into over thirty languages. Her second book, *The Sun and Her Flowers*, was published in 2017 by the same publisher. It made it into the top ten on the *New York Times* best-seller list.

I begin this chapter with rupi kaur's poem "there is nothing purer than that" because it contains, in a nutshell, the chapter's core argument:

how neoliberalism, which governs the working of the digital platform that kaur uses, functions alchemically to turn pain into gold—which in this capitalistic society means capital, currency, money—and turns her, a decolonial feminist, into an entrepreneur who projects the neoliberal self(ie) gaze. To a certain extent, her feminist social media practice exemplifies what political scientist Michaele Ferguson identifies as one of the three core concepts of neoliberal feminism, "liberation through capitalism." Of course, when kaur uses the word "gold" in her poem, she does not use it to refer to money. She provides a context to frame the meaning of "gold" by writing a caption to her Instagram posting that says, "you were pure gold yesterday southern California ♥ thank you for your hearts." In this context, she uses the word "gold" to refer to the pureness of one's heart and of her Southern California fans who came to her show. It is my analysis of her poems and Instagram postings in the context of social media as phantasmagoria[3] that yields a reading that makes visible how, in the process of sharing poems ("content") and selling products on social media, kaur's social media activism projects a neoliberal self(ie) gaze.

The above poem is also useful in exemplifying the ways in which kaur reimagines pain in the context of her feminist activism and illustrating the depth of her relationship with it. That is, racialized, gendered, and generational pain plays a central role in kaur's poems. She explains:

> my experiences have happened to my mother and her mother and her mother before that. it is *generations of pain* embedded into our souls. . . . i write to document we were here. (https://rupikaur.com/faq/#writing, emphasis mine)

Thus, for her, poems function as a vehicle to speak about and hold a space for those "unspoken moments of pain" (Botoman). She uses pain to carry and amplify her voice, deploying it as a site of protest and reclaiming a feminist voice. Through her poems, which often circle around the pain of sexual abuse, body-of-color images, broken hearts, and immigrant lives, she insists that pain matters and that the mattering of pain comes from its ability to do the work of (neoliberal) mobilization in the name of feminist activism. In turning pain into a feminist object, kaur is successful in mobilizing her fans and followers to show up at her sold-out talks around the world, including the one in Southern California, to gather around this feminist object.

The success of kaur's phantasmagoria indeed relies on her ability to reimagine pain as a poetic territory without a psychological and political boundary. In her poems, particularly as they are posted on her social media/phantasmagoria, pain becomes lost as an object of grief and emerges as something gorgeous, magical, empowering, soothing, and healing. Her poems create an opening as a way to enter pain, enter with pain, and enter from pain. Through her poems, she is able to rupture the relationship between pain and victimhood that is often constructed as an inseparable pair in feminism—the kind of feminism bell hooks criticizes as being based on "shared victimization" (*Feminist Theory* 45). kaur's postings do not turn her, as political theorist Wendy Brown has cautioned us against, into a wounded subject, whose identity is based on "states of injury," and who is "invested in [her] own subjection" ("Wounded" 403; *States of Injury*). When the sufferer demands political rights by insisting on evidence of suffering of the self, the sufferer remains in the suffering state, where pain becomes a "'wounded attachment' that inadvertently preserves rather than challenges the point of injury" (Philipose 64). Instead, by using social media to take back the meanings of injury and demand that the public recognize her pain, and speaking from the standpoint of a "subject speaking *grievance*," rather than an "object bearing *grief*," kaur challenges the traditional scripts of "victim feminism" (Cheng 174, emphasis original). For instance, in the first poem that kaur posted on Instagram (the first, at least, that can still be viewed on her account, which dates back to 2013), she speaks of sexual violence: "you trace the bruises on your ribs/with nervous fingers/before he swings/at your startling face." She ends the poem with: "you are not a rehab clinic for addicts/your body is not a prison." Here, as kaur engages with pain from a feminist perspective, "the pain of a female body in patriarchal culture" (Forte 252), she breaks free from the dominant view that considers the body in pain as the property of a victim. Thus, through the merging of pain, trauma, healing, and empowerment in her poems, kaur is able to untangle pain from victimhood subjectivity. Pain is reimagined as a transformable and transformative object, one that can turn something or someone into gold.

Through her works of reimagining pain, kaur reorients feminist scholar Sara Ahmed's question about *what emotions do* to the question of *what one does with emotions* (in this case, pain). Rather than giving up on pain, kaur works *with* pain. Nonetheless, in working with pain, infusing it with and turning it into gold, kaur's social media is disciplined by the neoliberal imperative of projecting a positive affect (in this book, what I call a "neoliberal self(ie)" gaze). That is, in her phantasmagoria, pain becomes a captivating story, but a neoliberalized (in its plastic and porous meanings) story nonetheless.

In what follows, I discuss the production of the neoliberal self(ie) in kaur's Instagram account and how social media functions as neoliberal alchemy. My analysis then moves to how kaur employs racial oscillation on her social media as a technology of the neoliberal self(ie). Finally, this chapter speaks to why it matters to critically analyze social media as phantasmagoria: because of phantasmagoria's ability to produce sensory distraction and have an anesthetizing effect, it reproduces "affect alienation"—how people are further alienated from their own feelings. That is, if the goal of feminist activism is to make structural and significant changes, then the production of phantasmagoria is troubling as it only further alienates its audience/Instagram followers from their own feelings. Such affect alienation, functioning as anesthetic, merely soothes and then paralyzes them from doing activism work outside of phantasmagoria—actions that could eventually move them toward achieving social justice.

The Production of the Neoliberal Self(ie) in kaur's Phantasmagoria

To be effective and affective in the digital world, or to have any currency or visibility on social media, one needs to have the ability to craft anything (the "X") that they post and turn it into a spectacle, an affective atmosphere, a phantasmagoria. First of all, relying on spectacular images in digital media is important. As information system and computer scientists Gerald Kane and Alexandra Pear point out, "image really is everything to the digital economy" ("The Rise"). For the purposes of marketing, "posts with visuals receive 94% more page visits and engagements than those without and elicit twice as many comments on average" (Kane and Pear). For an image to gain currency, however, it can't just be *any* image. Mastering the technique of turning an image of X into phantasmagoria is indeed a technology (or articulation) of the self in the neoliberal and digital world. I call this technique of the self on social media the "neoliberal self(ie)."

I frame the neoliberal self(ie) as a symptom of digital phantasmagoria. That is, in digital phantasmagoria, the self or the X must first be represented through a neoliberal self(ie) gaze—that is, turned into a spectacle, which, when viewed along with other images as one scrolls through social media, then becomes phantasmagoria—for it to gain any currency. Here, allow me to clarify that although spectacle is an important element of phantasmagoria, I do not conflate spectacle with phantasmagoria. Phantasmagoria encompasses "technical environments, tactile as well as visual, tectonic, multi-sensory, and multi-medial, reflecting the vastly superior power of present-day technology," and relies on "affective atmospheres" where commodities are "several stages further removed from their context of production," compared to spectacle, which relies on "material commodities" (Andreotti and Lahiji 128).

An example might be useful here. If someone were to post their breakfast of an açaí bowl they had while vacationing in Hawaiʻi on social media without positioning the bowl and the background of a Hawaiian beach to make the food look appealing, without narrating a compelling story of what makes that particular breakfast at that particular ocean-front restaurant special, and without using the phone's filter app to make the color of the fruits in the bowl more vibrant, that is, to not employ the neoliberal self(ie) gaze, the image won't evoke strong affective responses in the audience. For a breakfast to be social media worthy, it first needs to be turned into a spectacular image or a visual spectacle. And then, when that image is posted with captions, and other people view it along with other images as they scroll through their social media, that image and other images viewed *at the same moment*, are *collectively* transformed to create an "affective atmosphere," a phantasmagoria, providing its viewers with overstimulation of the senses and sensory distraction. Phantasmagoria therefore *cannot* be produced out of a single image or a single posting alone. Moreover, at the level of phantasmagoria, what is sold or considered a commodity is no longer clear: is it the fruits, the açaí bowl, the restaurant, Hawai'i as a tourist destination, traveling as a lifestyle, the smartphone with an advanced filter app, or the person who as a neoliberal subject has their own brand on social media (as a travel blogger)? The commodities, whatever they may be—the fruits or açaí bowl—are already "several stages further removed from their context of production."

Similarly, this is how social media as a neoliberal technology turns kaur's pain (the "pain" here does not literally or necessarily mean her actual pain, but rather pain both as a feminist object and a product of value in the neoliberal market economy) into phantasmagoria. Posting a poem about pain, just like posting an image of an açaí bowl, on social media does not automatically turn it into phantasmagoria. There are several layers of production that need to be added to create an affective atmosphere. For instance, the very first poem that kaur posted on her Instagram (at least, the one that was available when I accessed it) was a screenshot of a Word doc file, with a gray Word toolbar visible above the poem. Her second poem (like her third, fourth, and fifth), however, was no longer a screenshot of the Word doc file. Instead, the poem was now posted on a blank white background. This adds a layer of production in the process of turning the poem/pain into phantasmagoria. The sixth poem was posted on a largely white background containing her drawing of an eye and an eyebrow, sketched in a childlike scribble. Her illustration adds yet another step in the phantasmagoria production.

I would like to digress briefly here to make note of her sketches, which Priya Kudhail considers "childlike imagery." This imagery, combined with poems that often focus on issues of sexual violence, abuse, or heartbreak—this contradiction and juxtaposition—is what Kudhail calls a "technique of shock" that makes kaur's messages more effective (1). Or, to use the phantasmagoria metaphor, the imagery helps create the affective atmosphere. In short, weaving or juxtaposing abuse and affection (or abuse and childlike imagery) together may not only allow people who have never been in an abusive relationship to realize the intricate reality of abuse—abuse can be mistaken for affection and vice versa (2)—it can also create shock—the affective atmosphere that makes a phantasmagoria.

An example of this production of affective atmosphere is kaur's ninth poem that was posted on Instagram: "you/have been/taught your legs/are a pitstop for men/that need a place to rest/a vacancy, body empty enough/for guests 'cause no one/ever comes and is/willing to/stay—welcome." The poem is arranged in the shape of a diamond (with the word "you" at its zenith and "stay" on the bottom) and positioned in the middle of an image of a woman's vulva that kaur drew. The full image is of a woman's body, beginning with her breasts (thus without a face) and with her legs spread, providing a space for the poem. This posting that embodies the technique of phantasmagoria (of creating a spectacle out of X) certainly evoked more affective responses in the audience (5,080 likes) than did her first poem (2,806 likes).

It is how shock is woven into the everyday that allows phantasmagoria to be the norm, to absorb the totality of its effect. As critical theorist Jaeho Kang points out:

Benjamin finds that the experience of phantasmagoria coincides with a very central attribute of the modern experience of the spectacle, one which specifically depicts the shock penetrating into everyday life and the subsequent breakdown of communication. . . . The experience of phantasmagoria is neither partial nor transient but rather a general mode of modern experience arising from the expansion of the spectacle into all social communications. (165)

In other words, phantasmagoria is so commonplace that it becomes the language of the everyday; at the very least, it is an everyday mode of expression in the digital world. We live in a phantasmagoric world even without realizing it because it has been so naturalized and normalized in our daily lives.

The turning of pain into phantasmagoria is also done by way of kaur's being mindful about the sequence of her Instagram postings. A poem is always followed by an image. Thus, when a follower clicks on kaur's Instagram page, they can see how her phantasmagoria is created through juxtaposition, that is, carefully alternating between posting an image (usually colorful) and a poem (usually with a white background and black lowercase letters). Most of these images are of herself, but not always (there are also images of other women). The images that kaur posts have evolved as well. The first eighteen posts on her Instagram were all seemingly random and mundane images: of her painting something, of her paintings, of a self-portrait, of her art supplies, of a box of flowers, and of her standing or sitting down in everyday clothing, often denim. They have yet to embody the neoliberal self(ie) gaze. Then, after the nineteenth posting, which was a screenshot of her first poem, the postings consistently alternate between an image and a poem. The images also became more staged and symbolic, no longer of her or her artwork but of a hand holding a pink flower, or a vintage/artistic camera, or two hands seemingly trying to reach something.

Her recent (2018–2019) images are captivating and intriguing—they are taken from the neoliberal self(ie) gaze in that they pay excessive attention to the narrative of the self as appealing, inspiring, and entertaining, projecting an image of a successful, glamorous self that holds economic currency in the visual digital marketplace. For instance, an image was posted on December 13, 2018, of kaur in Vancouver, standing on a rock in front of a body of water. She is wearing fancy gold, shiny heels. Her long dress is green with shimmering sequins with a cut up to her thigh, although her position allows us to see only her left knee. The image was taken from a low angle and captures her looking down at the camera, which has the effect of putting her in a powerful position where the viewer is looking up to her. There is no smile such as is often used to represent feminine coyness. Rather, she has a stern and powerful look. Another image is of her in Toronto, also in front of a body of water, with the city skyline—the cosmopolitan icon—seen behind her. She is wearing another long dress, bronze and silver in color, with a pair of shiny heels. Similar images can be found of her traveling, working, or doing shows in Japan, the United States, Italy, the United Kingdom, and Cuba. Her cosmopolitan figure was validated by an image she posted of herself on the cover of *Cosmopolitan India*. These images of her in stunning outfits all over the world (often taken right before or during her talks) tell stories of kaur as a successful cosmopolitan woman who travels the globe and is empowered, confident, and strong—poses that are quite a contrast to the poems that speak of abuse or being in (or leaving) an abusive relationship.

This alternating between images of a glamorous cosmopolitan woman and poems of pain exposes the aesthetic logic of the neoliberal self(ie) in social media: to carry an aesthetic value, even pain must be able to enchant (provoke positive affect in) people. These glamourous images of kaur as a strong, powerful, and cosmopolitan woman function not only to challenge representations of South Asian women as the nonwhite Other (on social media or elsewhere), they also provide a strong affective juxtaposition (that is to say, "shock effect" and "affective atmosphere") to the pain that she describes in her poems. In other words, the painful poem is followed not by symbolic images that signify pain (such as blood, a broken heart, or the like) but by a beautiful, powerful woman in a glamorous dress posing all over the world. Seen together, *simultaneously*, from a panoptic gaze, the images and poems of pain become entertaining and enchanting.

In deconstructing the meanings of kaur's images on Instagram, we need to acknowledge, first, that it matters that a young South Asian woman occupies these transnational public spaces of theater, cityscape, and digital phantasmagoria. Her racialized and gendered presence challenges the invisible whiteness that has become the norm even in digital space. Second, as literary scholar Eleanor Ty has observed, the images kaur posts "are aesthetically beautiful, but do not rely on the sexualization of women's bodies" (215). This is powerful because to the extent that female bodies are allowed in digital space their acceptability is often predicated upon their sexual objectification status. This is not the case with kaur's postings. For example, kaur posted an image of a woman's body part—her bottoms, from the side angle that shows her cellulite—to challenge the ideal of women's perfect skin. The woman's body is not there to sexually arouse men or be sexually objectified by others. Rather, it is there to celebrate the authenticity and integrity of women's bodies.

Third, kaur thinks carefully about the representation of South Asian women. One of her poems explicitly addresses how "representation is vital/otherwise the butterfly/surrounded by a group of moths/unable to see itself/will keep trying to become the moth." Her beautiful images are meant to inspire, to provide a representation of powerful and glamorous South Asian women, which we don't see too often in mainstream North American media. As she writes on her official website, "i need access to words written by people *who look like me* writing about the things i am going through. at that moment i realize the importance of representation and know this must be different for my children" (https://rupikaur. com/faq/#writing, emphasis mine).

Fourth, kaur's use of Instagram, to a certain extent, actually does challenge Instagram's vision of how the platform should be used. For instance, her popularity first owed to taking the feminist issue of menstruation to Instagram. She posted a series of menstruation pictures (originally her college project) in which she was seen sleeping on her side with a red bloodstain in the middle of her pajama pants and another stain on her bedsheet. Her images were considered "offensive" and taken down by Instagram. Twice. It was not until the images and Instagram's censorship went viral on Facebook that she was allowed to repost the images (Ty 215). Moreover, on a platform that capitalizes on images, kaur emphasizes words and poems (although she also posts images of herself and others) to enact the political potential of pain. She explicitly envisions Instagram as a space for young women "to heal and to feel closer to one another" ("How Poet"). I therefore agree with feminist scholars who categorize her as a "decolonial feminist poet," courageously decolonizing poetry, technology, and patriarchy—spaces where women of color barely exist. kaur's phantasmagoria is thus powerful and progressive even as it projects a neoliberal self(ie) gaze, an uncovering that is made even more important *because* of the profound power it (and she) embodies.

Social Media as the Neoliberal Alchemy

Neoliberalism, as anthropology and geography professor David Harvey defines it, is the "maximisation of entrepreneurial freedoms within an institutional framework characterised by private property rights, individual liberty, free markets and free trade" (145). Not simply registering at the level of the political economy, neoliberalism matters because it has become hegemonic—it provides us with a lens to make sense of the world we live in (3). Neoliberalism influences how we do almost anything, including how we practice feminist activism, how we think about pain, suffering, and healing, and how we share emotions on social media.

For instance, in one of her poems about healing, kaur imagines healing as "every day work." She writes, "i woke up thinking the work was done/i would not have to practice today/gone were the moments i'd/split into tears because my past cracked open/how naïve. to think it was that easy./healing has no end point/no summation/no finish line to cross/ healing is every day work/the act of dedicating the self to/surviving what happened to me." Healing is positioned here as *work* that someone does continually and consistently, possibly, for the rest of their lives, on themselves. Because, in the neoliberal world, "work" is understood as a personal responsibility/endeavor, it is not a surprise then that healing practice involves focusing on the *self*, working through what happened to one's self, and on "*self*-love" and "*self*-care." As the caption that goes with this poem suggests: "healing—like self-love and self-care is an every day practice." Because neoliberalism considers that solutions to any problem are registered at the individual and not the institutional level (Stuart and Donaghue), the process of "healing" becomes an individual practice, an individual work, and an investment in the self. Here, kaur's emphasis is on healing the self rather than changing the structure of violence.

This focus on the self rather than the structure can also be seen in another poem: "to heal/you have to/get to the root/of the wound/and kiss it all the way up." Here, healing is not about rebelling or changing the structures; it is not about burning the root, but having the individual learn to adapt to the structures, kissing it all the way up—embracing it. Puerto Rican Ashkenazi author, activist, and artist Aurora Levins Morales would call this process "reclaiming the wounded erotic," which is done "against the backdrop of rape, abuse, and trauma" (284; Ibrahim-hakkioglu 186). In decolonial feminist poetry, including kaur's, healing is often imagined as "embracing life in the face of suffering" and "remaining 'soft' despite hurt and trauma" (Ibrahimhakkioglu 179). As kaur's poem further advises, "do not look for healing/at the feet of those/who broke you." Thus, healing is not found elsewhere, let alone at the mercy of those who hurt us. Although this suggestion is powerful, because to look for healing at the feet of others is to give our power away, it implies that the work of healing is based on going inward and within, which through a neoliberal lens can be seen as accepting "personal responsibility."

However, and to reiterate my earlier stance, kaur should not be conflated with a neoliberal feminist doing work that solely focuses on individuals or the self. kaur aims to cultivate a community of women. For example, many of her poems focus on women as a collective: "we all move forward when/we recognize how resilient/and striking the women/around us are"; "our work should equip/the next generation of women/to outdo us in every field/this is the legacy we'll leave behind"; and "my heart aches for sisters more than anything/it aches for women helping women/like flowers ache for spring." In this spirit of women helping women, her Instagram often highlights other women's work, such as thanking "@--- and @--- for the wonderful production on this photo series. @--- your photography made the delivery warm and full of ease. @--- for painting the cover on my back. @--- and @--- for hair and makeup. @--- your work is incredible and amazing. @--- who held down all the development on the website. the behind the scenes folks are the real heroes. i couldn't do this without my team. today is the first day of a brand new journey. you better believe it's going to be so fun." However, in kaur's thanking them, this collective body of her community of support received mentions, or in traditional media lingo, free advertisements for their brands. Thus, even as she aims to cultivate a sense of community, the neoliberalizing machine of social media—which functions as the phantasmagoria's magic lantern with its own goals—limits and co-opts the possibilities for community building because the users end up speaking through the language of commodification. Indeed, this is what phantasmagoria does: it "cut[s] the flâneur from himself, [and] lead[s] to the loss of his narrative capacities" (Tremblay 37). That is, kaur's efforts to build community are limited by the language of digital phantasmagoria. The apparatus of the magic lantern (social media) shapes what can be seen and shown in her phantasmagoria.

Through kaur's account on Instagram—the neoliberal alchemy machine—pain is turned into phantasmagoria (as products that can eventually be turned into gold): her poems of pain are commodified in the form of a poetry book, an audiobook, and canvas art. Her canvas art that features her poem "what is stronger/than the human heart/which shatters over and over/and still lives" exemplifies the working of neoliberalism as an alchemy that turns feminist healing poetry into a product that can be hung in one's home or other personal space. Rather than inspiring/enacting social change, feminist activism becomes a beautiful, artsy house decoration. In selling house decorations (even with feminist messages), the feminist figure has now become an entrepreneur whose existence further legitimizes capitalism and capital accumulation (Čakardić 39–40). To borrow from one of her Instagram followers' words, kaur is making "a business out of poetry." Although kaur may have posted thought-provoking poetry and comments about violence on social media, it does not necessarily translate into revolutionary change, because in the phantasmagoria, creative "production can very quickly be wrapped into the capitalistic machine" and have its subversive and critical possibility be co-opted (Tremblay 39–40). The digital platform as a neoliberal machine curbs, absorbs, and alchemizes kaur's feminist activism.

In addition to these products, kaur also offers poetry readings/shows and "trauma and poetry" writing workshops that further her stature as a good neoliberal subject. For instance, as kaur announces on her Instagram, "We will learn how to use the art of writing as a tool to heal. As aspiring writers you'll be given resources, tips, have the opportunities to ask questions, share your work, and walk away with your own poetry after the session." These kinds of workshops as well as others that focus on the self and tools for the self without *also*[4] asking participants to make structural changes function as the "neoliberal technologies of responsibilization" (Stringer 115). These workshops hint that it is our responsibility to learn the tools so we can heal ourselves (or to borrow from kaur's previously mentioned poem, to learn to kiss the roots all the way up).

Her workshops also reveal the neoliberal logic of futurity; as feminist theorist Catherine Rottenberg deftly observes, "the mobilization of futurity [i]s key to producing th[e] neoliberal subject" (94). In the example above, kaur's followers are addressed as "aspiring" writers—note the *futurity* of such an address. Neoliberal technology of the self is indeed "structured through futurity" (332). As Rottenberg points out, "neoliberal feminism is producing a new form of neoliberal governmentality for young middle-class and 'aspirational' women, namely, a governmentality structured through *futurity* and based on careful sequencing and smart self-investments in the present to ensure enhanced returns in the future" (15–16). kaur's workshops thus become an investment in the self whose benefits can be reaped in the future. Futurity is linked to capitalist profit in that it ensures that the market never runs dry.

If people are always "in the process," then they always need to purchase new goods and services or enroll in various workshops. As philosopher Ankica Čakardić helps us understand: "neoliberalism sees the individual as endless possibilities of activating the entrepreneurial spirit, as variable bundles of human capital, and counts with the interests of the individual always changing, mediated by the market and its values" (37). Workshops thus become spaces where women are transformed into "neoliberal human capital, a process that is ongoing but as yet incomplete" (Rottenberg 332). This notion of good neoliberal subjects as never complete and always in the process of improving themselves echoes kaur's previously mentioned poem on healing as "every day" work with no end point. From neoliberal and capitalist perspectives, it is much more profitable if individuals continually work on themselves. Healing as part of a neoliberal project cannot therefore ever end. Moreover, this form of empowerment works alongside neoliberalism. That is, as media scholar Holly Thorpe, sociologist Kim Toffoletti, and sport media scholar Toni Bruce point out, "within the neoliberal context, empowerment appears to have become 'a matter of reshaping responsible selves,' with such women increasingly 'internally driven to improve themselves' as they become 'entrepreneurs and consumers enmeshed in a global market'" (375). In other words, it is up to successful individuals such as kaur to keep improving themselves and help others to succeed, too.

↳ In a sense → Causing/ asking for people to hold themselves accountable

When these workshops that she offers are read against her poem "of course/i want to be/successful but/i don't crave/success for me/i need to be/successful/to gain enough/milk and honey/to help those/around me/succeed," they can be understood as a means to neoliberal success. In neoliberal terms, success is registered at the individual level: one person who is successful (kaur) can help others around her to succeed, too, rather than demand that a systemic effort for equity in distribution be made. Her project "a dinner of Queens"—where kaur would go to "the bougiest place where there's no people of colour. We're just going to sit down looking so fly and have a really expensive dinner" and "negotiat[e] with multimillionaires because we as brown women can and should. We're allowed to be in these spaces" (Kassam)—exposes the aspiration of occupying white wealthy spaces with brown bodies; think of Ferguson's notion of "liberation through capitalism." That the solution involves injecting the self, the brown self, the queen brown self, into expensive places and thereby changing these spaces, speaks, once again, of change that happens at the individual rather than the structural level— the level at which these white wealthy spaces are produced to begin with. Here, empowerment has in some sense been neoliberalized. As Thorpe and colleagues point out, neoliberal feminism operates when "gender inequality is being called out (rather than repudiated) but responses and reactions to such inequalities are framed by neoliberal discourses of individual entrepreneurialism and economic independence only. Simply, women who are able to individually overcome structural inequalities and obtain economic independence and success are celebrated as feminist subjects" (372). In other words, although through her poems kaur vehemently calls out gender and other forms of inequality, at a deeper level her economic independence and entrepreneurialism work to soothe the pain of the inequality that she fights against.

Moreover, the pervasiveness of neoliberalism as a governing logic of social media can be seen in how kaur's attempts to make visible the writing process through her social media are absorbed into the totality of phantasmagoria. For kaur, the process of writing itself, as she shares through her poems, can be painful. She writes, "the thing about/writing is i can't tell/if it's healing or/destroying me." In the digital world of phantasmagoria, the painful writing process is turned into a spectacle. kaur has even posted pictures of herself working and writing as part of this painful process. For instance, she posted a picture of herself at the library, hunched over on a desk with her face covered, signifying exhaustion or frustration, and captioning it: "what 80% of writing #thesunandherflowers looked like 😩." In one of her captions, she writes,

. . . for months i pored over which chapter should come first.
what they should be called. what themes would occupy each.
dozens of drafts later we arrived at:
  🥀wilting🥀: . . .
  🍂falling🍂: . . .
  ⚫rooting⚫: . . .
  🌱rising🌱: . . .
  🌼blooming🌼: . . .   #thesunandherflowers releases october
3rd. preorder at rupikaur.com to be the first to receive a copy

When we examine all of her pictures and captions critically, they suggest how even as she was conscious about making the process of labor production visible, this process is nonetheless being absorbed in its totality by the neoliberal phantasmagoria of social media. kaur turns the production of labor into spectacle by using social media/Instagram. Rather than seeing the production of labor as gruesome and feeling the pain of the process, her Instagram followers' senses are tricked into seeing something that is desirable/aesthetically beautiful—the process *has* to be represented as something that is desirable and beautiful, otherwise the followers won't preorder the book. At this point, the phantasmagoria is complete because "the phantasmagoria is the image as the result of the experience one has in identifying oneself with the commodity" (Pascucci 43). kaur becomes her poems, her products, her politics, all of which can be turned into a commodity. What is sold here is no longer just the book but also all that kaur does as part of her brand. Self-promotion is indeed encouraged under the logic of neoliberalism.

The neoliberal digital platform turns kaur into an entrepreneur when she invites her followers to preorder her book so they can be "the first to receive a copy." Selling her book on social media is part of being a good neoliberal subject. When the selling of the book happens, the alchemy is completed: pain is turned into gold. Here, "gold" is produced in the interaction between kaur and Instagram (which provides the apparatus for the phantasmagoria's "magic lantern" but which needs the user— kaur—to make it work, and yet, has its own goals and motivations). Both the user (kaur) and the technology (Instagram) are producing value ("gold") for themselves, and sometimes at cross-purposes.

Racial Oscillation on Social Media

In Canada, the history of South Asian migration began around the early twentieth century (Dua 447; Rajiva 18). By the end of 1908, there were approximately 5,179 people from India, who came mostly to British Columbia (Ralston 33). However, South Asian immigration to Canada was "severely restricted" (due to racism) until after the 1960s, when a point-based system that rewarded people with education and skills was instituted (Dua; Rajiva 18). Then, the Immigration Act, 1976, created, among others, a "family class" that allowed family members to reunite with their relatives in Canada (Atkey 61, 66).

Understandings of race in Canada shifted during the 1970s and 1980s, as they acquired new meanings under the rubric of multiculturalism. The Canadian Multiculturalism Act, passed in 1988, was designed for immigrants to preserve and promote their cultures through various policies and programs (Fries and Gingrich 43). When kaur and her family moved to Canada in the mid-1990s, multiculturalism had become mainstreamed and incorporated into Canadian electoral politics (Shariff 54).

In today's Canada, South Asians are one of the largest immigrant groups (making up 25 percent of the "visible minority") (Statistics

Canada 2016). Nonetheless, they still experience institutional and social racism (Poolakasingham et al. 195). For example, although they are more likely to hold postgraduate degrees than whites (13.16 percent vs. 6.0 percent), they still earn less than whites ($31,102 vs. $37,752) (Poolakasingham et al. 195). When high-skilled, highly educated South Asian engineers, doctors, or other professionals move to Canada, they have to undergo retraining if they want to stay in their professions (Rajiva 18). A study that looks at undergraduate South Asian Canadian students shows that these students regularly experience racial micro aggressions as a result of being *"perceived as fresh off the boat, excluded from social life,"* are seen as liabilities because they are brown, are assumed to have ties to terrorism, are presumed to be *"cultural expert[s]"* or stereotypically intelligent, or are *"treated as invisible"* (Poolakasingham et al. 194, emphasis original). South Asian Canadian girls experience extra pressures due to family expectations that they will excel in school, pursue careers in a limited range of acceptable fields, and perform culturally expected gender roles (Ghosh 63). As feminist and gender studies scholar Mythili Rajiva observes, South Asian Canadian daughters "carry part of the emotional burden of immigration" (19).

kaur's poems function as a form of carrying this gendered emotional burden of immigration. Her poems often illuminate the "ordinary trauma" caused by "the violence of everyday racism," migration, and being a part of a diasporic South Asian family (Rajiva 21). For example, in her poem "accent," she illustrates how the racialization process is registered and expressed through the body, most specifically the mouth and (metaphorically) the tongue: "my voice/is the offspring/of two countries colliding/what is there to be ashamed of/if english/and my mother tongue/made love/my voice/is her father's words/and mother's accent/ what does it matter if/my mouth carries two worlds." Although many of her followers expressed their appreciation for this poem that seemingly empowers people who speak two or more languages, some read the way she marks racism, sexism, and anti-immigration sentiments in/through her poems differently. A few of her followers criticize and objectify her, for example, by pointing out, "sis you have a whole ass canadian accent," "maybe she thinks indians living in india don speak english or something lol," and "I think it's attractive if you can speak two languages." From sexually objectifying those who can speak multiple languages to dismissing the issue of how racial discrimination often happens simply because of one's accent, these comments exemplify how, in the social media world, race is easily oscillated, sometimes intentionally, although not always, by both users and followers. Race is stripped of its context, decontextualized/recontextualized, repackaged, dismissed/embraced, or whichever way it can be oscillated, for the sake of existing, participating in, and benefiting from phantasmagoria. The apparatus of social media encourages this: to be shareable, to go viral—that is, to be successful—a posting must be able to survive different contexts. For instance, kaur's drawings, which once created a space for her to escape English and whiteness—her mother taught her to draw when she was a child, had just moved to Canada, and couldn't speak English—no longer carry their racialized history, as they are shared by her followers (including white followers) without this context. After all, social media is a space where the less context the better.

Nonetheless, I would insist, race always matters in any and *all* encounters. Consciously or unconsciously, we always try to "read" and therefore provide meanings for the other's race and racial signifiers, from name to facial features to skin color to accent. Racial ideologies always inform how we read others' bodies (whether they are overtly marked/racialized as such or not), but these racial ideologies are not always apparent. When we read anything, such as a book or a body, we need appropriate contextualization to help us better understand the meanings of what we're reading. However, on social media, the familiar "contexts" within which we read each other's bodies or postings are not always present, and even when they are, they may not be registered as such by others/followers. Racial oscillation thus speaks specifically about whether or not a content provider/user/follower/digital flâneur provides a *context* for others to read their body/race. It describes how

⤷ how Racism can be found present in social media via oscillation.

race becomes an object that can oscillate between being present/legible/visible (when a context is provided by the person who posts on social media so others can read their body as racialized as such) and absent/illegible/invisible (when a context is not provided or is not decoded as such) at the point of interaction on social media.

Race is both a visible and invisible element of kaur's social media success and journey to Instafame. First of all, kaur turned to Instagram because there was no place for a brown woman like her in traditional publishing. As she observes, "There was no market for poetry about trauma, abuse, loss, love and healing through the lens of a Punjabi-Sikh immigrant woman" (Kassam). Second, it is her ability to "racially oscillate" between writing about women as women (universal, nonracialized) and as women of color that affords her popularity as a feminist poet of color among multiple audiences of various racial backgrounds.

For example, according to writer and comparative literature scholar Chiara Giovanni, kaur presents a different "face to each market." Giovanni observes,

> On her website, she states that she writes in exclusively lowercase using only periods to pay homage to her mother tongue, Punjabi. But in a January 2015 interview with the mainstream feminist website HelloGiggles, she gives her love of "branding," "visual experience," and symmetry as the reason for her stylistic choice, with no mention of her mother tongue or the Gurmukhi script. It is a watered-down version of her explanation on her website, and one designed specifically with a white audience in mind. A love of symmetry is, after all, easier to identify with than a loyalty to a specific South Asian script. ("The Problem")

kaur thus racially oscillates between the nonmarked whiteness of symmetry of letters for the white audience and the marked Gurmukhi script for her non-white audience; and she oscillates, as well, between being the "'the patron saint of millennial heartbreak' (for her white audience) and 'a representation of their desire for diversity in the literary world' (for her people of color audience)" (Giovanni). After all, in phantasmagoria, what is important is the ability to turn anything—not least race—into a spectacle, a commodity, and eventually, phantasmagoria. In doing so, kaur is able to navigate the various layers of phantasmagoria production in constructing race as something that is entertaining and appealing for different markets. That is, it is her ability to "racially oscillate" on social media that leads her to being lovingly embraced by different audiences.

An example that speaks against racism, colorism, and sexism but was not necessarily registered as such by her followers is a poem titled "women of colour" that was reposted on March 3, 2019, garnering 293,199 likes: "our backs/tell stories/no books have/the spine to/carry." The caption kaur wrote for this poem was, "i will spend my entire life writing. i will leave behind volumes upon volumes of work. and they will barely scratch the surface." First, the issue of race is evident in the poem's title: "women of colour." The trope of "our backs" to illustrate the burden that women of color have had to carry is famous from a foundational text in the field of women's studies, *This Bridge Called My Back: Writings by Radical Women of Color*. Through her poem, kaur acknowledges the *collective* pain of women of color and the ways in which the literary world has forgotten the stories of/by/for women of color. Although there are comments that make race visible, such as "As a woman of color, I really feel this post," there are posts that subtly downplay race in their comments, such as "I'm not a woman of color but I identify with this," or those that completely erase the racial aspect of kaur's poem and end up literally focusing on back pain instead, such as "I have scoliosis too, I went to a spinal surgeon the other day and they said they can't do surgery for me cause I've stopped growing now." In other words, in the process of interacting with one another on social media about race, race gets oscillated between being legible and illegible, absent and present.

Another example is kaur's poem that celebrates her brown body: "it is a blessing/to be the color of earth/do you know how often/flowers

People read into posts differently — some acknowledge race & others don't

confuse me for home." Yet a comment on this poem addressed the sentiment of being in nature: "It describes very well a feeling/desire that I often have when I am walking around in Nature, melted with her. And it seems perfect to me even for a Brazilian friend of mine, to whom I want to dedicate it." In this sense, even Asians can simply be likened (or oscillated) to Brazilians.

In phantasmagoria, where the neoliberal self(ie) has to be projected as a spectacle—someone who is appealing and entertaining—a racial subject must thus learn to racially oscillate to accrue affective and economic currency, knowing when and where to mark (non-)whiteness. Racial oscillation is an integral part of phantasmagoria because when the neoliberal self(ie) has to be projected as entertaining, appealing, and inspiring, their race must also be represented and positioned as such. Race has to be absorbed into the system that turns X into spectacle and constructed through the lens of the neoliberal self(ie) gaze for it to gain any currency. Racial oscillation thus explains the process whereby race can be turned into a certain spectacle that fits a specific audience's taste, and transformed into another spectacle for a different audience.

Affect Alienation: The Digital Politics of Anesthetics

Phantasmagoria reveals and reproduces the condition in which people are alienated from their own feelings—what I call "affect alienation." The concept of affect alienation is different from the condition of those whom Sara Ahmed calls "affect aliens": "those who are alienated from the nation by virtue of how they are affected" ("Not in the Mood" 13). In affect alienation, people enter phantasmagoria "in order to be distracted. Within these *divertissements*, to which the individual abandons himself in the framework of the entertainment industry, he remains an element of a compact mass" (Benjamin 18, emphasis original). In the context of social media, people enter this digital phantasmagoria in order to be distracted *from their own feelings*. That is, people who seek out phantasmagoria *do* want to feel; however, rather than feeling their own emotions directly they want to feel what others are feelings, *as others*, or *through* others—the (socially) mediated feeling. Although these feelings may be felt as their own, these feelings are distractions that further alienate them from their own feelings and experiences and from the structure of their lives. "*Phantasmagoria functions to alienate people from their feelings*"

Before I discuss how phantasmagoria functions to alienate people from their own feelings, it is important to first clarify a concept that I have discussed elsewhere: digital media as a "space of affective simulation" (Saraswati, "La Douleur"). This concept underlies the working of phantasmagoria as it produces affect alienation.

In the digital world, the invitation to click is an invitation to feel and to express that feeling (by way of emojis, comments, etc.). By signing in, we agree to be affectively simulated/stimulated by what is projected from the Internet. People go to social media sites to be connected, get information, and eventually *feel* something (e.g., loved, inspired, connected, disappointed, and so forth). In the case of kaur's phantasmagoria, people go there to feel the depth and intensity of pain and healing—her poems tend to revolve around being able to walk away from or rise above abuse or a broken heart, and they are known to be "very spiritual with healing capabilities" (Gardner).

Arguing that digital media is a space of affective simulation, I insist that we do not see it as merely a medium (albeit new) of representation. That is, digital media is not simply a "window" into another world; rather, it has become a "virtual invader" that both "mediates" and "generates" reality (Vanderbeeken 247). In other words, it provides us with another *layer* of reality—think of reality here as consisting of layers rather than two different realities juxtaposed: the material and the virtual. As a mediator of reality, the screen provides us with virtual experiences that then "eclipse" and "overshadow" our physical-world experiences (248). As a generator of reality (and, in this book, of pain), the screen produces new images that function as simulacra and hence produce "a surplus of reality" (251, 253). Digital media culture scholar Nishant Shah offers a related, if much differently worded, perspective, viewing the screen as the "hole" through which "Alice" (of the Wonderland kind) has to fall to access the reality down below—a layer of reality that is perceived to be more real than the interface itself (353).

What is the difference between simulation and representation? Here, I rely on sociologist and philosopher Jean Baudrillard's argument:

representation vs. Simulation

> Representation stems from the principle of the equivalence of the sign and of the real (even if this equivalence is utopian, it is a fundamental axiom). Simulation, on the contrary, stems from the utopia of the principle of equivalence, *from the radical negation of the sign as value*, from the sign as the reversion and death sentence of every reference. Whereas representation attempts to absorb simulation by interpreting it as a false representation, simulation envelops the whole edifice of representation itself as a simulacrum. (6, emphasis original)

In this sense, representation assumes that there is the real truth to be re-presented in the media/new media. Simulation, however, accepts the premise that the real is already absorbed into the entire system of representation as re/production. Thus, in the study of representation, the questions that are often asked are: is the representation faithful to the "real" image, and what are the consequences of these representations for the "real" image/subject's life? Answering these questions involves measuring the proximity and truthfulness of the copy to the model and assessing its effect. Simulation detaches itself from and even challenges the question of the real. As Baudrillard further states, "It is no longer a question of a false representation of reality (ideology) but of concealing the fact that the real is no longer real, and thus of saving the reality principle" (13). As such, questions such as "Is kaur *really* in pain? Is her poem *really* about her pain?" are irrelevant. The "real" is irrelevant because "the real is no longer real" to begin with.

As a side note, kaur is often asked whether or not her poems are really about her. To this question, in an interview with a feminist magazine, *Bust*, kaur answers, "I would be lying if I said that it wasn't me, but it's not *all* me. People are like, 'Is this 100% biographical . . . ?' It's not, but the emotion is, and a lot of it is. *Milk and Honey* is the dissecting of emotions that I've carried all my life, but it's also the emotions that the women around me have carried" (E. Smith). Although she admits that the pain in her poems is not hers alone—her poems are not always autobiographical—she recognizes that it is irrelevant whether or not her poems speak only about her life and that what matters is the emotion (particularly of the gendered and generational pain—the collective pain—of racialized women in a white patriarchal culture) simulated and documented in her poems.

What kaur highlights here—the importance of the emotion simulated in her poems and phantasmagoria rather than the realness of her poems—has been articulated by various scholars. For instance, philosopher Slavoj Žižek, speaking about "the paradox of cinema," states, "I know very well it's a fake but, nonetheless, I let myself be emotionally affected" (*The Pervert's Guide*). Whether or not the word/image is real is irrelevant to the fact that it has emotional and affective ramifications. Information studies scholar Annette Markham and performance studies scholar Sharon Lehner also assert that "when experiences are experienced, they cannot be 'not real'" (Markham 120) and that the existence of images that can create emotional responses that drive viewers to action indicates that images have real affective consequences (Lehner 659). Similarly, Tremblay points out, "the spectacle of the feeds functions as phantasmagoria in their masking and distracting, but as simulation in their productions of 'real' psychological afflictions" (54). Lastly, media theorist Vivian Sobchack argues that any technologically based text is always read "through our perceptive sensorium, through the materiality (or *immanent mediation*) of our own bodies" (139, emphasis original). All of these scholars highlight the importance of the affective responses of the body and the ways in which experiences and emotions are resurfacing the materiality (rather than the "realness") of the body that *feels*.

To a certain extent, and to go back to the phantasmagoria trope that I have been working with, it can be said that spectacle is the representation and phantasmagoria is the simulation/hyperreality. Representation can be understood as spectacle to the degree that its production involves turning a product into a commodity, or an image into a spectacle, or an X into its representation, X-1 (copy). Simulation can be registered as phantasmagoria in the way that both involve several layers of production and have been "several stages further removed from their context of production." Simulation is a copy of a copy of a copy of a copy, which no longer has an original (the X) or a reality—rather, it has a hyperreality. Nonetheless, I argue, this space of simulation carries with it an affective charge. It is this affective charge that I center in understanding how social media as phantasmagoria can create affect alienation in its audience/Instagram followers. For instance, when followers read kaur's poems about her broken heart, their body may produce affective responses that signal that they are feeling kaur's pain as well as their own broken hearts. It does not matter whether or not kaur's broken heart in one of her poems is real. It does not matter whether or not the affective responses in kaur's Instagram followers come from an actual or imagined past or a present broken heart. What matters is there *is* an affective response that in social media has the space to be expressed, externalized, and circulated, by way of emojis, comments, share features, and the like. In the world of phantasmagoria, however, this affective response can be felt only for as long as the audience remains inside this phantasmagoric world. The spell is broken outside of this world. This is the condition that I call affect alienation.

In the digital world, a viewer enters into a state of feeling mostly *by choice*—the user chooses to enter the world of kaur's poems, for example, knowing that their affect will be triggered in a certain way, although of course no one can guarantee *how exactly* a person will be affected. On social media, users tend to "curate" their feeds by following people or hashtags that are affectively pleasing or intriguing to them (and unfollow them whenever they choose to)—even the advertisements that may pop up have been personalized to each specific user's taste. The algorithms in social media are induced to produce affect alienation. Indeed, one of the affective functions of media throughout its different forms has been to take viewers/readers to different worlds where they can escape and feel better (Radway). What is distinct about digital media is not simply its never-ending supply of content—television provides viewers with effectively endless choice if they subscribe to hundreds of channels. What makes it distinct from previous forms of media, rather, is, first, the algorithm system of curation that helps us sift through this endless content and facilitates our being sucked into its world that provides us with continuous, affectively pleasing-to-us content and, second, users' ability to actively, a/synchronously, immediately engage with this content, express opinions and emotions, and co-construct this phantasmagorical world.

The fact that we can click and enter a world to be affected in a certain way, yet know that we can log out at any time and even choose to hide our offline identity behind our avatar, establishes a condition of affective possibility that may be different from other ways of being affected in the physical world. First, it is different in that users feel a certain sense of control based in their capacity to create and curate the social media world that they are participating in, versus a film they are watching or a book they are reading. (To a certain extent, this is because, as mentioned previously, users have been tricked by the magic lantern/social media into believing that they have control over their own social media production/consumption and that they are benefiting from their social media involvement—that they can use social media to sell commodities, without realizing that while they use the magic lantern to trick others, they are also being tricked.)

Second, it is also different in that digital media both prompts and demands affective responses immediately after one encounters an object, and the platforms limit the range of affective responses. When we view something on social media we are prompted to make an immediate affective response: do we like it? If so, how would we externalize it through the symbols provided on the site (e.g., heart emojis)? One of the unique features of digital media is an interface that allows us to "externalize" our experience *with* an audience (Sperb 127); experience happens as we externalize it. That is, in the digital world, we make sense of our experiences as we socially mediate and publicly share them online. When people interact in the "physical" world, they are not constantly being prompted to immediately produce or articulate an affective response. Yes, an individual might be surrounded by people making comments about what they are seeing that might affect that person's feelings. However, this is very different from what occurs when one goes to an Instagram post and sees that it has two thousand likes or just five; and, again, the digital platform itself is structured to encourage viewers to externalize their feelings (by way of clicking a like button or leaving a comment). In this sense, then, the affective atmosphere of digital phantasmagoria is different partly because of the asynchronous experience of products that social media platforms allow, and the ways in which social media platforms prompt their users to give immediate affective responses within a prescribed and limited range of possibilities. Thus, the digital space itself, while not necessarily transgressive in terms of producing a different kind of affectivity, does create an affective performativity that is distinct in being produced under the constant surveillance of the omnipresent, always-being-recorded, and externalized-for-the-audience-to-see gaze (the neoliberal self(ie) gaze).

Third, digital media is different in that the affective environment is more overt and mediated. That is, when a person is in a roomful of people who are experiencing affective responses, that person has to interpret their responses through their facial expressions and words/actions. These responses are more varied, nuanced, and harder to read than the range of affective responses that are marked by emojis and clearly marked by recognizable symbols (e.g., a sad face emoji). In short, the platforms both limit the range of affective responses and prompt users to record their affective responses immediately and publicly.

Phantasmagoria has the ability to produce a "deceptive experience" (Tremblay 22). Deception here is understood as "a multi-sensory experience that at once plays upon the audience's sense of the real and the imaginary. It is the dazzlement of the commodity's social and exchange value, the fantasies produced and desires manipulated when that dazzlement takes root, it is the 'luster with which the commodity-producing society surrounds itself'" (22). This means that, in the world of phantasmagoria, even our desires and fantasies—our feelings—have been manipulated by the luster and distraction of the commodity that appears both real and imaginary at the same time. When a person within a phantasmagoria interacts with an object, that person thus interacts not so much with it as a material object but rather as "the object's abstractions and significations" (23). For instance, when a person is exploring kaur's phantasmagoria and interacts with her poem and feels affected by it, it is not kaur's pain or their own pain that they are engaging with. Rather, it is the poem's "abstraction and signification" and the ways in which the value of the poem as a commodity has been hidden. It is not a surprise then, that a few of kaur's followers wrote these comments on her Instagram: "I seriously want to get this illustration tattooed on me" and "I want this drawing as a tattoo so bad." These tattoos become "souvenirs," so to speak, for people who are doing "trauma tourism" (Jones 47) inside the world of kaur's phantasmagoria. Pain and/in poem have been abstracted and signified as tattoos and become part of the dazzlement in this neoliberal, "commodity-producing society." How we feel, how we express our feelings, and how we relate to others through these feelings are mediated through commodities (in this example, tattoo as commodity). Even feeling itself functions here as a public commodity.

kaur's poems have the ability to soothe preexisting affect alienation (e.g., through escapism and simulation of affect) as well as reproduce affect alienation that people experience. A follower comments that one of kaur's poems is "right in the feels." Indeed, kaur is intentional in creating "a positive reader experience. This is something [she] learned in school. [Her] major ended with the art of persuasion—how to pull emotion out of people—and so [she] think[s] that's been a big part of [her] poetry. [She] always ask[s] [her]self, 'Okay what does a reader experience? Is a reader able to understand the emotion of the speech?'" (Parsons). In being able to "pull emotion out of people," her poems, as philosopher

Theodor Adorno writes about Wagner's music, can "warm up the alienated and reified relations of man and make them sound as if they were still human" (Buck-Morss 26). However warming or soothing to the alienated souls these poems and music may be, they nonetheless do not address or dispel affect alienation. Allowing us to feel something or other in the moment does not erase the fact that these feelings are "distractions" from the feelings and experiences in our own lives. It does not make visible the neoliberal/capitalist structure of emotional hegemony that governs what to feel, why we feel the way that we feel, and how these feelings are gendered, racialized, and sexualized.

For instance, capitalism tells us that to feel happy we must purchase the latest smartphone, to feel healthy we must run with the latest Fitbit, or to feel sexy we must wear Victoria's Secret lingerie. Neoliberalism teaches women that to feel good they must take care of themselves first (i.e., self-love, self-care) by getting a massage treatment (a commodity), for example. Such narratives have contributed to the condition of affect alienation—how we feel is mediated by capitalism, neoliberalism, or other forms of hegemony. When we go to the digital world of phantasmagoria and feel something, our pain is being "warmed up" or soothed to the point that we believe we are still humans who can feel. But these feelings remain a distraction from accessing and processing the emotions in our body that stem from ideologically, politically, and structurally influenced experience. kaur's phantasmagoria reveals what scholars have argued before: how "human being[s] posses[s] a striving to create a space in which pain . . . can be regarded as an illusion" (Ernst Jünger quoted in Buck-Morss 33) and how "viewers have become fascinated with the screen as a medium that can communicate suffering. Images of fictitious and actual pain are turned into a spectacle" (Gerbaz 164). In other words, neoliberal phantasmagoria shows how pain becomes desirable when it can be consumed or felt as an illusion or spectacle. Phantasmagoria makes us feel (good) because of its entertaining and enchanting qualities. Yet affect alienation remains. kaur notices this as she observes: "What happens when you're so connected with other people through these things [social media], you become so disconnected with yourself, and we find it so difficult to just sit with ourselves and just be alone" ("How Poet"). That is, connection with others on social media may paradoxically produce disconnection (affect alienation) between a person and their own feelings. In some ways, this can be explained through the phantasmagoria metaphor: Benjamin emphasizes this paradox and ambiguity in his discussion of Paris arcades, where flâneurs are surrounded by people but are alone and alienated. They are seemingly insiders, part of the arcade, because they can see the commodities through the glass enclosure, yet they are really outside because the glass functions as a border between them and the shop. There is a similar ambiguity with Instagram, where kaur's poems seemingly register as private experience, although they are public, and seemingly address our feelings, even as they distract us from actually dealing with them. Thus, in the world of phantasmagoria, people *do* feel (even seemingly feel more), yet, ironically and paradoxically, they are more alienated from their own feelings than ever before.

Let's turn to another example to understand this point better. kaur writes about loneliness in two poems: "loneliness is a sign you are in desperate need of yourself" and "fall/in love/with your solitude." In both of these poems, the antidote to loneliness is constructed as going within and reconnecting with oneself. Yet these poems do not question how emotional hegemony shapes our feelings, why the feeling of loneliness exists to begin with, how living and social arrangements in capitalistic society or the neoliberal ideology of individualism contribute to one's loneliness, and how existing ideological narratives of the self and self-love contour how loneliness is experienced, mediated, and remedied.

The comments posted on kaur's Instagram often demonstrate how her poems make her readers feel. But they do not show affect alienation being dispelled. For instance:

I read this and just started crying

@— . . . everything makes me cry

@— feeling feels yet?

Me for the past 4 years. Alone, transformed, grateful. This triggered me hard

All of these comments highlight how kaur's poems allow her Instagram followers to feel and perform these feelings on social media. First
of all, these kinds of comments are revealing of the condition of digital
media as a space of affective simulation where people go to feel (or even
cry). These comments also expose the kind of "self" that neoliberalism
creates: a "self-centered self." Particularly on social media, what one
posts is often about what one does, eats, thinks, or is interested in. The
above postings reflect how the self experiences loneliness or is being
triggered or grateful. As someone else commented: "She is amazing &
will make you feel so much better about yourself. She understands!" To
this follower, what makes kaur amazing is her capacity to make "you feel
better about yourself." The insistence is nonetheless on the individual—
"you." This exemplifies how neoliberal logic shapes and limits how affect
is experienced and expressed in public. Neoliberalism creates an ironic
kind of loneliness that will never be resolved because loneliness becomes
something that is the responsibility of the individual to resolve—by reconnecting with oneself. As with all neoliberal products, the goal is not
to solve the problem because solving the problem would destroy the
market. Fixing the structures that create loneliness would lessen kaur's
popularity, negating the value of her commodity. Tapping into this conundrum of loneliness, kaur writes, "the irony of loneliness/is we all
feel it/at the same time—*together.*" Yet the real irony is not that people
are experiencing loneliness together, but that the experience of feeling
lonely together is distracting them from the processes and actions that
would actually address the causes or experiences of their loneliness in
an impactful way.

Second, these comments also show that the production of kaur's
phantasmagoria relies on her followers doing the affective work of ex-

ternalizing their emotions via emojis and affectionate comments on her Instagram, and collectively creating that phantasmagoria together with her. As architects and critical theorists Libero Andreotti and Nadir Lahiji argue, phantasmagoria in the present day relies on "the *means of transmission* through which subjects 'actively participate' as autonomous agents in the construction of phantasmagorical dreamworlds" (129). It is this collective and interactive co-creation of phantasmagoria that distinguishes twenty-first-century phantasmagoria from its previous incarnations.

Moreover, pain felt as an individual experience is evidence for how we are alienated from our own feelings. In another one of her poems, kaur writes, "you break women in like shoes." The poem's caption reads:

> this is what being in an abusive relationship felt like. he'd kick me so hard my legs would crack and i'd fall to the ground. then he'd demand i stand up. only to kick me down again. and again. and again. till i got so tired of collapsing i decided it was easier to give in. do what he was asking. become malleable. mouldable. his idea of "the perfect fit." #thesunandherflowers

Comments on this poem include:

> thanks for making me cry

> Your words are so painfully relatable

> I lived with this for 3 years in my 20s. I finally knew on one not even special day that I was done forever and left. The part about fighting and then the giving in to it . . . very well expressed.

> I'm in this situation right now. So happy to hear you came out on the other side. ❤

> Wow I can relate to this, I've been in abusive relationships also and I felt the same exact way (that it was easier giving in) until I learned I was much stronger than that. It may not always be easy, but there's always a way out of anything that doesn't do us any good. Thank you for sharing your beautiful soul to the world 🙏❤

Taken together, the poem, caption, and comments show us how patriarchy alienates women from our own feelings, how kaur's poem makes her followers believe that they are being reconnected with their feelings, how pain is the medium through which the audience is reached, and how affect alienation is not dispelled even when women feel as if they are being reconnected with their feelings through this poem. Let's unpack this.

Patriarchy—the culture that endows men with power—alienates women from our own feelings. The caption of the poem exposes how an abusive relationship molds the woman and her behavior into what *he* wants her to be and do. It does so by disconnecting women from our will to fight back and to feel, and even from our own bodies. Distancing ourselves from our body and emotion is a mode of survival. We walk around feeling numb or deadening our feelings. Then, reading kaur's poem allows us to believe that we are being reconnected with our pain, which was once too much to bear. kaur's pain seemingly becomes a bridge to access that pain as it makes us cry, even though it may be the simulation of pain that we are experiencing. In this case, pain merely becomes "the medium by which the spectator can be reached best" (Zimmermann 38). That the pain that is felt is simulated pain means that this pain that we feel *distracts* and *alienates* us from our own pain. It leaves our pain intact in its cocoon (created by alienation). As can be seen from the comments, kaur's followers focus on what *I* am feeling, what *you're* feeling, or what *she's* feeling after reading the poem. Beyond those moments when they feel good after reading kaur's poem, nothing else seems to happen at the fundamental/structural level that could eventually transform that pain. The trauma is still there, the problem is still out there. The poem becomes a new distraction from the structure that alienates them from their feelings in the first place. That is, reading and commenting on feelings may distract and alienate people from their own feelings. Remember, phantasmagoria is a place people enter "in order to be distracted" by the entertainment value of something that has been turned into a complex spectacle (Benjamin 7). People go to phantasmagoria and "surrende[r] to its manipulations while enjoying [their] alienation from [themselves] and others" (Benjamin 7). This alienation is what is entertaining and enchanting: people can delight in the contradictory tension of being able to feel, yet be alienated from their feelings at the same time. People do not see these poems, postings, and phantasmagoria as distractions, but rather as enchantments. Phantasmagoria functions to "dazzle and mask the reality of both the user's life and the lives of other users" (Tremblay 53). In this world, people experience "intoxication" of the senses by "turning reality into a phantasmagoria" (Buck-Morss 24).

Digital phantasmagoria produces "affective intensities" rather than "stable symbolic structures of knowledge," and these affective intensities do not provoke critical thoughts about people's interactions, but create "a logic of drive" that is about "excess" and "viral proliferation" in digital media (Andreotti and Lahiji 129). Digital flâneurs (social media users) care about what can make their products go viral. They are not necessarily interested in pointing out the specific ways in which the patriarchy, neoliberalism, and digital phantasmagoria that produce and reproduce affect alienation can be exposed and defeated. They do not question what we are healing from, what we are healing toward, or what "okay" looks like beyond the neoliberal imperative to focus on oneself and practice self-care and self-love—the imperative of affect as disciplinary apparatus. They do not explore how commodification and technology pave the way to further one's affect alienation. One's pain can never be fully felt and released in phantasmagoria until one is free from one's own affect alienation. Simulated pain becomes something, a distraction, that keeps our affective registers occupied. And because there is always a lack—the inability to subvert one's affect alienation—those in a phantasmagoria will always come back for more (feelings). They keep searching for the next poem, the next shiny spectacle, the next phantasmagoria to feel again. The search continues, the addiction remains, and the market continues to be profitable.

One may suspect that kaur is intuitively aware of the affect alienation related to social media when she deletes social media apps from her phone, recognizing that "social media, the thing that first connected her work to the world, can also be a cause of the pain that so many young people feel today" ("How Poet"). Nonetheless, she uses Instagram through other devices to post her poems. In the social media world, where everyone is encouraged to focus on themselves, their products, and the benefits for them, everyone continues to use social media, exploring what it can do for them, *despite* knowing that its manipulations can be harmful.

Phantasmagoria is addictive and often likened to a narcotic, even a sedative. As Andreotti and Lahiji argue, "the phantasmagoria of an architecture that *incorporates* digital technology is not only incapable of undoing the alienation of the corporeal sensorium but becomes a means to further *anaestheticize* it in the interests of greater social control" (146, emphasis original). That is, the phantasmagoria keeps people in their alienated state of being/feeling—and one may make the argument that this makes it easier to control and make money off them. Phantasmagoria is an enchantment that distracts people from truly understanding the neoliberal logic of public affect and the articulation of affect in public/digital/neoliberal spaces. This addiction is also fed by the algorithm system that curates and provides us with content that is affectively pleasing. The more affectively pleasing content we view, the more of it is provided for us, the more of it we watch, and the cycle continues. Yet people remain alienated from their feelings and what they have to go through in a given day: dealing with an abusive partner or feeling lonely, for example. The irony and paradox of phantasmagoria is its capacity to allow us to escape from our feelings,

↳ So, is phantasmagoria good or bad?
Both.

from things we have to do and feel at the moment, only to, yet again, feel, even if it's (through) someone else's feeling. It is the ultimate affect alienation experience. Although kaur's poems and pictures have the appearance of allowing readers to feel their emotions, they also work to re-alienate them from their own feelings, prompting them to seek new sensory distractions so they can feel again. And the cycle continues.

Conclusion

This chapter shows the ways in which social media platforms and their users, through the process of neoliberal alchemy, turn pain, first, into phantasmagoria, then gold. It demonstrates how when a decolonial feminist poet, rupi kaur, uses the apparatus of phantasmagoria's magic lantern (in this case, Instagram), the trajectory and language of activism is co-opted, limited, and shaped by the neoliberal logic of social media. In this phantasmagoric space, empowerment happens when one purchases kaur's canvas art piece with an inspiring poem printed on it, or when one enrolls in a writing workshop that teaches how to heal from trauma, for instance, but does not extend beyond it.

It bears repeating that what I am criticizing is *not* rupi kaur the feminist figure, the person, her poems, or her Instagram postings per se. Rather, it is the ways in which feminist activism, even when it was not originally founded on neoliberalism, is carried out on digital platforms governed by neoliberal values of personal responsibility, entrepreneurship, and liberation through capitalism and by the neoliberal logic of the visual-economy marketplace, which limit and shape the trajectory and practice of feminist activism in this domain.   ← her main argument in this chapter

The master's tools (the magic lantern/social media) *can* dismantle the master's house (phantasmagoria), as long as they are used *against* the master, of course. However, when healing is imagined as individual work, it can never free us from the pain that we feel or, worse, from the pain of alienation. Revealing and challenging various structures that contribute to one's inability to be reconnected to one's feeling and to fight back, understanding how the structure works in creating affect alienation and producing disempowered citizens, and working toward structural change and community (rather than *only* individual) healing are what may eventually dispel affect alienation.

3

Masking Pain, Unmasking Race

Sexual Harassment, Shaming, and the Sharing Economy
of Emotions

Mia Matsumiya, Japanese American violinist, born in Massachusetts and currently based in Los Angeles, became "social media famous" after creating an Instagram account, perv_magnet, where she posted some of the screenshots she saved over a ten-year period of more than one thousand online sexual messages from "creeps, weirdos & fetishists" (as Matsumiya calls them on her Twitter profile).[1] These messages ranged from "catcalls," to "low grade micro-aggressions," to "I know where you live and I'm going to rape you" (Guillermo). Her Instagram quickly went viral and was featured in many online news outlets including www.cosmopolitan.com, www.nbcnews.com, and www.washingtonpost.com. When asked in an interview on www.dazeddigital.com why she created perv_magnet, Matsumiya answered:

> I want to start a dialogue by sharing, commiserating, and discussing these messages. I hope to make aware that this is the way some people—a lot of people—act behind their computers. (And often in real life too.) Personally, I don't know any woman who hasn't been the recipient of creepy behaviour. It's unacceptable and so depressingly rampant. I want my account to be a place where women can commiserate and men to just learn what women can experience online. I don't know yet what can be done about it but I feel like the first step is definitely to shed light on the issue. (Ewens)

In this way, Matsumiya's social media campaign does the feminist work of consciousness raising and embodies the same spirit as the

#MeToo movement. Her account was created in September 2015, two years before #MeToo went viral in 2017.

In the preceding chapter, I focused on the neoliberal aspect of entrepreneurship and "liberation through capitalism"; in this chapter, through an examination of Matsumiya's social media campaign, I shift my analysis to another aspect of neoliberal feminism, what political scientist Michaele Ferguson identifies as the "privatization of political responses" (230). This term refers to the ways in which people seek private means and funds to respond to political issues. For instance, rather than demanding that the state improve public transportation, a neoliberal response to the lack of reliable and accessible transportation is to establish a ride-sharing system, such as Uber or Lyft, that turns citizens into "entrepreneurs" who run a business by capitalizing on their own private cars.

In this chapter, I want to think with this same logic of the neoliberal sharing economy to make visible how neoliberalism seeps into and shapes Matsumiya's feminist activism on social media. Matsumiya's campaign is embossed with a neoliberal signature of the sharing economy in that rather than demanding that the state/system (legal, social, political, financial) be improved to deter people from sexually harassing others in the digital space, it establishes an emotion-sharing system in which she and her Instagram followers collaboratively process and externalize their feelings about these sexual harassments[2] and shame the perpetrators on her social media. (She indeed stated that she wants her account to be a space where women can "commiserate.")

It is this practice, which I call "the sharing economy of emotions," that I explore in the first part of this chapter. This sharing economy is evident in the ways in which Matsumiya is "crowdsourcing" emotions from others on social media: she calls on other Asian American women to share their screenshots of sexual harassment with her so she can post them on her Instagram account; in turn, these posted harassment messages provoke emotions in her Instagram followers, who then share and externalize their emotions on her social media (mostly in the form of online shaming the harassers).

The second part of this chapter teases out another property of neoliberalism that is at work in Matsumiya's feminist campaign: how she strategically (and, if I may add, quite brilliantly) redeploys *kawaii* aesthetics, the culture of cuteness, operating in the harassment messages she received, to talk back to the harassers in an entertaining and witty way. In doing so, she inevitably projects a neoliberal self(ie). Here, I purposefully evoke the trope of masking—a trope that English professor Traise Yamamoto argues operates in the writings of the Japanese American women that she studied (selected Sansei and Nisei autobiographies, fictions, and plays, and contemporary Japanese American women's poems)—as I want to dig deeper into the ways in which Matsumiya's redeployment of kawaii aesthetics functions as a mode of masking and unmasking race in social media interactions (that is, her way of performing racial oscillation as a technique of the neoliberal self(ie)).

Still working with the trope of masking, the last part of this chapter takes us to the ingenious way in which Matsumiya uses sarcasm as a strategy of resistance to mask her emotions, thereby preserving the "impenetrability" not only of her Japanese American feminist agency but also her neoliberal self(ie) on social media. As a whole, this chapter thus carefully charts how neoliberal ideology operates as the underlying structure in Matsumiya's feminist activism on social media: (1) by way of her practicing the sharing economy of emotions; (2) by way of her redeploying kawaii aesthetics as a technology of the neoliberal self(ie) to racially oscillate on social media; and (3) by way of her using sarcasm to mask her emotions and thereby protect and project her neoliberal self(ie).

The Sharing Economy of Emotions

The sharing economy is a term that is used to describe the peer-to-peer activity of sharing services or goods for a fee, or for free, that is enabled by digital platforms, such as Uber (sharing rides) or Airbnb (sharing accommodations) (Albinsson et al. 4). As information and communication technologies scholar Leslie Regan Shade states, "the sharing economy emanates from ideals surrounding collaborative consumption . . . , the ethos of open source communities . . . and modes of peer production" (35). The sharing economy is also known as "crowd-based capitalism" (Arun Sundararajan quoted in Shade 36) or the "gig economy"—indeed, "sharing" seems a disingenuous way to characterize the corporate and capitalistic culture of this economy.

Sociologist Juliet Schor has identified four broad areas of the sharing economy: (1) the "recirculation of goods," such as on eBay or Craigslist; (2) the "increased utilization of durable assets" as facilitated by companies such as Uber and Airbnb; (3) the "monetization of the exchange of services" through the outsourcing of jobs via businesses such as Task-Rabbit; and (4) the "sharing of productive assets via cooperatives, peer production sites, shared workspaces and at technological spaces like hackerspaces and maker labs" (quoted in Shade 37–38). In none of these four areas is emotion mentioned.

To contribute to this area of study, provide a more comprehensive understanding, and emphasize the importance of emotion in the sharing economy, I thus propose the concept of "the sharing economy of emotions." I define the sharing economy of emotions as the ways in which digital media enables, encourages, and provides us with a means to *publicly share and socially mediate* our emotions in online spaces. It is conducted peer-to-peer, often among strangers, and enabled by digital platforms. In the sharing economy of emotions, rather than sharing access to services or goods, people share their emotions on digital platforms and process them together with others.

The Sharing Economy of Emotions

As a theoretical concept, the sharing economy of emotions allows us to comprehend the *sociality* of emotion: emotion as a social (not only individual) feeling, and as publicly shared and socially mediated. The term "sociality of emotion" directs us to a fresh perspective of emotion as a cultural, social, and ideological phenomenon that is processed and practiced on social media as "feeling-with-other-ness." That is, as we share our feelings publicly with others on social media, others share their feelings about our feelings and in turn socially mediate how we feel about our feelings. In this digital environment (where emotion has to be *externalized* to be legible for others to read/see/understand), emotion is processed as an *interactive* and *collaborative* practice, something that we feel together *with* others—the "feeling-with-other-ness." Here, "with-other" becomes a way to highlight the *other-ness* of one's feeling when one's feeling is immersed with others' feelings through this process of emotion-sharing on social media. This process then allows people to socially recalibrate their emotions as the event unfolds.

The end goal of the sharing economy of emotions is not always about the monetization of these shared emotions, although it is possible. For instance, Matsumiya wrote a caption on her Instagram to accompany a screenshot of sexual harassment that another Asian American woman shared with her:

My artist and model friend @– is extremely sick right now—she's been battling muscular dystrophy for most of her life and is experiencing epileptic seizures. She can't work so she can't afford to pay her medical or dental bills—her front teeth are falling out— and she received this abhorrent and twisted message. It makes me feel so nauseated that someone would try to take advantage of her situation like this. If you'd like to help . . . pay her medical bills out of the kindness of your heart and not because you expect predatory sex in return, please visit her GoFundMe page here: . . .

In this example, the sharing economy of emotions involves a financial motive of pooling individual economic resources. Interestingly, the donation is collected on another neoliberal platform: GoFund*Me*

(I emphasize "me" here to highlight the "me"—the self/individual—as a key player in the neoliberal economy). Donations and charities that rely on individuals' resources (or the "kindness of [one's] heart") distract us from insisting that the structure (in this case, the unaffordable health-care system in the United States) be changed.

In Matsumiya's phantasmagoria,[3] the sharing economy of emotions works in two ways. First, she crowdsources emotions by way of asking other Asian American women to send her their sexual harassment screenshots so she can share them on her Instagram account. She posted, "I don't know if you knew this already, but I accept submissions for Perv_Magnet! Please tag me or DM me the disgusting messages you've received. I'd love to post them to get a more complete picture. Thanks SO much for all the overwhelming support and positivity about my project! Xoxo." Note here how she emphasizes the positive affect, a disciplinary tool of the neoliberal self(ie), to highlight how she turns "disgusting messages" into a project that receives "overwhelming support and positivity." In this world of social media that is governed by neoliberalism, her Instagram followers are also expected to show up with their positive affects and externalize them in the comment box— that is, to perform as good neoliberal self(ie)s.

Matsumiya practices the sharing economy by way of what Schor identifies as the "recirculation of goods," except here it is the recirculation of emotions simulated by the solicited screenshots[4] of sexual harassment that is at work. The logic of the sharing economy is this: if a person doesn't have X (a car, a room, a particular emotion, etc.), others who have access to it may be able to share it with that person for a fee or for free. Moreover, in the sharing economy of emotions, if a person experiences something (such as sexual harassment or anything at all) and would like to process the emotion of that experience with other people, they can "crowdsource" others to share their emotions about the experience so as to better process the emotion collectively (the "feeling-with-other-ness"). For instance, when her followers commented "Nasty perv 😖" or

"F%cking disgusting f%cking PRICK 😡" to condemn the harassers, they provided Matsumiya with *their emotions* (e.g., by showing angry emojis and angry words). In this case, Matsumiya is crowdsourcing emotions from other people when she posts the screenshot of the harassing message on her Instagram to solicit other people's emotions.

In this sense, what social media does is it makes it acceptable for and even encourages people to air their "dirty laundry" publicly, so to speak. The degree of intensity of the emotions that are recirculated in the sharing economy then determines the value/currency of one's connection with one's followers/friends (as well as with oneself). It is this currency as a form of (social and emotional) capital that can be transformed into a different form of (possibly economic) capital (such as in the posting above, where Matsumiya asks others to donate to her friend's cause). In other words, by sharing and crowdsourcing emotions, a person may accrue some currency in the sharing economy of emotions, which can be accumulated and subsequently exchanged for other benefits.

Of course, people may share emotionally laden or emotion-provoking experiences on social media because it is cathartic for them to do so. Studies have found that venting or disclosing personal information on social media may help people mitigate stress and maintain better relationships with friends (Wendorf and Yang 273). As a side note, whereas women tend to disclose more about themselves, men tend to focus on other subjects; women also tend to speak more about their emotions than men in this space (Walton and Rice 1466, 1468).

However, when we crowdsource emotions from others, we never know who will arrive with what kind of emotional baggage and how they will then shape our emotional landscape. For instance, Matsumiya received a comment that says, "your on tinder what do you expect you attention whore >_>," which certainly projects a victim-blaming perspective and further harasses her. In this regard, Internet technology can be thought of as creating conditions of possibility where people can be more insensitive about how their words may affect other people's emotions. In an interview, Matsumiya mentioned how easy it is for people to be hurtful online:

> I definitely think it's true that people are much more open and aggressive online than offline. I think when there's no one standing in front of you giving you an emotional reaction, it's easy to forget you're talking to a human being. You might strike more viciously because of that, whereas in real life, you might just have a dark thought, but not act on it. (Guillermo)

What she is pointing out here is how our *sense* of reality (and not necessarily the reality itself) is altered when we are online. These historically specific technologies, materialities, and discourses inevitably help reconfigure human experience (Somaini 7) and the different ways in which we process our emotions.

On social media, as I argue throughout this book, emotions (or anything at all) have to be turned into a spectacle and phantasmagoria to gain any currency. When experiences and emotions are turned into and registered as a spectacle, or phantasmagoria, their end form and meaning will inevitably change. They may even be unrecognizable to the person who experienced them firsthand. A room will be less likely to be booked on Airbnb, for instance, if it is not adorned with beautiful decorations. Similarly, for screenshots of sexual harassment to have any currency on social media, they have to be turned into a spectacle and a phantasmagoria. To this end, Matsumiya does the work of curating—crowdsourcing, choosing which screenshots to post, and providing them with witty captions that appeal to her audience. Indeed, as she admits in one Instagram posting, "This one is so grim and repulsive, I actually can't even come up with a good caption for it." Matsumiya's note suggests that she actually takes time and effort to craft a "good caption" for each awful screenshot. She doesn't just randomly come up with them. For her Instagram to be successful and have many followers so that her anti–sexual harassment campaign can take off, Matsumiya has to do this work. As a result, the emotion originally attached to the screenshot is changed and now acquires different (if more entertaining, spectacular, and polished) meanings.

Here I touch upon one of the ramifications of the sharing economy of emotions: the absence of emotion's coarseness on social media. (When emotions appear on social media as a spectacle, they have to go through several layers of production.) My goal in pointing this out, however, is not to salvage the rawness of emotions, as emotions are always ideological and never "raw" as such (Ahmed, *Cultural Politics*). Rather, I am interested in querying the corollaries of the emotions' contour and content once they go through the process of being shared on social media, that is, after they enter into the sharing economy of emotions. I am intrigued to know what emotions we hide, repress, and let die because the neoliberal logic that governs this space dictates what emotions are deemed valuable and worthy of being externalized (and how to externalize them) on social media. What are the languages (modes of communication) and emotions that are lost when this is how we relate to each other on social media? Why do we post an event that evokes (or, in the neoliberal language, "crowdsource") emotions from others?

Certainly, in face-to-face interactions, people do share emotions with each other. The sharing economy of emotions on social media is different from other forms of interactions in that it is done virtually, and peer-to-peer, at times with virtual strangers, people with whom we have become "friends" or fellow "followers," even when we have never met them in person and therefore have no context for understanding them well. The scope of the interactions on social media is so much larger than that of face-to-face interactions, and when a person posts something on social media, they never know who will respond and how. Moreover, with social media, people have the ability to process their emotions instantaneously with others as they experience an event via live-tweeting or Facebook Live. In this sense, the act of sharing one's emotions online "live" can provide an emotional feedback loop that inevitably helps shape how a person processes their emotions in that immediate moment (the feeling-with-other-ness). Lastly, because the virtual technology creates a *sense* of distance, one may feel more comfortable in sharing an emotion that they may not have felt comfortable sharing in person. People do confess their love for the first time in a messenger/chat room, or, indeed, break up with their lovers via text message.

To claim that the emotions being re/circulated on social media function as a system of the sharing economy is to seek an understanding of their value, currency, and ramification. It is to question: if a system of economy suggests that what is being exchanged is not free, then what is the price we pay for entering into this economic system? Because an economic system can only thrive when there is an excess of value, where does the excess lie, or who accumulates this excess of value?

Throughout this book, I address these questions by asserting that even if a content provider accrues values by being able to sell their products on their social media or acquiring fame as a currency, it is the digital platforms (as the ultimate magic lanterns/tricksters) that often accumulate the most capital. I also caution us about how phantasmagoria reproduces affect alienation and narrows down both *how* we externalize our emotions and *which* emotions and emotional discourses are worthy of performing (and therefore become dominant) on social media.

Online Shaming

The second way the sharing economy or crowdsourcing of emotions operates in Matsumiya's phantasmagoria is through online shaming. Computer science scholar Amy de Vries provides us with a useful description of how online shaming typically unfolds:

> a person uploads material (e.g. screen shot, photo, video footage, texts) to popular social media sites (e.g. YouTube, Facebook) of some behaviour they have captured (or identified through other means) of someone behaving in a particular way that they disapprove of, or perhaps is deemed (by the person who uploads the material) to be contravening some form of expected social norm. As a consequence of the material being uploaded

to online sites, the behaviour is exposed, judged, and disseminated to the wider public; who may then respond in various ways. . . . The use of "online" infers the use of social media to facilitate this shaming process, however the behaviour open to "Public Shaming" can be online or offline in nature and the "shamed behaviour can be legal or illegal." (2055)

Thus, online shaming often targets individuals and is done by other individuals, not by institutions. It relies on the "audience" to amplify the shaming by commenting, sharing, or even adding to the shaming content (Detel 94–95; de Vries 2055). As such, the audience/followers on social media hold a key role in this aspect of the sharing economy of emotions. Without them, online shaming would not be as effective or as affective.

For instance, Matsumiya and her followers work together to shame the harassers she posts about. In the comments section, different followers call the harassers names:

Gross idiots

What an insect!

He's one of those losers who has to post a fake name and picture to shame women because he can't get a gf. Get a life, coward!

Dudes are shitty

What a piece of crap. That guy is going to rot in hell

What a loser

These comments exemplify how Matsumiya's Instagram followers go to her specific account to be affectively simulated[5] by the sexual harassment postings—they go because they want to *feel*. They want to access the emotions felt when reading these harassments, but from a safe distance. (The harassments are not addressed directly at the followers.) In accessing these emotions by way of going to Matsumiya's phantasmagoria and being affectively simulated by her postings—through the recirculation of emotions—they are participating in the sharing economy of emotions. Then, as they externalize their emotions by posting their comments, they further their participation in the sharing economy of emotions—they provide more emotions for others to feel with them.

Simultaneously, their comments show their disapproval of harassing behavior and work to "punish" the harassers by publicly humiliating them. Attacking a person's morality and employing naming and shaming techniques have often been used in media as ways to punish[6] an offender (de Vries 2056). As a form of punishment, shaming is understood as "a social act" (often hostile) that aims to express community disapproval of certain behavior and to give the shamed person a chance to apologize, correct their behavior and then be reintegrated back into the community (A. Cheung 304; de Vries 2054, 2056; Tarnopolsky 5). It is this social aspect of shaming that lends itself as a practice that can be easily adapted to a social media environment.

As a social and "public" act, shaming has historically been registered as a form of spectacle. In the Western past, for example, public shaming often went hand in hand with inflicting pain on the offenders and turning it into a public spectacle. In the seventeenth and eighteenth centuries, the pillory and stocks were common punishments for criminals (Whitman 1061). Punishments as public spectacles—hangings, for example, sometimes took place at carnivals—were used as deterrents in the eighteenth century (Morris 178). In nineteenth-century France, a convicted offender would have to perform a public apology in front of a crowd (Whitman 1061). By the mid-nineteenth century, however, with the rise of "human and civilized taste" and decency, public shaming spectacles as a form of punishment came to an end (Whitman 1072, 1075). As philosopher Michel Foucault describes, modernity and its notion of respect for the humanity of criminals contributed to the shift from public (usually corporal) punishment (pain as punishment and public spectacle) to the prison system (Foucault; Karavanta 210; A. Cheung 305).

In contemporary American society, punishment that operates by way of shaming continues, albeit in different forms, such as making offenders wear shirts that describe their crimes or posting YouTube videos of sentencing hearings that aim to shame criminals for their crimes (A. Cheung 304). If in the past, with the pillory and stocks, the crime was written beneath or near the body and the body had to take abuse in real time, in online shaming, words become a proxy for the body and the perpetrator may never need to actually experience the shame (i.e., he might never see Matsumiya's Instagram). In both cases, however, the use of shaming to solidify community values is the same. It is in the act of shaming that users reaffirm the community and its values (and hopefully deter others from whatever behavior has been deemed shameworthy).[7]

Its history as spectacle positions shaming as a perfect tool for the social media environment of phantasmagoria, where spectacle is an integral and imperative aspect. In Matsumiya's phantasmagoria, in addition to her witty captions, her posting of the images of the harassers can be considered an example of how she turns her screenshots into spectacles. In many cases of online shaming, when posting evidence of the harassment they experienced, women leave out their harassers' names and other private information. Maggie Serota, for example, when tweeting disturbing messages sent to her OkCupid account with her own #OkCupid hashtag, didn't reveal identifiable information or signifiers that could be traced back to specific individuals (Dewey). Matsumiya's online shaming, however, goes further. When posting screenshots, Matsumiya includes the names, sometimes email addresses, and oftentimes photographs of the harassers to expose and shame them for their behavior. Out of 102 of her repostings, 42 include the harassers' photos, email addresses, and/or names.[8] This strategy works to turn the screenshot into a spectacle and adds to the production of phantasmagoria.

The decision to expose harassers' faces and identities also reflects how the sharing economy works: it relies on a "reputational economy." This means that being shamed online undermines the harassers' ability to accumulate "reputation capital" (Shade 38). In a neoliberal economy, the main incentive to perform a good behavior or service is often to receive five-star evaluations on one's digital site. This ubiquitous rating system—and the obsession with receiving excellent, publicly available feedback from customers it promotes—functions as "the digitization of word of mouth" (Dellarocas 1407). Especially because the Internet and its technological apparatus make it easy for a shaming post to be spread globally, quickly, and permanently, it can truly affect one's reputation (A. Cheung; Detel 93).[9]

The popularity of online shaming[10] in the twenty-first century as a system of punishment and spectacle is indeed enabled by the technology of social media. It is this technological invention that allows Matsumiya to strike back. As she has acknowledged, prior to Instagram, although harassment made her "really angry," she didn't do anything with the messages she saved. She had planned to create "a coffee table book" out of them but never "had the courage to do it" (Ewens). When Instagram came along, with its ease of use, availability, and affordability, she decided to open an account and post the messages there. As Instagram is an image-based digital platform, it provides Matsumiya with a perfect venue to share her saved screenshot images. It was only after Instagram came into being that she was able to turn to social media, not only to provide "proof" of how racism and sexism exist in our society but also to express her feelings and strike back at harassers (Bahadur). Because of Instagram, she can online shame these offenders by revealing personal identifiable information to humiliate, socially condemn, and punish them. The offenders in turn become "transgressor-victims" (A. Cheung 302), as the plot thickens: the harassed now harasses back.

Feminist theorist Gayatri Spivak argues that it is the conditions in which the subaltern speaks but cannot be heard that raise the question "Can the subaltern speak?"; I argue that digital media provides a different condition of possibility for the subaltern (at least the subaltern who has access to social media) to talk back in ways that can finally be heard. Prior to Instagram, Matsumiya wasn't able to speak out and demand an apology; since she began posting, she has actually received apologies from some of the men who harassed her. After receiving an apology, she blurs[11] the personal identification of the individual to save them from being shamed any further.

Arising not only as an effect of technological innovation, online shaming also emerges as a direct result of the lack of institutional support for women.[12] Women find that sharing evidence of online harassment—irrefutable screenshots—with the police almost never leads to any changes (de Vries 2057). Their attempts to turn to institutional structures is often met with resistance or, worse, further harassment. This is why online shaming, particularly the shaming of sexual harassers, continues to rise, riding on the waves of the #MeToo movement. Indeed, "the primary instrument of redress in #MeToo is public shaming and criminalization of perpetrators" (Tambe 200).

When Matsumiya first received a threat, her initial response was to turn to the state and its apparatus, to seek institutional support. She called the police, but did not receive any assistance:

> They were unhelpful, telling me to just turn my computer off, as if this person was an imaginary being that lived in my hard drive. People didn't commonly use the internet back then, so I think the police didn't entirely get it. I ended up leaving the country for half a year to hide out. That person eventually ended up realizing the fear he had been causing me, and wrote to me with an apology, saying it was a joke and he had "just" wanted to scare me. (Guillermo)

This problematic police response, unfortunately, is a common one in a patriarchal society, as feminist scholar Kimberly Williams observes:

> The obvious question, often leveled at girls and women by everyone, from their harassers to the police officers they call in to stop the abuse, is, "If

you're being harassed, why don't you simply get off the Internet?" The in-
herent problem with such a suggestion is that, just as men do, women use
the Internet for work and play, and it has become a constitutive part of most
of our lives. . . . The suggestion, then, that women should get offline in order
to avoid being the victim of eVAW [electronic violence against women] is
akin to warning them to stay home in order to avoid being raped. (498)

Even on her own Instagram account, Matsumiya received this message: "but I don't understand why u don't just keep ur profile on private??? And block every one??" This comment, which once again puts
the responsibility back on to the woman to avoid harassment, was
quickly challenged by another Instagram user, who responded, "so we
should just all live in the safety of our house and never go out because
men can hurt us. . . . Why should WE hide, when we have done NOTH-
ING to deserve this kind of behavior." (This latter comment is interesting as it unintentionally hints that there may be women who actually do
"deserve" such treatment.) The rhetoric that asks women to get off the
Internet or to change how they dress so they can stay safe perpetuates
the victim-blaming perspective. Women, rather than the structure that
creates a rape culture, are once again viewed as the ones who are responsible for what happens to them. To demand that women stay away from
the Internet is to bar them from accessing this public space and to force
them to miss out on the many opportunities of being, living, and working in the digital world of the twenty-first century.

By first turning to the state to provide her with protection and justice, and—after it failed—undertaking consciousness-raising activism
to illustrate the systemic, racialized, and gendered ways in which Asian
American women are sexually harassed, Matsumiya certainly cannot
simply be likened to the neoliberal feminists that law professor Hila
Keren discusses in her article:

as a result of its privatized and individualized framing, neoliberal feminism follows the general neoliberal rationality in posing minimal de-

mands on the public state. Neoliberal feminists do not seek budgets for their projects; they go to Shark Tank and pitch their innovative ideas with graceful passion until they raise the millions they need. . . . The state, it is important to notice, is completely out of the picture, rendered insignificant and unnecessary in this privatized feminist journey. (91)

As Matsumiya tried to seek help from the police when she first received a threat, she does not render the state or the collective completely insignificant. However, the dominant cultural narratives provide her with a script for how to respond when the structures don't work: fix it yourself—it is your personal responsibility. In taking care of the issue herself by turning to social media, Matsumiya was indeed creative in finding a different resource to combat sexual harassment. Nonetheless, what "resources" look like is shaped by the neoliberal logic that is the dominant logic of the time. Thus, although Matsumiya might have other choices when institutions fail her, her sense of these choices is constrained by neoliberal ideology.[13] Neoliberalism tells women that when institutions fail to provide them with justice, they need to take matters into their own (virtual) hands—exemplifying the "privatization of political responses." When we contextualize Matsumiya's strategic resistance within the larger structure of power, we see a manifest example of how structure limits one's strategy.

How can we think, therefore, beyond online shaming harassers on an individual basis? If we continue focusing on harassers as individuals, without contextualizing their behavior as the product of a problematic culture that needs to be changed, we may foreclose the possibility of framing sexual harassment as a systemic issue of racism, sexism, and heterosexism. I thus wonder if instead of calling names, or calling oneself things like #pervmagnet,[14] perhaps the hashtags that are used to highlight sexual harassment should emphasize the importance of education, transformation, and *systemic* violence such as #StopSexualHarassment, #StopOnlineHarassment, #ThisIsHarassment, #racism, #sexism, or #SystemicViolence. As it stands, even the #MeToo hashtag still underscores the "me" of the neoliberal self(ie). Indeed, that is perhaps one of the reasons for its success: it speaks to the neoliberal self(ie)'s sensibility of focusing on the self, although it perhaps intends to highlight the systemic condition of sexual harassment, by the inclusion of the "too" in its hashtag. The #MeToo movement, while seemingly individual ("me"), is also a *collective* movement. It's the "too" that allows women to name their pain within a collective naming. Nonetheless, although it is arguably one of the most successful and global women's movements of our time, #MeToo has not been able to dismantle the structure of violence because the problem is still framed in individual terms, "*MeToo*," and therefore the solution is still registered at the individual level. The #MeToo movement successfully brought down famous NBC news anchor Matt Lauer, for example, but it let NBC off the hook for enabling a hostile work environment for women in the first place. While some individuals have fallen from grace, the structure remains standing strong.

We therefore need to collectively demand a better politics of accountability that imposes structural, legal, and financial (not just moral) consequences in online spaces to regulate behavior and deter users from sexually harassing others. We need to query: what better apparatus could be put in place in online spaces/social media so that this sexual harassment doesn't happen in the future? Perhaps, instead of having only the "like," "haha," "sad," and other existing buttons on Facebook and other social media, we could demand they have a button that represents "that's sexual harassment" to make it easier and less time-consuming for women (or anyone) to report and flag harassment when it happens. In other words, there may be ways to use social media to combat sexual harassment beyond the neoliberal mode of focusing on individuals.

As we aim for structural change, would it be possible that when reposting images that wound (e.g., screenshots of online sexual harassment), perhaps instead of ending our efforts there, we could simultaneously call people's attention to online harassment *laws* and *policies* and demand change by, for instance, providing a link to an online petition or other "action" activism that would help end sexual harassment? Perhaps what we need is a simple next step that would eventually weaken the violent patriarchal structure. Perhaps we are still in the process of unfolding, and it may be too early to tell what these movements against sexual harassment will end up accomplishing.

Kawaii Aesthetics, Racial Oscillation, and the Un/Masking of Race

The production of the neoliberal self(ie) in Matsumiya's phantasmagoria relies not only on online shaming as a form of the sharing economy of emotions but also, I argue, on the working of racial oscillation. Specifically, through the ways in which Matsumiya redeploys kawaii aesthetics (in this chapter, of cuteness and smallness) to mask and unmask her "race" as a Japanese American woman, she is able to cleverly and entertainingly strike back at her harassers and project her neoliberal self(ie).[15]

What is distinct about Matsumiya's Instagram campaign, and how it differs from the #MeToo movement, is the ways in which she highlights the deeply racist articulation of those sexual harassments that are uttered specifically to Asian American women. These messages, such as "Hey Asian whore want to get raped? I know where you live" or "People who like you, They probably have ugly Asian wife or watching AV video from japan. And they see that in your picture, you slut," purposefully deploy race as it intersects with gender and hetero/sexuality to produce harm and evoke emotional pain. Matsumiya is thus intentional in emphasizing the racialized nature of these harassments, commenting, "The messages I've published demonstrate specifically the experience of being an Asian-American woman online and the disturbing, predatory behavior that comes with that territory" (Guillermo). An Asian American woman, according to her, is seen as "submissive," and this seems to give these harassers permission to send whatever messages they want (Guillermo). She stated, "the Asian fetish factor definitely brings out the worst" in people (Guillermo). (A man with an Asian fetish who sexually harassed her was arrested because he was stalking another Asian

American woman, for example [Friedman].) In the American context, the representation of Asian women as sexually available, sexually "exotic," and docile has a long history and serves to uphold white supremacy, racism, and male dominance (Chou). Thus, through her Instagram page, Matsumiya aims to reckon with the political history of Asian American women's sexuality as "a site of victimization and pain" (Duncan 174) and exercise her feminist agency and her rights to demand public recognition for what happens to Asian American women, thereby providing an "intervention in the history of racism" (Cheng 174).

The history of Japanese and Japanese Americans in the United States has been filled with perpetual challenges. Between the late 1860s and 1880s, only a few hundred Japanese arrived in the United States (Glenn 22). Around that time, Japanese (as well as Chinese) immigrants worked jobs that were considered "too dirty, dangerous, or degrading for white men" and were paid less than whites (Glenn 24). One of the first groups of Japanese people to migrate to Hawai'i arrived in 1885 (E. Lee 111). In 1890, there were 2,039 Japanese in the continental United States (Takaki 180). Between 1908 and 1920, around 20,000 Japanese women traveled to Hawai'i and the United States as picture brides (E. Lee 113). Japanese women at the time primarily worked in agriculture or domestic service for white families (S. Lee 78). The Immigration Act of 1924 created a quota system based on national origin and excluded entry of people from countries deemed ineligible for citizenship (such as Japan). Thus, Japanese were barred from legal entry to the United States (Nakano 31, 104; Glenn 22).

In 1942, with the signing of Executive Order 9066, over 112,000 Japanese and Japanese Americans who lived in Washington, Oregon, and California were forced into concentration camps (Nakano 131). In 1945, these detainees of Japanese descent were finally allowed to return to their homes on the West Coast as the camps were ruled unconstitutional (Nakano 64). It was not until 1952, with the passing of the Immigration and Nationality Act of 1952, that Japanese (and Koreans) became "the last Asians to receive naturalization rights" (Nakano 67; Okihiro 73).

The anti-Japanese sentiment can be contextualized against the larger historical backdrop of Japan being perceived as a threat to the United States and the West as a whole. Through the image of the "feudally loyal samurai, the fanatically nationalist kamikaze, and the aggressively acquisitional corporate executive," as well as the "Sino-Japanese war, Japan's colonialist aggression in the Philippines and Korea, Pearl Harbor and the 'economic miracle' of the 1970s and 1980s," Japan was perceived as a force that could challenge the dominance of the West (Yamamoto 11). The notion of the "yellow peril" that began in Germany and became a global discourse in some ways emerged out of this "threat of Japan and the threat of Japanese immigrants" (E. Lee 122). In the United States, this Japanese threat was framed as a concern about "settlement"—when Japanese immigrants became "landholders," they were "entitled to a wife" (most often through the picture bride) and began to start families (Takaki 204).

To undermine and defuse this threat, since 1853, the West has actively otherized, orientalized, infantilized, and feminized Japan. In this process of feminization, the figure of the Japanese woman is constructed to represent the Japanese national, cultural, and racial identity (Yamamoto 5). In the process of romanticizing and exoticizing Japan, Japanese women are ideologically constructed in the American imagination as embodying different variations "of the geisha stereotype" throughout various historical periods (Yamamoto 24). Between 1860 and 1900, for example, the Japanese woman was constructed as "the sensual geisha girl" and "the devoted woman" simultaneously; then, between 1910 and 1945, as "the heathen woman, oppressed by Japanese men and Japanese culture, who must be saved by enlightened Christianity"; between 1945 and 1960 as "the emancipated Japanese woman, freed by postwar Occupation-style democracy"; and between 1970 and 1990 as "the empowered Japanese woman, recuperated through a combination of new social history and cultural feminism" (Yamamoto 23). In addition to these stereotypes, and within the context of the civil rights movement in the 1960s, Japanese Americans emerged as part of "the model minority" represented in popular media as "a uniformly hard-working, quiet, law-abiding people who managed to achieve economic success without governmental help despite being subjected to deplorable racism" (Niiya ix). This image appeared in the context of representing Japanese as obedient, nonthreatening figures.

To infantilize the Japanese, they were constructed to have a "physically childlike dimension"—when Japanese people spoke English, it was likened to the "garbling of toddlers"; the West touted Japan as a "paradise of babies" and reduced it "to a country of childlike women" (Yamamoto 11, 16). Japan has thus been de/historicized as "the timeless land of harmless, cute little people" (Yamamoto 17, emphasis mine). This concept of "cute little people" who are sexualized/romanticized is unsurprisingly found in the harassing messages that Matsumiya received and posted on Instagram.

The history of kawaii as "an aesthetic of smallness, weakness, and helplessness" can be traced to the post–World War II "trauma of the atomic bombing and Japan's diminished sense of itself as a military power" (Tran 21). Since the 1960s, however, Japan has rebranded kawaii and now successfully exports culturally "deodorized" products (a process that erases any traces of racial otherness) for global consumption (Tran 21). Kawaii no longer registers as a "symptom of an infantilized, feminized postwar Japan" but instead as representing Japan's "soft power" and ability to navigate and negotiate the complex global market (Tran 21). Kawaii has reached global and popular commercial success, relying on "visual commodity culture, the hyperfeminine, the infantile, and its Japanese origins"—it is known as a "'cute' aesthetic commonly associated with Japanese anime, manga, and *shōjo* (girl) culture" (Tran 19).

English professor Sharon Tran offers a different interpretation of kawaii—as "an Asian American feminist politics that both accounts for and accommodates vulnerability, dependency, and emotional liability. Kawaii attunes us to conditions where hard power cannot be mustered or would prove to be counterproductive" (35–36). A tension is thus embodied in kawaii aesthetics: it is a site of infantilization and exoticization and simultaneously a site of the "critical imaginary for developing a more nuanced theory of agency that complicates the binary logic of resistance and acquiescence" (Tran 36). However, unlike Tran, who sees kawaii aesthetic agency as a site to "theorize an Asian American feminist politics that contests a neoliberal logic of individual empowerment, choice, and responsibility" (20), in this chapter I still consider the kawaii aesthetics as being strategically employed *within* the construction and articulation of both the feminist *and* the neoliberal self(ie).

More specifically, Matsumiya redeploys and reoccupies kawaii aesthetics as a form of masking and unmasking race in social media interaction and as a way of performing her feminist subjectivity and neoliberal self(ie). For example, on November 10, 2015, she posted a screenshot of an online message that she received: "Very funny micro penis in ur face but i would not be the one cus my penis will take up ur entire face haha." She then wrote a caption to go with this posting: "Even if it did take up my entire face, my face isn't very big. Just saying. #pervmagnet." Using her caption, Matsumiya redeploys kawaii aesthetics by reclaiming how small her face actually is—and therefore the man's penis would still be considered small—to undermine his masculinity. The kawaii aesthetic of smallness is employed here to provide her with the weapon to strike back at the harasser and articulate the type of Asian American feminist agency that Tran alludes to. Matsumiya emerges here as a neoliberal self(ie) who is witty, independent, and equipped to defend herself against the predatory harasser.

That kawaii aesthetics is the *dominant* logic operating in the harassing messages that Matsumiya received can be seen from another posting of a screenshot of a harasser contacting her on social media: "You're so cute and tiny. I just want to shrink you down and keep you in my pocket! xD." The caption that Matsumiya wrote to accompany this posting was: "Want to know about an unusual fantasy/fetish that Im often approached about? Microphilia is a fascination with or a sexual fantasy involving tiny beings, usually beyond normal human size range. The fantasy typically involves one or more larger beings dominating a smaller being. ☺." In noting the pattern of harassment, Matsumiya is aware that fascination with smallness or "tiny beings" functions as a fetish that the harassers often subject her body to. Here, the Japanese-ness of her body is registered as a kawaii object (that is cute and small). Rather than projecting their Asian/Japanese fetish, the harassers use kawaii aesthetics (smallness/tiny being-ness) that is mapped on to the infantilized/romanticized/sexualized/feminized Japanese woman's body to mask the racialized process of this hyper/sexualization and harassment. In other words, the kawaii aesthetic masks the racial undertone of these harassments. It makes visible *how* these harassments are racist: by way of the deployment of kawaii aesthetics as a mask for racialized fetish and (racist) encounters. Reading these messages without the context of kawaii aesthetics, one might consider such a fetish as harmless/nonracialized, as one of her followers commented about this posting: "This honestly doesn't seem that creepy/Pervy to me." This comment also evidences how racial oscillation takes place during social media interaction: how some encounters are encoded as racialized/racist and yet are not decoded as such by other social media users.

A kawaii aesthetic is also at work when Matsumiya is likened to a schoolgirl (girl culture and schoolgirls are a significant part of the kawaii aesthetic), even though she is already in her thirties. A harasser wrote to her, "I tried watching Japanese porn, but it didnt work . . . cuz you're not in them!! i dont like you because you're Japanese, or you're this Music Star, or even because you're beautiful [. . .]. but because when i imagine walking through school, and seeing how groups gather against other groups, I know that I would've walked right up to you and grabbed your hand [. . .]." Here, the harasser takes pains to explain that Matsumiya's race, her Japanese-ness, is not the reason why he's interested in her. He doesn't have an Asian fetish. It is sexually fantasizing her as a schoolgirl that excites him. Yet framing a thirtysomething woman as a schoolgirl once again exposes the kawaii aesthetic that is at work, functioning here as a mask for the racialized way in which such people sexually harass Matsumiya.

This insistence on portraying Matsumiya as a very young girl can also be seen in many other postings, from "You seem like a spoiled racist little Japanese child!" to "U r trying to be 12 here. Mentally, u are sick.

Stop trying to be a little girl. Were u abused? Do u get pleasure being submissive? It's weird." For the latter posting, Matsumiya wrote a caption: "I've never seen anyone react so violently to a picture of me with pigtails." Here, the original picture that the harasser was commenting on was, according to the caption, Matsumiya in pigtails, a hairstyle that is popular among young girls in Japanese anime and manga—a dominant genre in which kawaii is the operating and dominant aesthetic. As a follower chimes in, perhaps sarcastically, "Cause only the Japanese wear pigtails, yup, #truth." Matsumiya deploys the kawaii aesthetic both in the original picture (her in pigtails) as well as in her caption (explaining that the comment was made in regard to her pigtails). And in responding to the violence of this racist harassment by stating, "I've never seen anyone react so violently to a picture of me with pigtails," Matsumiya redeploys, once again, kawaii aesthetics in calling out the racism of the harasser, but without calling the person racist as such. Matsumiya, through her caption, seemingly represents the violent words from the harasser as about pigtails rather than "race." The kawaii aesthetic—the mentioning of pigtails—allows Matsumiya to racially oscillate between unmasking and masking race in this interaction. For people who are not aware of the association between pigtails and Japanese kawaii aesthetics embodied in young female characters in anime and manga with this hairstyle, this conversation then becomes simply about hairstyle and not about race. A follower even asks, perhaps naively, "am I missin something? how is this nitwit a 'racist?'" This comment demonstrates how the kawaii aesthetic can be used to mask the issue of race and racism (that is, to racially oscillate) in these social media interactions.

The kawaii aesthetic can also be seen operating in "sadistic" and aggressive messages that Matsumiya frequently receives. Some examples of these messages from different harassers are:

after i dissect you i'm going to cook and eat your upper lip first

Damn you look good enough to eat! lol <wink

use crest and you'll be alright . . . can I tie you up and brush
your teeth?

In 6–7 years i will come to America and I'll try to find you . . .
mark my words

SO STUPID, MAN JUST FUCK YOU. SO SUCK WELL? WHEN I
SEE YOU, YOUR EYES SAID ME: YES I PRETTY YOU WANT ME

In these messages, as English professor Sianne Ngai suggests, the
kawaii aesthetic, or cuteness, may provoke "ugly or aggressive feelings,
as well as the expected tender or maternal ones. For in its exaggerated
passivity and vulnerability, the cute object is as often intended to excite a
consumer's sadistic desires for mastery and control as much as his or her
desire to cuddle" (816). These postings indeed hint both at the violence
the harassers want to enact upon her body as well as how cute she is—
she looks "good enough" to eat, or one will brush her teeth while tying
her up. In this way, "kawaii entails and seemingly invites violent forms
of objectification" (Tran 32). Being positioned as sexual objects furthers
the stereotype of how the "Japanese woman has been constructed not as
a subject with subjectivity but as a subject of serviceability. She has been
granted agency only insofar as it has served the interests of those other
than herself" (Yamamoto 60). For these harassers, Matsumiya is there
simply to serve (or to "suck" and "fuck").

What these sadistic messages also reveal is that the racist stereotype
of Asian bodies as "extraordinary" superhuman (or subhuman) bodies
that are represented to have a different relationship to pain from that of
Western bodies (which is then used to justify the inhuman treatment of
Asians) is still alive. As English and gender studies professor Rachel C.
Lee argues, the necropolitical theory of race governs how some bodies
(such as Asian bodies) are "construed as biologically distinct species-
beings that are assumed not to suffer or feel pain in the same way as
the valued humans of the global North or Western metropole do" (216).

Thus, the messages that articulate a fantasy of tying or cutting up Matsumiya's body may subconsciously carry the stereotype of Asian bodies as extraordinary bodies that do not suffer or feel pain.

The deployment of the kawaii aesthetics as a form of masking race in social media interaction allows Matsumiya to racially oscillate between marking/unmarking her body as racialized/Japanese and between calling out/toning down racism. In doing so, she manages to "construct the self as a subject within a society that constructs them as objects without agency" (Yamamoto 4)—in this context, the construction of the neoliberal self(ie). In other words, when these harassers always and already position Matsumiya as a sexual object embodying the kawaii aesthetics, her redeployment of the kawaii aesthetics to strike back at them, even as she projects a neoliberal self(ie) in the process, can be quite powerful as it allows for an articulation of antiracist feminist subjectivity, without her having to be explicit about it.

Masking Pain: Protecting and Projecting the Neoliberal Self(ie)

In addition to un/masking race, Matsumiya projects her neoliberal self(ie) by way of masking emotion, specifically through the deployment of sarcasm as her strategy. I would like to note here that the technology of masking, especially of emotions, can be employed as a form of racialized and gendered resistance. In the Japanese American women writers that Yamamoto analyzed, masking—be it psychological, narrative, or metaphoric—is employed as "a psychological defense mechanism" and a form of "resistance" (127). Moreover, because "the unreadable surface of Japaneseness" may be considered threatening by the dominant power, "the strategy of masking feelings" can function as "a way of protecting 'that other, private self'" (118, 119).

I need to make clear that in working with the trope of "masking," I do not mean to suggest that there is a "true" essential self underneath the mask. All selves (including the neoliberal self(ie)) are performative. Following in Yamamoto's footsteps, I thus consider "masking as a double-sided trope" that allows Matsumiya to "preserve a sense of dignity and selfhood" and "construct, protect and give voice to 'that other, private self'" (Yamamoto 117, 140). I refer not to the "private" self as the ultimate true self of the author/Instagram user/trickster/ Matsumiya—as if there is such an essentialized self to begin with—but, rather, to the private/privatized neoliberal self(ie) whose performativity needs to be protected to remain entertaining and appealing for it to have any currency and value in the phantasmagoric world of social media.

In Japanese American women's literature, the masking of emotions as racialized and gendered can be seen through the absence of the characters' facial (or verbal) expressions. Asian American literary critic King-Kok Cheung, in examining Hisaye Yamamoto's fiction, uses the term "articulate silence" to demystify the "Japanese American preference for nonverbal or indirect communication," through which Hisaye Yamamoto's characters "transmit" and "trans-mute" their "unspoken emotions" (219, 292). Rather than seeing the nonprojection of someone's feelings on their faces as a lack or repression of emotions, both Cheung and Traise Yamamoto invite us to imagine "masked" feelings as a different way of communicating or asserting one's agency. To claim or embody the mask as one's form of agency or to be articulate in one's silence is to insist on the impenetrability of the person's selfhood.

For example, a harasser sent Matsumiya this note:

When I saw your picture on your page, my first reaction was "DAMN!" Then I took a closer look and ended up going to your other pics to get a better look. What struck me in all your pictures was what I see in your eyes. . . . You portray yourself as this confident self assured woman but I can see the little girl hiding behind those eyes. I can see you hoping for the right person to look below the surface and see what a wonderful person you really are. I just thought you should know, I "see" you. I see past the façade, past the bluff, past the style, past the exterior (nice as it is), I can see that you that you protect. I just thought you should know that there is one person in the world that sees the you that you "should" be.

First of all, this note certainly provides further evidence for the working of the kawaii aesthetic: the harasser insists that Matsumiya is really just a "little girl"—that's who she *really* is—instead of the self-assured woman that she is projecting herself as. Second, the harasser claims that he can see the "you that you protect." Here, he is hinting at the ways in which Matsumiya uses a mask to protect "that other, private self," and how *he* is so special and thoughtful that he can see behind the mask. Instead of being seen as thoughtful, however, his gesture can be read as a move to assert his dominance over her—even as she's trying to hide the real her, he can see her—and as a way to manage his own fear of not being able to read beyond her mask (if, in fact, she has one).

For Matsumiya, this move can simply be seen as creepy, something that a pervert would do. In her Instagram response to this message, she wrote a caption that says, "This one sees me for who I really am, guys; the real me. #pervmagnet." Here, she uses sarcasm to poke fun at and undermine the harasser's self-proclaimed ability to see her for who she really is. Through her sarcastic manner of communication, she reframes his behavior as rather creepy—he is the perv to whom she is a magnet, rather than the sensitive soul who really sees her. In this way, Matsumiya deploys sarcasm as a way to mask her emotion and protect and project her gendered and racialized neoliberal self(ie) in the aftermath of sexual harassment.

If the harasser is correct in pointing out that there is a process of "masking" taking place, he is incorrect in locating where it is and pointing out its function. The mask is not, as he claims, evident in the pictures that she posted; it also does not function to hide her "true" or "private" self: the little girl hiding behind the mask. Rather, I argue, the technology of masking is registered in the caption of her postings—where instead of projecting the anger, pain, and hurt that she feels after receiving these messages, she projects the mask, the neoliberal self(ie) who is entertaining and funny, that hides these feelings. Matsumiya admitted in an interview that these messages make her "really angry" (Bahadur.) Yet had she projected that anger, instead of the sarcastic humor that she employs, her Instagram account might not garner as much attention as it has, because it would be less entertaining and therefore accrue less value in the phantasmagoric world of social media.

Indeed, sarcasm works well in Matsumiya's case because "sarcasm allows speakers a nonviolent means of expressing anger. . . . Speakers can vent their frustration and still remain polite" (Rockwell and Theriot 45). For instance, Matsumiya responds to a harasser who asked her, "Niiiiiiiiiice girl don't you thiiiiiiiiink you should knooooooooow meeeeeeeeee. . . . ," by saying, "Soooooooooorrrrrrrrrrry but nooooooooooooo." In this example, sarcasm works, as it often does, by way of "quot[ing] or otherwise repeat[ing] other people's words . . . and, by repetition, draws attention to their peculiar inappropriateness" (Haiman 25). This strategy is efficient (and humorous) in mimicking the harasser's writing style and thereby exposing its peculiar inappropriateness. In addition, instead of projecting the anger that she feels, she can remain "polite." In sum, Matsumiya strategically and successfully uses sarcasm on social media to speak about the pervasiveness of online sexual harassment and strike back at the perverseness of the harassers, all the while remaining polite, funny, and entertaining—once again projecting and protecting her neoliberal self(ie).

It is this tension that her Instagram account embodies, between being horrific yet humorous, that her followers find valuable. As they have commented:

I read the screen shots and I'm horrified. Then I read your captions and I laugh hysterically

These messages are terrible but your captions are hilarious

These posts are hilarious and horrifying. Stay safe!

Super creepy yet entertaining.

I think I am enjoying your responses to these creepers even more than the actual proof!

Anyone who's ever done online dating has hundreds of these messages and worse. I like her captions tho. Funny.

These comments show that, although the screenshots of the harassment Matsumiya experienced and posted on Instagram are not unique, how she frames them is perceived as entertaining and funny. Her wit and humor function not only as a technology of masking pain or anger but also as a mode of projecting the neoliberal self(ie) who her followers call "entertaining."

By way of employing sarcasm, Matsumiya is nonetheless able to strike back at the harassers as it is "a form of hostile humor" (L. Huang et al. 163). It is often used to wound another (Rockwell and Theriot 45). Education professor Cate Watson even defines sarcasm "by its intention to wound. . . . Sarcasm therefore may be open to the charge of offering merely gratuitous insult" (143). Communication studies scholars Patricia Rockwell and Evelyn M. Theriot similarly point out that sarcasm is uttered with a flair of "contempt or mocking, either of the listener or someone else 'in an attempt to wound'" (45). Indeed, Matsumiya often mocks the harassers, especially for their lack of intelligence. For example, responding to a comment that says, "i masterbated to yuo," she wrote, "I feel pretty bad for Yuo," to poke fun at the misspellings. If we carefully examine her captions, many of them can be read as hurtful, as they attack the *individual's* intelligence or character. They are funny as they make the "perv" the butt of the humor, as it were.

In this way, sarcasm can be used as a productive strategy in feminist activism as it subverts the power hierarchy and dominant structure (Douglas 95). For example, Matsumiya writes:

A message @— received on OkCupid. REAL male chivalry means asking if you want a dick pic before you send it, obviously. So polite! #pervmagnet

Here, she makes fun of the pathological and toxic heterosexual masculinity and "male chivalry" in a patriarchal society that creates a culture in which men would feel comfortable sending unsolicited pictures of their penis. Her sarcastic humor functions as "a form of resistance"—it reveals that it is "not women who are ridiculous (in the sense of being easy targets for ridicule), but the culture that has subjugated them" (Walker 143; D'Enbeau 26). As feminist media scholar Suzy D'Enbeau argues, feminist humor can be used not to trivialize the cause of pain but rather as a form of feminist strategic resistance to it (30–31).

Conclusion

This chapter speaks to the troubling ways in which neoliberalism shapeshifts Matsumiya's social media feminist activism, from aiming to raise consciousness surrounding sexual harassment against Asian American women as a systemic issue to being carried out in and having currency as a neoliberal self(ie). It focuses, first, on how Matsumiya's campaign operates under the system of the sharing economy of emotions. Then, it explores the working of racial oscillation as a technology of the neoliberal self(ie) in Matsumiya's Instagram—more specifically, how she redeploys kawaii aesthetics to mask and unmask race as she strikes back at harassers through her captions. Lastly, this chapter delineates her use of sarcasm as a strategy to mask her emotions, thereby allowing her to protect and project her neoliberal self(ie).

My analysis alludes to the ways in which, by attacking/shaming/making fun of the harassers as individuals and using social media strategies that widen her activism's reach, yet narrows down its effects, Matsumiya's campaign tiptoes around the structural violence that provides the conditions of possibility for the kind of harassment she encounters to happen in the first place. Feminist political scientist Jessica Megarry raises this issue with a Twitter campaign, #mencallmethings, that highlights sexual harassment in public spaces, similarly arguing that these hashtags do not challenge the structure that is conducive to creating this problem (52).

As a final and clarifying note, this chapter does not function as a plea to stop sharing our emotions on social media—or elsewhere, for that matter. It is the ways in which this practice is being appropriated and capitalized on by the neoliberal sharing economy that I find troubling and see as shortchanging our feminist movements. Social media should not simply be a container (and thereby shaping and limiting the expression) of emotions. Instead, we should consider social media as poetry, when it works as a site to excavate deeper layer of truths through languages that have the capacity to make us feel more and to expand the repertoire of our emotions, and as something that allows us to experiment and experience new, previously inexpressible, never-before-felt emotions. Social media as poetry also means that social media, like poetry, should function as a site where we can work through the difficult and impossible emotions and questions we have in and about our lives. Rather than sharing emotions on social media as a form of "investment" in ourselves and others (which is what neoliberalism teaches us), we should approach it as a form of loving interest in each other and in the ecology as a whole. (I speak more about love as a progressive social media practice in chapter 5.) It is through continuously seeking for a radical antidote, an alternative practice that can be a potential force of resistance, that we may eventually take back social media and challenge the entire patriarchal system.

4

Silence as Testimony in Margaret Cho's #12daysofrage

On November 1, 2015, Margaret Cho, one of the first and most success-ful Korean American women comedians in the United States, launched a social media campaign with the hashtag #12daysofrage in which she shared her sexual abuse story and asked others to tell theirs on social media using the hashtag. Cho created the campaign as she believes that "sexual abuse becomes self-abuse if you don't murder the rapist inside you. So it's about encouraging people to get rid of those awful feelings and express your rage. I think cathartic rage has to have voice."[1] In doing so, she carried forward the feminist tradition of speaking up as a path-way to liberation and healing. Simultaneously, she enacted the political potential of pain by demonstrating how powerfully connective it can be when women hold, support, and amplify each other's pain narratives.

In this chapter, as in previous chapters, I examine how the neolib-eral discourse, in tension and in conjunction with feminism, shapes and limits Cho's feminist social media activism. Specifically, I turn to what political scientist Michaele Ferguson identifies as one of the three core concepts of neoliberal feminism, "individualization of persistent gen-der inequality" (230). The tweets analyzed in this chapter will illustrate how sexual abuse is framed as an individual issue. When sexual violence is interpreted through a neoliberal lens, it is seen not as a structural expression of gender inequality and toxic masculinity, but rather as a result of "bad luck" or "bad choices" that certain individuals make. The solution then rests, once again, on the individuals who experience these abuses.

Unlike previous chapters, this one focuses not only on postings that *do* share sexual abuse stories but also on tweets that respond to Cho's in-vitation to share stories of sexual violence by *not* doing so. I thus explore the theoretical possibilities not only of speech but also of the spaces of silence (what I call "silence as testimony") surrounding the hashtag #12daysofrage. In other words, when Cho's attempt to socially mediate and publicly share her pain is met with the unwillingness of others to share their stories, this silence as testimony may tell us something important about the complex ways in which we engage with pain, with each other, and with each other's pain on social media differently. To understand silence in this way is to comprehend the currency of silence in the sharing economy of emotions. It is to build our capacity to find refuge in silence when speaking up about one's sexual violence on social media becomes compulsory and therefore a form of violence in itself.

I offer the concept "silence as testimony" to name the ways in which silence can function as a *collective testimony* when a group of people perform such silence on social media. Certainly, feminist scholars have discussed the usefulness of silence. (I will explore this scholarship later in this chapter.) In some ways, this chapter draws on and aims to extend existing scholarship on feminism and silence by interrogating silence as it is practiced on social media and from a digital media perspective. I intend to show how social media allows us to perform silence in a different way—that is, not as a mere absence, but rather as an unwillingness to engage with the invitation to tell stories of sexual abuse on social media. Silence as testimony can be understood as a form of holding space, as a different way of being present online, and as a form of witnessing. Through this concept, I want to illustrate that when it is intentional, the space of silence can be quite powerful.

Silence as testimony is also useful in shifting our understanding of feminist agency, which is often constructed through "voice" or "breaking the silence." Here, I offer the possibility that collective silence can be a feminist option—that is, registered as a vocabulary within the repertoire of feminist agency—for responding to others' invitation to tell stories of sexual violence on social media or to participate in online campaigns. To exercise this option is to challenge the hierarchy of voice as having more value than silence. Of course, this does not mean that we should stay silent in the midst of injustices, but rather that silence can remain a possibility in the midst of the imperative to speak up as a way to prove one's feminist agency, especially when it may not be safe to do so. This is why I prefer to call it "silence as testimony," rather than simply "silence." Silence as testimony allows us to reveal the problematic patriarchal structure that conditions the very production of that silence. Functioning as testimony in this way, silence can be powerful when performed *collectively* on social media.

In this chapter, I theorize *with* silence by carefully examining what is unsaid. First, I examine the ideological silence (i.e., what cannot be said because it is so much a part of the thought of our era that we can't see or talk about it) of neoliberal discourse that informs Cho's online feminist activism and, in particular, her notion of healing and her feminist goal to end sexual violence against women. Second, I explore the silence that is performed through the tweets and the ideological work that it does (i.e., functioning as a testimony). And lastly, I lay out the ramifications of theorizing through and with silence in rethinking feminist agency. Before proceeding with these analyses, I will provide a brief context for Margaret Cho and her #12daysofrage social media campaign.

Margaret Cho's #12daysofrage

Margaret Cho was born in San Francisco in 1968, three years after the US Congress passed the Immigration and Naturalization Act of 1965, which led to the first big wave of Korean migration to the United States (Min and Song 46; Kim and Grant 236). Korean Americans can be considered one of "the newer immigrant groups" who moved to the United States after the act was passed (Kim and Grant 236). Prior to 1965, Koreans migrated only in small numbers, as "diplomats, students, and merchants landed in Hawaii" around the 1880s and laborers for sugar plantations starting in 1883 (Okihiro 133).

There were disruptions to the flows of migration from Korea. In 1905, due to reports of Korean migrants being mistreated in Mexico, their government stopped sending workers to Mexico and other places, including Hawai'i (Chan xlii). Additionally, there was pressure from Japan to close the emigration office as their workers were competing against each other. In 1907, due to Executive Order 589, which barred migrants' movement from Hawai'i to the mainland—targeting Japanese and Korean laborers—migration was further interrupted (Chan xlii–xliii).

What is especially important to note here is that the troubled Japanese-Korean relationship shapes Korean immigrants' experiences in the United States. For instance, when Korea was under Japanese colonial rule between 1910 and 1945, Koreans who were abroad became "stateless exiles" (E. Lee 145). Around 1930s, anti-Japanese sentiment was observed in the Korean immigrant community (Takaki 281). In addition to the problems they had to endure because of Japan's colonial power, Koreans also experience racial discriminations in the United States because Americans "associate[d] them with the Japanese" (Takaki 271). That Koreans were often mistaken for Japanese was intimately detailed in Mary Paik Lee's *Quiet Odyssey: A Pioneer Korean Woman in America*: when she asked her doctor if something was wrong with her newborn son's eyes (she found out six years later that there was), he dismissively responded, "All you Japs have small eyes. What are you worried about?" (Chan 114).

By 1990, the Korean population in the United States had reached over 700,000, from less than 100,000 in 1970 (Min and Song 46). Nonetheless, representation of Korean Americans in popular culture was almost nonexistent, as had been true throughout the twentieth century. The first (and at the time only) TV sitcom to feature a Korean American family was *All-American Girl*, and Margaret Cho was its star. Unfortunately, the sitcom ran for only nineteen episodes (1994–1995) as the Asian American community criticized it for perpetuating "orientalist stereotypes" (Danico 890). In playing the stereotypical Korean American lead character, Cho was criticized for not being Asian enough. Network executives then hired an "Asian consultant" to help her be more "authentically" Asian (i.e., to better represent a stereotypical Asian);

additionally, they also hired a group of people to help coach Cho to lose weight as her producer told her that she was too fat and her face took up too much space on the screen (R. Lee, "Where's My" 119–120; Pelle 25). His exact words, Cho reported, were: "The network is concerned with the fullness of your face. They think you're really overweight [. . .]. And do me a favor, do not wear a mini-skirt in public again" (quoted in R. Lee, "Where's My" 119). Although, at first, Cho did lose weight at an unhealthy rate, when the show was cancelled, she went on a self-inquiry quest that eventually led her to embrace her weight and herself, and to create a show and a biography that assert her self-acceptance, titled *I'm the One That I Want*.

Cho is a self-proclaimed feminist. As she shared on xojane.com, "my feminism—it's kind of necessary. I don't want to feel like I am less than anyone, and so I have to label myself in order to be ready for the fight." Cho also identifies as queer, "beyond bisexual," a "fag hag," and a "slut" (Reed 763). She often uses her jokes to challenge heteronormativity and express her antiracist, antisexist politics. Through her comedy sketches, she shares intimate moments of sexual pleasure and racial pain in ways that "alleviate the shame she once felt for her 'inauthentic' racial performance and her 'excessive' face, vagina, and body size that were threatening to 'take over America'" (Pelle 33). In this way, Cho sees herself doing feminist and activist work, refusing to be controlled and contained by the norm.

Some of Cho's activism takes place through her Twitter account. She's a prolific user, having tweeted over 28,500 postings as of May 3, 2019, at which point she was following 97,600 people and being followed by 489,000. She tweets on almost every subject possible, from politics to food to hair to clothing to dogs, with much frankness and humor. The hashtag #12daysofrage and the YouTube videos that accompany the Twitter campaign are only some of her critical online feminist activist endeavors to end rape culture and other forms of violence. Through the hashtag that she created, Cho aims to hold a space for women to take back their stories and lives.

In some ways, Cho's #12daysofrage campaign is similar to Matsumiya's Instagram perv_magnet account. They were even launched around the same time: Matsumiya created her perv_magnet account in September 2015; Cho posted her first #12daysofrage video on November 1, 2015. They both share their own as well as ask others to share their stories of sexual harassment/violence/abuse. From her very first tweet, Cho invited others to post their stories: "Coming soon #12daysofrage I'm posting short videos about sexual abuse and encourage everyone to do the same! 1st one up shortly!" Her second tweet specifically asked people to send her their stories: "#12daysofrage send me videos telling me your stories of sexual abuse. There's no shame in what happened to us, so let us all come together." While Cho's campaign, unlike Matsumiya's, does not focus solely on Asian American women, she nonetheless hints at the racialized aspects of sexual harassment in some of her videos.

Through her #12daysofrage videos and tweets on YouTube and Twitter, Cho is deliberate in creating a buzz, a spectacle, and phantasmagoria. For example, the choice of "twelve days" was not random. She wanted to reference the "Twelve Days of Christmas" and so, for twelve consecutive days, from November 1 to 12, 2015, Cho posted one video each day on YouTube. These amateur/raw videos of Cho, mostly from a headshot camera angle, recounting the horrific occurrences of her sexual abuse, are short, from twenty seconds to just under a minute, each focusing a specific event that happened to her. On day six, for instance, Cho shares: "When I was a little, little girl, an old white man and his granddaughter grabbed me in a swimming pool, he put his fingers in my anus and my vagina and lifted me up out of the water and he said, 'I caught a fish,' and [the] lifeguard and my family laughed." And on day seven, Cho recounts another story: "When I was in South of France, a family of four chased me down. The father and mother grabbed me by the arms, the son pushed his fingers in my vagina. The daughter bit my arms and spit on me. They looked very wealthy, like they were having fun. And I ran into a store and they came in and they were looking for me and I found a back entrance and I escaped." The stories Cho shares are heartbreaking—a few times, she tears up or has a hard time speaking as the pain of the trauma she is describing overwhelms her.

In the above videos, race functions as a structure on which the narrative of sexual violence hangs. Through her #12daysofrage YouTube videos, Cho, an antiracist feminist activist, told stories that mark and unmark race throughout, hinting at how the intersection of race and gender colored her sexual abuse: it was "an old white man" and a wealthy family in Southern France, presumably white, who sexually assaulted her. In this case, sexual violence/assault/harassment *is* racialized. However, tweets from Cho's followers do not necessarily pick up on these racialized observations. There could be many reasons why people do not feel compelled to respond to the racial aspect of sexual violence. The invitation for her hashtag activism was open to everyone, of all genders, races, and sexual identities. Nonetheless, the response (or lack of it, in this aspect) provides us with more evidence of "racial oscillation": how in the social media world, users and content creators may oscillate between marking and unmarking someone's race, the self or others, as they see fit.

After posting videos for twelve consecutive days, on the thirteenth day, Cho premiered her song "I Want to Kill My Rapist" on YouTube as a finale, so to speak, for her #12daysofrage social media campaign. Her phantasmagoria was thus created through multiple platforms. Collectively, the YouTube videos and the hashtag campaign on Twitter function as a phantasmagoria that turns narratives about sexual violence into a "spectacle" that people all over the world literally watched. Each of her #12daysofrage videos were seen by 3,200 to 8,500 viewers.

For this chapter, I used the Twitter search app with the hashtag #12daysofrage and collected all tweets that were available posted from November 1, 2015 (the first day of the twelve-day series) to November 13, 2015 (the day Cho posted her "I Want to Kill My Rapist" video). I collected a total of 1,926 tweets over the thirteen-day period the campaign took place. All tweets with the hashtag that appeared in the Twitter timeline during this period were then manually logged and discursively analyzed. Rather than simply finding the most common pattern within a particular discourse, I also looked for a pattern in which *silence* exists in the texts. I paid attention to the unsaid, what text cannot say, and how ideology limits what text can and cannot say.

Healing in Neoliberal Times: The What and Why of #12daysofrage

At the core of #12daysofrage is an invitation to "heal." As Cho tweeted, "You can be conservative + hate rape. You can be liberal + hate rape. This is not political in that way. It's about us healing #12daysofrage." Healing thus emerges as the ultimate and necessary goal: it drives the campaign. Cho, however, is very particular in suggesting *how* healing can take place. She tweeted, "We are only as sick as our secrets. Let's heal. I'm healthy now. #12daysofrage." Through this tweet, Cho insinuates that keeping secrets makes us sick. To heal and be healthy like she is now, we need to tell our secrets. But why, one may wonder, does telling our secrets lead to healing? Why is healing (presumably, to be free from pain) the goal? What kind of healing is the goal? Is there not a different way of healing or even of engaging with pain? The answers to these questions, I argue, rely on our ability to situate Cho's online feminist activism within a neoliberal context. In Cho's campaign, as is in kaur's (see chapter 2), healing as a process becomes "work" that a person is responsible for. It becomes our *personal responsibility* to share our secrets, speak up, and listen if we want to heal. I would argue that secrets make us sick only if we assume that to stay silent is to contain the rage and bury it until it "threatens to destroy the narrator and the life she has rebuilt" (Duncan 78). This is the assumption of Cho's campaign, that there is no healing possibility outside voicing our rage and that there is no possibility of having a meaningful relationship with our pain that does not involve healing.

Neoliberalism indeed demands that we see healing as "work" (of tending to the materiality of pain and the commodification of healing through "pain-killing" products, for example) and an "investment" in one's self. A neoliberal healing practice is registered through narrativization about overcoming adversity through the individual's hard work. The key words and key works in a neoliberal process for healing seem to be "self-transformation" and "self-reliance" (Windle 253). A tweet from a follower addressed directly at Cho exemplifies this line of thinking:

> @margaretcho I got therapy and have let go of so much. Life is good now. We can thrive #12DaysOfRage

The values associated with the neoliberal economy are at work when citizens as consumers are asked to participate in a lifelong learning process (both in the formal and informal sense) that is self-motivated and self-funded (Windle 252). As suggested by the example above, women are asked not only to have the motivation to go into therapy but also to pay for it themselves. (Wouldn't it be interesting if rapists, as part of their punishment, had to pay for therapy? Or, better yet, the government, for failing to provide safety for its citizens, could pick up the tab.) Addressing this issue of healing as individual work, psychologist Sharon Lamb suggests that we need to focus on a cultural rather than an individual approach in dealing with abuse, which means involving and paying attention to boys, not only girls, and to stop asking women to focus on how they resisted rather than how they were violated (132, 133).

It is also important to note here that putting together and posting videos about sexual trauma online are forms of "work." There are different kinds of work that are involved here that should not go unnoticed: from emotional work to recording work to posting work to "promotional" work to campaign work (e.g, being interviewed on television) to mobilizing-through-digital-platforms work. All of this took place on Cho's own time and dime, so to speak. This exemplifies how neoliberalism's solution to sexual violence is to turn to individuals, to individual women, to do the work of healing *and* the (activist) work of ending sexual violence.

Neoliberalism also frames, based on my analysis of #12daysofrage tweets, how women interpreted what happened to them. For example, the tweet "#12DaysofRage I was raped by my boyfriend when I was thirteen, he was almost seventeen. I didn't tell anyone. I hated myself so much" shows how one woman blames herself for what happened to her. Another tweet, "I've been sensitive & emotional the past couple days. Let's remember to self care through our #12daysofrage #healing @margaretcho," exposes the belief that caring for ourselves is our personal and not a communal or an institutional responsibility. As American studies scholar Catherine Rottenberg argues, "self-care work [is] necessary to cultivate a 'mature' and positive neoliberal feminist subjectivity, whose objective is not only balance but also—and crucially— 'presenting' happiness" (113). In other words, under the neoliberal logic of affect as a disciplinary apparatus, a person's unhappiness (or unbalance) is their own responsibility or fault: they did not do the work of self-care. To post on social media that one does self-care work (or to remind others to do so) is to perform happiness in this space—that is, to project the neoliberal self(ie).

Another tweet, "@margaretcho Let's exercise COmPassion by kindly educating those who say 'Get Over It' w/Patience & Self-Love in our telling! #12DaysofRage," demonstrates how one person encourages Cho and others to educate other people about sexual violence in kind and compassionate ways, the way a good neoliberal subject who is disciplined through the affective apparatus would do. Individuals, rather than institutions, are again the ones being asked to do the work of teaching others about sexual violence. Neoliberalism equips us with blinders that make invisible the ways in which the power structure helps shape individuals' life experiences and how interdependence works among individuals and institutions.

To further break down the working of neoliberalism in framing Cho's feminist online activism, and how it helps shape the Twitter responses to it, I will share a few more examples. First, within the neoliberal structure of power, individuals become subjects who know what's best for them. Rather than focusing on structural inequalities and institutions, they see what happens to them as their own responsibility. It may be useful here to restate what geography professor David Harvey has pointed out, that neoliberalism has become a hegemonic power by becoming the invisible lens through which we make sense of the world we live in (3). As a hegemonic discourse, neoliberalism shapes the prevalent view that healing rests on the shoulders of individuals. Hence, when Cho proposes that to heal we need to speak up, speaking up is formulated within the "neoliberal technologies of responsibilization" that frame how fortune and misfortune are related to the individuals' personal responsibility (Stringer 115). If you don't speak up and you don't heal, then it's your fault—that seems to be the implication. The following tweets show how neoliberalism shapes Cho's Twitter followers' responses:

> Been raped 3 times, sexually abused as a baby and young child & used in human trafficking. I am strong & wise. #12daysofrage @margaretcho

> Confused. Angry. Sad. Scarred. Scared. But most importantly, here. Survivor. Conqueror. Healing. #12daysofrage @margaretcho

> #Isurvived because I am more than the sum of my traumas. I'm a kick ass woman of infinite possibility #12daysofrage @ margaretcho

What these tweets suggest is that the narrative of sexual violence becomes a narrative of the individual self as a "strong & wise" woman, a "survivor" and "conqueror," and a "kick ass woman"—the neoliberal self(ie). None of these tweets, however, criticize the structure and technology of patriarchy that create rape culture in the first place. Not only that, in a neoliberal world, women are being asked to do the *work* of healing, that is, to be the best version of themselves against all odds and structural barriers (e.g., "I am more than the sum of my traumas") and to share their victories on social media, which is the imperative mode of performing the neoliberal self(ie). As law professor Hila Keren argues, "the neoliberal feminist project requires each woman to cope with gender inequalities by working on herself and pushing through gender-related obstacles with confidence and determination" (90–91).

Another example of how these Twitter responses reveal neoliberal ideologies at work is how Cho is put on a pedestal—the individual cast as a hero. The following tweets exemplify this:

thanks @margaretcho for challenging the typical rape victim construct with art & humor. you are my hero! #Iwanttokillmyrapist #12daysofrage

I have a hero. It's nice to have a hero. You should get a hero. It's helpful. #12DaysOfRage #HERO

#12DaysofRage @margaretcho leads rape survivors in a cleansing. [link]

@margaretcho I want to commend you for #12daysofrage. This discourse has to happen. Sexual violence is too prevalent and nothing is done.

Thank you, @margaretcho #IWantToKillMyRapist's 4 minute runtime did more for my healing than countless hours of "therapy". #12DaysOfRage

I'm very grateful to @margaretcho for #12daysofrage. Thank you for taking on such a huge weight and for making the world a safer place.

@margaretcho You're the voice of our revolution. I'm healing through my story of abuse & thank you for uniting the survivors #12daysofrage

Oh man I've always been a fan but this is straight up healing beauty—I think you'll get your fucking parade #12daysofrage @margaretcho

@margaretcho is an angel of love and understanding. Follow her feed for stories of strength & survival. #12DaysofRage

@margaretcho @—Margaret thank you for caring and united us all in pain, survival and rage [heart emoji] #12daysofrage

There are several layers to peel back here. First, these tweets clearly show that Cho is hailed as a hero. This narrative coincides not only with the appealing, empowering, and inspiring neoliberal self(ie) but also with the uniquely individualized superheroes of mass culture. I am reminded of critical development studies scholar Ilan Kapoor's argument that one of the prominent features of neoliberalism is "individual initiative and heroism" (46). The thread that runs most strongly through these tweets is that Cho, "an angel of love and understanding" and "the voice of our revolution," becomes the individual with the capacity to make a change: while "sexual violence is too prevalent and nothing is done," she is "taking on such a huge weight and . . . making the world a safer place." Certainly, these tweets do not intentionally erase the unwavering work of so many activists and organizations who have been advocating for an end to sexual violence for a long time. However, when neoliberalism becomes a hegemonic lens through which we see the world, we become blinded to interactions between structure, individuals, and collective work. We focus on particular individuals, such as Cho, highlight their individual initiative, and put them on a pedestal as our "hero" who has the capacity to "car[e] and unit[e] us all in pain, survival and rage." And, of course, if you don't have a hero yet, as one of the tweets suggested, "You should get a hero. It's helpful."

The narrative of heroism meshes well with the "I am a survivor" narrative. For, as a "survivor," the victim becomes an agent, a resistor; as

Lamb in critically examining new notions of victimhood writes, "whatever she did, whether it was to dissociate, kill her oppressor, dress up for him, or not tell her mother, she did this to 'survive'" (119). Even Cho herself uses the term "survivor," as in this tweet: "Send me your videos— tell me your story. #12daysofrage I was a victim of rape for far too long. Now I'm a SURVIVOR! Tell me how you lived." Focusing on one's survivor identity carries the residue of the neoliberal mode of viewing the self, in that it positions change as once again within the realm of the individual rather than the structural (Lamb 121). This narrative of "survivor" as inspiring, appealing, and entertaining is symptomatic of neoliberal culture, which focuses on *self*-transformation rather than community/ecological/structural change.

It is important to clarify here that my analysis should *not* be read as a criticism of these women, who not only have had to go through the pain of systemic sexual violence and different forms of injustices, but also have gathered the courage to transform their lives in spite of what happened *and* share this on social media. Rather, and most significantly, the analysis in this chapter (and this book, for that matter) is intended to show how neoliberalism shapes how we think about ourselves and how we engage with pain and the world, and how it limits our feminist social media practice and activism. It is the *neoliberal way of thinking* that is at issue here and that I am criticizing. It is the neoliberal discourses that shape the kind of feminist activism that Cho and her followers perform on social media, as well as influence how they engage with pain and healing, that I am challenging. The call here is thus not to abandon online activism, feminist activism, or women's voices. Rather, it is to make visible the ideological work that is somehow carried on through Cho's and other feminist campaigns on social media and to find an alternative mode of social media activism.

Another layer that must also be uncovered here is Cho's celebrity status and her online presence. Being a celebrity in a neoliberal culture holds its own currency. Indeed, the underlying milieu of Twitter culture is celebrity culture. When a celebrity sheds light on a particular issue, it may bring more attention to the subject matter (Gotham 98). In Cho's case, her celebrity status certainly boosted the success of her campaign, at least in the form of more media coverage.

Nonetheless, although celebrity activism has allowed for particular causes to receive wider attention, it also has led people to become more complacent. Celebrity activism helps create an affective structure within which we can feel good about ourselves and the social problems we are facing, because we think that someone else is doing something about it so we don't have to. This is deeply problematic, as this process not only shows how "ideology is externalized and materialized," it also creates an illusion that as a society we have progressed when in fact no significant changes have happened at the structural level (Kapoor 103).

The #12daysofrage tweets may be considered "pseudo-activity" that simply "mask[s] the nothingness of what goes on" (Žižek, *On Violence* 217; Žižek, *How to Read* 26). Although Cho's tweet "Xoxoxo #12daysofrage the video tomorrow for #killmyrapist will heal us all. I promise. And you are brave. I love u" promises that all will be healed, it actually "masks" the fact that no significant structural change has happened or even been called for. Not only that, this very narrativization of sexual violence becomes a spectacle that does not encourage further political participation (Evans and Giroux 32).

It is important that we recognize the power relationships that emerge out of these spaces of silence, speech, and suffering, and ask, *Who gets to encourage whose speech? Where and under what conditions can this speech be heard?* This latter question is of particular significance—as feminist scholar Sorcha Gunne reminds us, "to speak about rape in a space that is disempowering does not constitute healing" (168). As feminist theorist bell hooks similarly points out, "naming the pain or uncovering the pain in a context where it is not linked to strategies for resistance and transformation created for many women the conditions for even greater estrangement, alienation, isolation, and at time grave despair" (*Talking Back* 32). In other words, feminism may "create" even more pain when it provides women with a lens to see the problems they experience but does not offer them strategies for change at either the micro or macro level. As psychologist Dana Sinopoli states, "discussing one's sexual assault before the survivor is ready to retell her story can be damaging to the survivor and to her healing process . . . the healing process needed to have reached a certain point before the survivor felt ready to engage in this project" (37). This reminds us of the ethical issue involved in asking survivors to share their stories on social media when they may not be ready to do so.

The harder task here is to transform a public space such as Twitter into an empowering space. One might argue that a more private online group, mediated and monitored by a healthcare specialist or a spiritual leader or whoever is deemed able to provide loving and helpful assistance to these women, could be a safer space for them. The point here is to be mindful of the institutional and emotional support that women may need throughout the process.

Another suggestion would be to make sure that the process of telling stories about sexual violence makes the women who are telling the stories feel humanized. This can be done, for example, by allowing women to identify and express how structural oppression and "social toxicity" shape their daily experiences and how to reclaim their power in that context. When testimonies and storytelling are rendered "sacred practices" instead of tools with their own standard measurements used to simply help people heal, it can be humanizing and powerful (Pour-Khorshid 185).

It is also important to challenge the assumption that everyone wants to have the same kind of relationship with pain: to get rid of pain by way of healing and to do so through speaking up, which seem to be the goals of Cho's social media activism. The notion that speaking in groups about "personal" things can lead to collective political activism may be traced to some of earlier feminism's assumptions about consciousness raising and activism. However, instead of simply maintaining this assumption, we may want to ask these women: what kinds of relationship do they envision themselves having with pain? Perhaps some may indulge the idea of embracing pain rather than pushing it away, or of processing pain in ways that do not involve speaking up. We should not assume that healing is everyone's goal. For feminist theorist Gloria Anzaldúa, the ultimate goal should not be about healing but rather about feeling the pain and creating new meanings for it, so it can expand and lead us into new forms of being (Bost 24–26).

The assumption that talking to heal is desirable is problematic because that is not always the case. In some cases, talking can create even more pain, because "talk is performative. It creates that which it names. Not only does it not dispel pain by (perhaps impossibly) pinning it down with a word nor does it 'lead to less pain' . . . it makes more" (Polloc 169). To claim that speaking up is the path to healing is to acknowledge only *one* mode of relating to pain.

What about not speaking? Can it lead to healing? Can we have a different relationship with pain through *not* speaking? This is what communication scholar Kimberlee Pérez asks us to consider in arguing that a practice of silence would allow us "to recognize and honor pain as that which brings about healing, into living conocimiento [with awareness]" (208). Thus, how can we *also* honor silence in our journey to create new relationships with pain? What are we really (with)holding in our silence? These questions are an invitation to have a dialogue on how we can engage with silence and craft new relationships with pain as it is shared online. I turn to this issue next.

Silence as Testimony and Digital Spaces of Silence

In carving a theoretical space from the edges (rather than the center) of what is said, or rather, tweeted, I am thoroughly intrigued by tweets that force us to take into account the power of what is left unsaid, cannot be said, and will not be said. I am taking a lead here from literary critic Pierre Macherey's argument: "What is important in a work is what it does not say. This is not the same as the careless notation 'what it refuses to say,' although that would in itself be interesting: a method might be built on it, with the task of *measuring silences*, whether acknowledged or unacknowledged. But rather this, what the work *cannot* say is important, because there the elaboration of the utterance is carried out, in a sort of journey to silence" (97). It is this "journey to silence" as an ideological journey that I find intriguing.

In this section, I examine Cho's #12daysofrage Twitter campaign by critically reading those tweets that answered her call to share stories about sexual abuse with silence, or, to borrow literary theorist Trinh T. Minh-ha's words, with "a will not to say or a will to unsay" ("Not You" 373). I aim to understand the consequences and conditions of ideological possibility of speech that does the work of being *performatively* "silent." In other words, although people who tweeted that they cannot share their stories can't simply be categorized as being silent—if silence is defined as the absence of voice—because they *did* tweet, they nonetheless remain "silent" by not sharing their stories, thus straddling a line or occupying a space between speaking and not speaking.

Of course, silence is never *just* silence. Silence has multiple guises: "active," "generative," "creative," "expressive," "oppressive," "resistant," "political and ideological," and "meditative" (Clair 93; Fidyk 114). English professor King-Kok Cheung also differentiates between "the undesirable silences—the speechlessness induced by shame and guilt" and "enabling silences" such as the act of listening to another (20). There are silences, Cheung points out, that demand "utmost vigilance from writers and readers alike" and which "are the very antitheses of passivity" (20). Feminist scholars have taken on silence as a trope and discussed the multiple uses of silence in literature (and) history (Hedges and Fishkin; Olsen; Rosenfelt). Women's writing has often been "characterized by silence" in that silence is employed to "tell the forbidden and name the unspeakable" (K. Cheung 4). Some scholars, such as Hélène Cixous and Monique Wittig, uphold the idea that language itself is already and always patriarchal; to reject language is therefore to resist the patriarchy (Pfaelzer 1).

In this chapter, I aim to contribute to a new understanding and usefulness of silence by focusing on how it is performed on social media, the discursive stories it tells, and its function as testimony. Silence can tell stories and reveal something larger and more ideological than what is said. Silence can, according to Pérez, be used "as a practice and tactic for reading and producing narrative and relation" (204). Feminist scholars Aimee Carrillo Rowe and Sheena Malhotra argue that "as cultural workers we must become fluent in reading what is not said, or what is actively omitted, to unravel the imperative to domination embedded within any efforts to represent or know 'others'" (9). In other words, by examining what is not said, we may tap into the dominant ideology that produces silence (about the other) and thus understand the other better. By way of focusing on silence, I aim to signal a shift in direction: one that moves us toward what can be heard and understanding how to hear. We must mindfully ask, "what can we hear when words cannot be spoken or when words do not quite convey what needs to be communicated?" (McCormack 181). What institutional changes should be carried out so that what was structurally silenced can finally be heard? (40, 43).

Silence also reveals power relationships. In the classic 1982 Dutch movie *A Question of Silence*, the woman defendant who murdered a male shop owner remains silent because, as the expert psychiatrist attests during her trial, she finds no use in speaking. This sort of silence may become women's way of resisting power domination and patriarchy. The unwillingness to say what the subject is not willing to say or what the subject cannot say is a work of ideology. Silence and speech fracture and structure one's relationship to power. It is this ability of silence to fracture power relationships that I would like to focus on by proposing the notion of silence as testimony. In calling it "silence as testimony" rather than simply "silence," I want to make visible the usefulness of the works on *testimonio* to think with.

The Latina Feminist Group, in their book, *Telling to Live: Latina Feminist Testimonios*, provide us with an understanding of testimonio "as a crucial means of bearing witness and inscribing into history those lived realities that would otherwise succumb to the alchemy of erasure" (1). Testimonios are often told by "the disenfranchised to assert themselves as political subjects through others, often outsiders, and in the process to emphasize particular aspects of their collective identity. . . . These texts are seen as disclosures not of personal lives but rather of the political violence inflicted on whole communities" (Latina Feminist Group 13). Testimonio is a genre that produces narratives that are "lodged in memory, shared out loud and recorded" (Latina Feminist Group 20). Drawing from this theoretical genealogy of testimonio, I offer silence as a form of testimony in the way it can be used to bear witness to what happens and enable us to be present in history by telling our life stories (here, through performative silence) as an effect of the structural power hierarchy and stand for a collective community (rather than only for individuals) against systemic violence. The word "testimony" is also used in this chapter in the way that writer Steve Edwin uses it, to denote "the act of representing trauma itself" (14).

I argue that the ways in which certain tweets that claim that the writers "cannot" share their stories function as performative and collective silence: silence as testimony. These performative silences are unique in the digital environment, whose technology allows us to perform silence in a different way. Here are some examples of tweets that express how stories cannot be told:

@margaretcho I don't think I can, but I am so happy that you are doing this. :) thank you #12DaysOfRage

@margaretcho #12daysofrage Still can't talk about everything they did to me

@margaretcho I wish I had the strength all these other women have . . . it still paralyzes me. #12daysofrage

I'm not ready to publicly speak about my exp. except through my poetry BUT I SUPPORT! Everybody should follow #12DaysOfRage & margaretcho

@margaretcho I tried to tweet what happened when I was 5 . . .
I can't do it. Maybe I'm not better (never saw a shrink for it.)
#12daysofrage

Dear @margaretcho I am still not ready to talk. But I am with you
for #12daysofrage so hard!

I need to first acknowledge here that these tweets, as individual
speech acts, that express that the writers cannot or are not ready to
share their stories may not necessarily express an agency in themselves. On the contrary, they are expressing the writers' desire to speak,
if only they were brave or strong enough. But *collectively*, their silence
creates a narrative in which the magnitude of violence against women
can be read. The comments of the women who do not speak *do* document the horror of what happened (i.e., act as testimonio), but only
when read as a *collective narrative*. It is Cho's twitter campaign that
enabled the formation of this community and allowed these women to
read each other's comments. This is what social media allows us to do:
to see these comments *together* in one panoptic gaze. The Internet creates a discourse about the choice to remain silent. It is not silence per
se that is powerful, it is a collective silence performed together on social media that may enact the political potential of pain. Those tweets
that share the tweeters' inability to tell stories exemplify the notion
of silence as testimony: they bear witness to the structural violence
beyond individual acts of rape that provide the conditions of (im)pos-
sibility for telling their stories. These tweets can also be regarded as
resistance to the neoliberalizing culture of social media that focuses on
the "me-me-me" culture—the neoliberal self(ie). To refuse to return to
the neoliberal self(ie) as a point of narrative is to enact the possibility
of resistance.

These tweets insist that their writers' stories shall remain unspoken,
and therefore, in some ways, these women remain silent. Minh-ha argues that "silence as a refusal to partake in the story does sometimes

provide us with a means to gain a hearing. It is a voice, a mode of uttering, and a response in its own right" (*Woman* 83). Found within discourse rather than "outside of discourse," silence can become a way of "seeing (unseeing) and knowing (unknowing)" (Duncan 14–15). "Silence as testimony" thus refers to the ways in which silence *does* tell something: it testifies against the systemic violence that creates the conditions of possibility, first, for sexual violence to occur and, then, for the persistent feeling of endangerment that renders social media an unsafe place for women to speak about violence. In this case, their silence discloses the political and systemic violence that still exists in the moment of their disclosure—a testimonio that is articulated through collective and performative silence.

The tweets that do not speak in the manner that the invitation asks them to can be read as revealing women's need to care for their own pain and to carry the pain in a way that honors its presence in the body. Communication studies scholar Della Polloc argues, "not-speaking or keeping quiet in the particular sense of tending silence may be a way of realizing the relational subjectivity of pain. . . . The space between must then be carefully kept, swept and brushed, maintained, not so much against the unspeakability of pain but against the potential excesses of speech, the possibility of overspeaking it and violating the tender space it opens" (159). In this way, silence can be protective (Duncan 220). As these tweets suggest, these women needed to be in a space in which the wounds remain untouched. In this case, it is not speech but silence that may take them to healing (Malhotra 227).

This inability or unwillingness to participate can also be read as a rejection of complicity in demands that may hurt them or "in injurious interpellations or in subjection through regulation" (Brown, *Edgework* 97). Cho's tweet already interpellates these women as "survivors/victims" of sexual abuse who harbor rage. Her invitation does not allow—ideologically, that is—for their subjectivity to be articulated outside of this very narrative. By not recounting their stories, they may escape being positioned within the victim/survivor binary.

Emotions also matter in this politics of unsay-ability. For instance:

Still too afraid of putting it all out there, but, I'm thankful for
@margaretcho and all she's doing for us. #12DaysofRage
#rageisalllknow

@margaretcho Too horrific to recount but I'm proof that one
can survive & thrive. Know that it gets better. Find your healing.
#12DaysOfRage

#12daysofrage I'm far too anxious to make a video, but this cam-
paign means so much. I feel so much anger after what I experienced (cont)

@margaretcho I want to say thank you from those of us who
are still too scared, hurt, and ashamed to admit to more than
#12daysofrage

@margaretcho Too heavy for me to take on tonight, but know,
you & all those by our side have my complete support. Always
#SexualAbuseSurvivor

These commenters' unwillingness to participate is related to the too-
muchness of their feelings: "too anxious," "too afraid," "too scared," "too
heavy," or "too horrific." The excess of emotions becomes an excess of
speech, which is registered as silence nonetheless. Emotions structure
what can and cannot be said.

What kind of relationship is Cho offering to her followers when she
tweets, "It's ok to be silent. I am loud for them. #12daysofrage"? Certainly,
it is problematic to speak *for* others. Yet it is important to note that Cho
is a Korean American woman whose history of silence has preceded
her. Racism in visual media has also silenced Korean American voices
for so long (E. Kim 275). Silence also has a sticky attachment to "Asian,"

sustained in the stereotypes of the "model minority" or the submissive and obedient woman. Thus, Cho's campaign is subversive when read through a lens that makes her Asianness visible: at a time when Asian women are still stereotyped as being silent, she lives her life and even makes money by being out (and) loud.

Carrying/Passing Pain, Moving beyond Voice as Agency

In this final section, rather than simply reiterating my points, I will explore the ramification of theorizing silence as testimony—the collective silence performed on social media platforms such as Twitter as a form of testimonio. Specifically, I argue, a critical engagement with silence and pain would allow us to move beyond the victim-agency debate that is often centered on the notions of "voice" and "choice." But first, I will expose the problems with existing notions of agency and then propose a new understanding of agency that relies on performative, collective silence—silence as testimony.

Problems with the Feminist Tradition of Voice in Formulating Agency

Central to the debate about agency in feminism is the notion of voice and speaking up. As Pérez argues, "To have voice is to utilize the agency to speak for oneself. Voice is agency, visibility, location, determination, and power" (202). Particularly for second-wave feminism, "voice" and "silence" were important both literally and metaphorically. Not speaking meant risking not being heard, not being seen. Speaking was thus "an act of risk and daring," especially in the context when one is not spoken to and when women's histories and stories have been repressed in the dominant narrative (hooks, *Talking Back* 5). When women share their stories about rape, they do not simply tell a story, they are also reclaiming the power of narrative for themselves. What Cho does effectively through her tweets is to intervene in the question of who has the power to tell the story/history.

I would like to shift the dominant trajectory by following in the foot-steps of feminist theorists before me who have highlighted the importance of silence in political movements and questioned "voice" as the sole path to liberation. I suggest that there are three problems with existing understandings of agency. First, in feminist discourse, agency is often constructed through "speaking up" or "breaking the silence." In looking at voice critically, I draw on Lamb who uses dress as a metaphor for voice. She argues, "voice becomes something of a dress that has been chosen from the cultural wardrobe according to the rules of fashion and decorum, which is then rewashed, pressed, and rehung on the victim by researchers, therapists, and authors according to similar but slightly different rules of fashion and decorum. What lies underneath the voice is not the naked truth but a body that also has been shaped by cultural rules and discourses. There is no concealed naked or unadorned truth" (Lamb 130). In other words, there is no deeper (truer) and more essential truth that lies within that which needs to be uncovered.

To articulate a feminist agency based on voice is problematic when we do not understand the complex processes through which stories unfold, such as how meanings are created and "altered," how certain conditions influence how a story ends up being told in a particular way, and how certain stories are more privileged than others because of the story-teller's "race, class, able-bodied, and citizenship privileges" (Russo 34). When certain Twitter users remain silent about their sexual abuse and claim that their lingering emotions inhibit their speech, it may not necessarily mean that they do not have a voice. Perhaps it is because the only discourse "in fashion" for representing their trauma simply doesn't "fit." Perhaps the language for their trauma eludes them.

Second, feminist agency has historically been expressed through speaking out *as a victim*. In the United States, the 1970s marked the era when conversations about sexual abuse and harm began to take place in the public arena (Lamb 113). With the publication of Susan Brownmiller's *Against Our Will*, the feminist anti-rape movement began to gain increased visibility (Chasteen 105). In the 1980s, however, the conceptualization of "woman-as-victim" came under scrutiny, with some arguing that discourses of "victimhood" (even "survivorhood") are disempowering because they position women as the victim, that is, an object, rather than a subject. Victimhood celebrates "the triumph of the weak *as* weak" (Stringer 89).

To be a "convincing victim," a person must prove that she experiences long-term psychological damage (short-term isn't enough). Further, "convincing victims" are often constructed as "pure, innocent, blameless, and free of problems (before the abuse)" (Lamb 108). Sufferers are framed in the language of morality, holding a "moral superiority" over the abusers and oppressors, the "morally inferior people" (114).

Third, agency is often constructed within a neoliberal framework. Since the 1990s in the United States, pop culture has popularized a version of feminism that is rooted in neoliberal values of "personal responsibility and individual transformation rather than collective politics and structural change" (Stringer 7). Social work scholar Laina Bay-Cheng even argues that agency in a neoliberal time has become a requirement, a "hegemonic imperative," and a "hegemonic institution," not ascribing to which will have serious social sanctions. In neoliberal times, sexual agency is no longer framed within "gendered moralism." Rather, as Bay-Cheng proposes, there is "the agency line," where girls are now judged by how much agency they have—they can be a virgin or a slut as long as it is because of their "unfettered free will," which within the neoliberal discourse of agency is considered the "ideal" way of being (280). It is interesting to note that white middle-class girls tend to have more agency than girls of other racial and class backgrounds (Lerum and Dworkin 321).

Rethinking (Once More) and Moving beyond Voice as Agency

By way of feminist theorizing from the margin and from the spaces of silence, I offer new understandings of agency that simultaneously allow us to question and move beyond voice as agency. First, I argue that rather than always having to be articulated through voice, agency could also be articulated by way of performing silence, both collectively and as testimony. Malhotra argues,

> there are different contexts in which silence can be an act of resistance, when silence can open up spaces that words would have closed out. Understanding the complex interplay between agency and silence is key to embracing the silences we engender, or that we encounter. (227)

Collective and performative silence, as I have pointed out throughout this chapter, can function as a site where one resists and asserts their agency. Here, I refer to the notion of agency as "the capacity of people to act purposefully and reflectively on their world" (Rebecca Rogers and Melissa Wetzel quoted in Kayi-Aydar 141). By purposefully and reflectively refusing to tell their sexual abuse stories and thereby performing their collective silence on social media, these women are exercising their agency.

These women are also performing their agency in that their silence goes against the grain of what Cho asks them to do. As Gunne highlights, "In the debate between speech and silence, to be told when, how, and to what end to speak represents total effacing of potential agency and subjectivity, even if that agency is narrowly and problematically defined as 'the victim'" (171). Silence can thus be a site of agency when a person refuses to speak under the terms that regulate the permissibility and desirability of such a speech. Moreover, these women may "claim rights to quiet" (Polloc 173) as a way to protect their pain and their own feelings. When others ask them to share certain aspects of their past and pain, that request is always embedded in power relations. To deny such a request can be read as subverting those power relations, although not always.

Furthermore, silence makes visible the disjuncture between agency and language (Gunne 172). Whereas language may fail, silence may succeed in preserving our ability to hold on to the integrity of pain in a particular way. Not engaging with language can even propel us to access and process a deeper level of pain that is inaccessible to language (Saraswati, "Why Non-Story Matters"), such as in cases where the "non-linguistic and abstracted modes of recalling and representing rape" can "transfor[m] memory" (Kabir 158). As Polloc argues, "talking does not so much 'give voice' to pain as it gives authority to the linguistic systems in which 'pain' is encoded" (169). Agency must therefore be articulated not only within but also beyond language to allow for frictional and fictional spaces where we can simultaneously recuperate and resist language.

It is in questioning silence, why we perform it, and why we exercise our agency through it, that we may come to understand the very structure that provides us with the conditions of *necessity* for such silence to be performed in the first place. In casting silence as agency, I add another experience to the biography of silence.

Second, I propose that we consider agency as being articulated at the site of the collective,[2] that is, as collective-based and virtual-based, rather than individual.[3] To listen to and through silence is to find new ways to connect, live, and feel-with-others. In digital media, even silence can be experienced together, with people who are thousands of miles away from us, or even with strangers. As Pérez points out, silence has often been constructed in our society as alone or lonely (200). However, as digital spaces and these tweets show us, they allow us to experience silence as togetherness.

In constructing the notion of agency as a collective, I evoke, once again, the spirit of testimonio, where narratives are spoken "not for the individual but for the experience of a community" (Latina Feminist Group 20). Certainly, people with power and privilege should never claim that they are speaking for others with less power and privilege. However, there are productive and critical ways in which others' voices can merge with ours, without our appropriating them and vice versa, as long as we are aware of where the flows of power go. These tweets exemplify my point:

> Out of shame and self-doubt, I've opted to keep my own experience with #abuse as a silent war. But, @margaretcho, your voice is now my own.

> @margaretcho you are a beautiful and powerful voice for women even those of us who aren't ready to tell our stories. Love you #12daysofrage

> @margaretcho this is for those of us that still can't bring ourselves to speak. #12daysofrage

> @margaretcho Thank you for speaking for those of us who can't! Xoxo #12daysofrage

> @margaretcho thank you for all you do & for being a voice for people who maybe can't be their own voice right now. #12DaysOfRage

These women who chose to be silent about their own stories are reclaiming Cho's voice as their own. Their speech acts do not rely on personal narrative, but serve as a testimony and a collective "social memory" (Haaken 25). The agency-as-collective highlights the togetherness of being in the stories, as speaking *with*. Rethinking agency as a collective articulation shifts the focus from the stories and the identity of the person telling the story to what the story, told collectively, allows us to understand and achieve (Stringer 109).

Agency as a collective frames togetherness as a source of power and empowerment. A tweet by Cho illustrates this point, "You are never alone. We survived and we heal together #12daysofrage."

Performing agency as a collective becomes a communal activity. Other tweets also further illuminate this idea:

> @— @margaretcho It has been healing to stand with men and women that share in this common atrocity. #12DaysofRage

> #12DaysofRage & @margaretcho are fueling all my Survivor Solidarity feelings, so many of us are still trying to heal: [link]

> Sending so much love to survivors of sexual abuse. This #12daysofrage by @margaretcho is much needed healing

> @margaretcho Thank you for sharing your story and giving others the courage to share theirs. #12daysofrage

What these tweets reveal is that trauma testimonies have power in creating meaningful relationships and connections among women. One woman's story becomes another's source of courage. It is in believing that there is power in articulating the self as a collective and in solidarity that healing and agency can be thought of differently, in a more transgressive and politically progressive way.

Considering agency as a collective also suggests how our sense of self can be "vicarious." A tweet acknowledges this:

> Vicarious trauma is real. Especially for survivors. Make sure you take good care of yourself when reading #12daysofrage [two heart emojis]

This tweet reminds us that digital media functions as a space of affective simulation, where pain is simulated and circulated, not only for the self but also for others to feel (see chapter 2). What happens to a person that is shared on social media, another person can supposedly feel it, too.

Rethinking agency as a collective articulation means that the agency is located not only when someone shares their stories on social media, but also when others respond to those stories. One of the tweets suggests this, "Sometimes how people respond to your attack/rape can be more traumatizing than the actual attack. It shouldn't be this way! #12daysofrage." As Polloc poignantly observes, "the communicability of pain thus has less to do with content utterance than with the *conditions of relation* in which it is spoken or given to be heard" (164, emphasis mine). People therefore construct stories and agencies through each other and through their relationships with each other. What this means is that in digital media, the self is often constructed in relation to the audience (Saraswati, "Wikisexuality"). The more "likes" or "retweets" they get from a particular kind of posting, the more similar postings people tend to post in the future. Too, the tweets that refuse to share their sexual abuse stories may reflect the fear of how the audience will respond to their tweets, if they were to tell them. In other words, what one decides to post or not to post often times depends on their assumption about how their audience (their social media followers) will react. It is in this *interaction* that agency is articulated on social media. Agency can therefore be argued to be articulated on social media at the point of the collective.

Third, I argue that agency, often attributed to a coherent self, should instead be understood as a result of a leaking self in the digital space. When people post things online, they may say things they probably would not say in person. For example, people would feel reluctant to show pictures of what they just had for breakfast or lunch to colleagues whom they barely talk to on a daily basis, or to rant about random things happening in their lives to just anyone. Yet they do that on social media. In other words, in the physical world, people tend to contain their self-image as a coherent self. On social media, which is but another layer of their lives, this coherent self is leaking by way of their postings, whose meanings cannot be fully contained or guaranteed by the speaker. When posting, the self leaves a digital trail or "footprint" of these leakages. Agency is thus found, I argue, not only at the site of the projected coherent self, but also at the site of these leakages. Sometimes these leakages are the speeches/postings people share online; other times they are the silences, as can be seen from tweets mentioned in this chapter.

Fourth, I propose that we consider agency in the form of carrying the pain. Agency, in relation to the pain, should not be thought of only as healing, repairing the wound, or as moving away from the pain. Tweets that question, "Why does it still hurt?" or claim, "But it still hurts," are not simply outside the discourse of agency. These statements are not a passive confession of experiencing pain. Rather, they hint at the ways in which they are still carrying the pain within. They are an acknowledgment that pain has the capacity to take us to a space where we can coexist with it, rather than pushing it away. Pain passes and moves through our body and onto other bodies. We are not better or worse, before, during, or after pain. Pain simply passes through.

Carrying pain as a form of agency can even be perceived as dangerous and thus in need of being trolled and controlled. International studies scholar Liz Philipose points out, "There are ways of embodying pain which fuel activism against the conditions that cause the pain, not just on behalf of one's self but potentially on behalf of 'other Others' who are similarly situated" (64). For example:

Marge, the only way ur gonna stop rape is if every female in the world looks like you #SorryNotSorry #12daysofrage [link]
Washed up comedian @margaretcho's #12DaysofRage campaign glorifies rape hysteria [link]

What these examples show is how, because Cho dares to carry, embody, and pass on her pain in ways that fuel activism, she (and others like her) have to be trolled and controlled. Carrying pain also allows us to further the theoretical trajectory that English professor Anne Cheng has set up, which is to consider subjectivity as "a convoluted, ongoing, generative, and at times contradicting negotiation with pain" (15). The carrying of pain in our bodies, on social media, and through our silences is also a form of asserting our agency.

In this chapter, I have illustrated the ways in which neoliberal ideology shapes and limits Cho's feminist activism online. Specifically, I query how neoliberalism informs the speeches as well as the silences in the #12daysofrage tweets, and how silence as testimony offers a renewed perspective in understanding feminist agency. I argue that performing collective silence—silence as testimony—can be powerful when it calls attention to and exposes the structure that produces both violence and silence in the first place.

I hope this chapter is not read as an instruction on *how* (not) to tell a story. That is exactly what I am working against. No one should invite others to tell a story in a particular way without querying how it changes the speaker's relationship to what happens and to the pain that they may be feeling/carrying. When a person reveals a fragment of their life through a pain narrative or when they invite others to tell stories of pain, we must contemplate what it is that they seek, for themselves and/or from the listener. What is it that they find compelling about the pain narrative and what it does? Perhaps by grappling with these questions, we may think into being other and more radical ways of incorporating stories of pain that can invigorate our feminist activism on social media.

This chapter is instead offered as an exercise to strengthen our muscles for silence, to increase our capacity for silence (rather than necessarily to *be* silent). It emphasizes the participatory and performativity of silence. It wrestles with the paradox of making visible silence as a public discourse and performed publicly on social media, while simultaneously recognizing silence as that which people turn to when they want to keep stories of their sexual abuse private.

Silence is not only paradoxical but also provocative. It incites new ways of thinking and theorizing. On the one hand, I acknowledge that we must always, always, always speak against violence. As feminist theorist Sara Ahmed argues, "Silence enables the reproduction of the culture of harassment and abuse. When we don't speak about violence we reproduce violence. Silence about violence is violence" ("Speaking Out"). We simply cannot stay silent. On the other hand, I point to the ways in which speaking about violence (or the imperative to speak to prove or perform one's feminist agency) on social media can also feel violent and violating when done in unsafe or toxic spaces. In this case, silence can therefore be a form of defiance, a way to protect and be faithful to one's own pain. Of course, not all silence is equal, and not all silence equals resistance (Gunne 165). Nonetheless, in however way we approach it, we should cultivate a reverence for silence as a tool of feminist activism.

Finally, I would like to end this chapter by explicitly stating that I do not advocate *a simple silence* over speech in regard to sexual violence, but rather seek to complicate both silence *and* speech and move us beyond this binary and oppositional thinking. It is also important to re-member here that it is not silence per se that is equated with subjectivity, but how *collective* silence is *performed* on social media (through silence as testimony) that is the basis for one's agency. Perhaps the hashtag we use when we do not feel safe to share our stories online, while highlight-ing our agentic and feminist silence, can be #SilenceAsTestimony. Such a hashtag would underscore how we can use the digital apparatus of a hashtag to perform and remain silent (as it has the safest consequence for us at the time) while being present in history and bearing witness and providing a testimony to systemic violence. In this chapter, I have demonstrated how people can engage with the pain of sexual abuse on social media differently, through silence, but a different mode of silence that functions as a testimonio—silence as testimony. This mode of si-lence can thus serve as an invitation to imagine a different way of relat-ing to pain that may not always involve speaking out or healing, but always working toward structural transformation and social justice.

5

What Else Might Be Possible?

Imagining Vigilant Eco-Love Practice

"What kind of online activism should we do that does not subscribe to neoliberal values?" A student at NYU Shanghai asked me this question after I presented my lecture based on chapters 2 and 3 of this book. This question is powerful in making visible the urgency to carefully think about an alternative that would allow us to escape the neoliberal imperative of the feminist social media practice of our time. It is therefore the question that I would like to grapple with in this chapter: "What else might be possible?"

In the previous chapters, I have demonstrated how neoliberal logic structures social media and hence limits and shapes feminist activism and practices on this space; in this chapter, I want to tease out a possibility of socially mediating pain and doing feminist activism online that could possibly override and subvert the limitation of the platforms and evade the neoliberal self(ie) gaze. This chapter thus serves as an invitation to envision what else might be possible and to consider activism as work that relies on the imaginative, on creativity and curiosity.

But this chapter may also serve as a reminder that we need to question this very desire for an alternative. That is, *Why do we imagine? Who do we imagine with and for? With which/whose tools do we imagine? How may we imagine outside the parameters of dominant discourses that provide us with the language/tool/cognitive machine for our imagination? Once we imagine "the otherwise," how may we call it into being? What exists in the crevices and cradles of the imaginary, and in doing feminist work as imaginary work? Is the "failure" of feminist activism on social media the failure of the imaginary?*

I bring up the issue of failure here to expose the dilemma, troubling logic, and possible limitations of imaginary work in feminism and social media. If failure can be seen as subversive, as theorist J. Halberstam argues in *The Queer Art of Failure*, and if we carry out activist work in the name of feminism that aims to subvert—that is, to "fail" that which is the dominant norm—then is feminist activism on social media already destined for failure from its very inception? Perhaps the *"success" of the feminist movement requires us to fail as neoliberal subjects, and to fail hard.* Perhaps the alternative practice that I theorize is already doomed to failure, if it were to ever spark any change and subvert the social media status quo at all.

Nonetheless, I insist that we dare to imagine in the midst of looming failure and propose some initial thoughts that may be built upon in future research. Specifically, I offer what I call "vigilant eco-love" practice as a possible alternative to the neoliberal self(ie) and as a promising and subversive mode of living and loving in a neoliberal, patriarchal, digital, racist, and capitalist age. To elucidate my points more clearly, I will turn now to the social media activism of Sahar Pirzada.

Sahar Pirzada, HEART, and Vigilant Love

Sahar Pirzada is a Pakistani American Muslim woman who is currently based in Los Angeles. Since 2016, she has worked as programs and outreach manager for HEART Women & Girls, an organization that "promotes sexual heath and sexual violence awareness in Muslim communities through health education, advocacy, research and training."[1] HEART was co-founded by Ayesha Akhtar and Nadiah Mohajir, a consultant for the Office on Women's Health at the US Department of Health and Human Services. In 2009, Mohajir was tasked to host a "health and wellness day for Muslim women" in Chicago. The big turnout for the event motivated her and Akhtar to form HEART. In 2016, Mohajir invited Pirzada to join the group as she was already actively tweeting about Muslim sex education and has a similar approach to

HEART's in that they both believe in cultural- and context-based sex education (J. Huang).

Pirzada also co-founded Vigilant Love, a "healing and arts-driven organization that counters mainstream narratives of insularity" through grassroots organizing, policy advocacy, and political education. It was founded in December 2015 as a response to the San Bernardino shooting and Islamophobia in Southern California and across the United States. Although it was established in 2015, Vigilant Love's history dates back to the aftermath of 9/11, when a coalition of Muslim American and Japanese American leaders was formed. From the very beginning, Vigilant Love thus embodied a kind of activism that is intersectional in its articulation. As a side note, Vigilant Love was the organization that led one of the largest nonviolent sit-ins and rallies at Los Angeles International Airport against Trump's Muslim ban in January 2017.

I would like to briefly contextualize Pirzada's work against gendered Islamophobia and sexual violence/health in Muslim communities within the larger history of South Asian American immigration, racism, sexism, and Islamophobia in the United States. As is the case with the Korean American immigrants discussed in the previous chapter, South Asian Americans also migrated to the United States in significant numbers only after 1965, although they had been arriving since the late eighteenth century, mostly as "indentured servants on the East Coast" (Rahman 12). In 1923, however, the Supreme Court of the United States ruled that South Asians were ineligible for citizenship (13). A new quota system in 1946 then allowed South Asian immigrants to enter the United States, albeit in small numbers (13). It was only after 1965, when the longstanding rule basing immigration on national origin was overturned, that immigration from South Asia rose from 769 in 1965 to 2,805 in 1966, and to 31,295 in 1984 (Minocha 348).

In 2001, in the aftermath of September 11, racial politics in the United States shifted, impacting South Asian Americans in devastating ways. South Asian Americans, as well as Arab Americans and Muslim Americans, increasingly became the target of hate crimes (Sthanki 70). South

Asian Muslim women who wear hijab are often mistaken as Arab Americans by much of the American public (Hermansen and Khan 90). This further entrenches racism, sexism, and discrimination against Muslims and Arab Americans (and people whose bodies are read as such) as the ultimate Other in the United States. It is important to note that although Muslims in the United States are often conflated with Arab Americans and vice versa, only more than a quarter of Muslim Americans are Arab Americans. African Americans make up one-third of the Muslim population, and South Asian Americans make up the other one third (Rayside 109, 112). Moreover, although the number of Muslims in the United States may seem large, they account for only 1 percent of the national population. These figures reveal the power of media and representation in constructing identities and narratives about specific groups of people.

The post-9/11 era was significant for South Asian Americans as it marked the normalization of violence against not only Arab American and Muslim American but also South Asian American men (Sthanki 70, 76). The American public even considers it acceptable to racially profile people "as long as it [i]s directed at Arabs and Muslims" (Maira 334). A 2004 Cornell study revealed that 44 percent of Americans "believe that the civil rights of Muslims should be curtailed" (Sthanki 71). In an effort to curb these citizens' rights, Congress passed the USA PATRIOT Act of 2001, which allows communities and the state to racially profile and systematically conduct surveillance against people who may be deemed "terrorists"—a term that has always been racialized, gendered, and religion-based (i.e., associated with Muslims). With the Patriot Act, South Asian Americans were increasingly scrutinized and their supposedly sacred and safe spaces of public gathering such as mosques became places that were heavily policed even by their own community members. It is within this hostile racial political context that Muslim American youth (such as Pirzada) have emerged as educators and activists, teaching the community about Islam against this state-sponsored gendered and racialized Islamophobia.

In this chapter, I discursively analyze Pirzada's activism, particularly as it was broadcast through her Twitter account from January 29, 2014, to May 3, 2019,[2] to theorize what alternative, non-neoliberal-infused feminist practice might be possible on social media. It needs to be noted here that Pirzada's Twitter postings do *not* always reflect a vigilant eco-love practice, and it is interesting to see how her tweets have evolved over time.

Early in her tweeting days, Pirzada, like others who use social media, projected a neoliberal self(ie) gaze—social media, as ever, shapes and structures how and what we post. For example, there is the very first tweet that she posted (that was still accessible as of May 3, 2019), on January 29, 2014: "I have a feeling this will be used to post Bollywood song lyrics stuck in my head. You've been warned." Other tweets around that time also focused on the self(ie) and what the self(ie) is interested in, such as posts on January 31, 2014: "Grocery shopping during CNY is never a good idea. Also why does cilantro have 5 different names?!"; on February 2, 2014: "Loved the coke ad from the Super Bowl! #AmericaTheBeautiful #ImAmericanToo"; February 5, 2014: "Where can I get Girl Scout cookies in Singapore?"; and February 25, 2014: "Just started watching True Detective. Good television makes me happy. #hbo." In all of these tweets, Pirzada highlights the mundane things of her everyday life: what the self is interested in, what makes the self happy, where/who the self is—for instance, a cosmopolitan American living in Singapore.

Starting in March 2014, Pirzada's posts began to focus more on her work as a sex educator. For example, on March 30, 2014, she tweeted, "I'm a Muslim hijabi sex educator and love my job #MuslimSexEd," "As a Muslim Sex Educator I promote safe and consensual sex between partners, regardless of marital status. #MuslimSexEd," and "Hoping that one day parents will start having open conversations about safety in sex with both their daughters and sons. #MuslimSexEd." In approaching sex education in the Muslim community, Pirzada teaches the idea that "Islam is a sex-positive religion." This view is certainly radical when read against the media representation of Islam in the United States, which positions it as an oppressive religion that limits women's social and political lives and, certainly, their sexuality.

Starting in August 2015, Pirzada's tweets became more about community activism. For example, on August 28, 2015, she tweeted, "Join us for a community forum tonight in Santa Ana about identity profiling! Also still taking sign ups for the DA!" It is these later tweets, which focus on her community activism both in terms of being a Muslim sex educator (through HEART) and community activist organizer (through Vigilant Love), that I examine in this chapter and that are the basis of my development of the concept of a "vigilant eco-love" practice.

Although I may have painted a picture of Pirzada's tweets as evolving linearly, her tweets do not always line up neatly in this way. There are moments when they are lodged in the contention and contradiction of practicing *both* the neoliberal self(ie) *and* vigilant eco-love:

Solidarity and not charity. Snaps to that! #muslimurbanjustice
For anyone who had questions about sex or their bodies growing up, appreciate @HEART_wg and donate today [link]

Y'all know the work we do is tough and underfunded. Help us #talkaboutsex and support our launch good! #showmethemoney

Yes and donate to muslim women organizations like @heart-togrow at the forefront of the Reproductive Justice movement for the Muslim community! #muslimsexed #genderedislamophobia

The neoliberalizing force of social media seeps through Pirzada's tweets when she asks her followers to donate, even as she previously tweeted, "Solidarity and not charity." She hints at the problems of charity (as it relies on individual rather than structural support) and suggests solidarity, which is based on collective effort, as a better solution. Nonetheless, she later asks people to donate to the specific organization where she works.

I will digress for a moment to acknowledge that funding for non-profit organizations is a contentious issue, as various contributors to the edited volume *The Revolution Will Not Be Funded: Beyond the Non-profit Industrial Complex* point out. One of the contributors, Dylan Rodríguez, argues that the creation of the "non-profit industrial complex" (NPIC)[3]—US nonprofits together would rank as the world's seventh-largest economy—functions to *impede* rather than further social justice (22). The NPIC, he writes, "serves as the medium through which the state continues to exert a fundamental dominance over the political intercourse of the US Left, as well as US civil society more generally" (30). This problem exists because, among other things, nonprofit organizations are often funded by big corporations' foundations, which dictate what programs and services can be carried out—as a result, these programs often do not benefit marginalized people nor are they aimed toward radical change (A. Smith 7, 9).[4]

It is not only funding from big corporations that is problematic but also funding from individual donors. Both operate with the same logic: "wealthy people should be the donors, and thus, inevitably, the controllers of social justice struggles" (A. Smith 9). The NPIC creates a conundrum inside the neoliberal capitalist economy in that the more nonprofit organizations do their work, the more the structure/the government does not have to change. People remain unaware of the (structural) problems involved. In other words, the inequality, the structural injustices, the status quo can be endured in part because of the nonprofits' existence.

In voicing concerns about the NPIC, I do not suggest that we forego social service or social justice work altogether. Rather, the call here is to do the work, while making social service agencies and nonprofit organizations accountable to social movements and not "an end unto themselves" (A. Smith 11, 15; Kivel 145). One of the alternatives to existing nonprofit organizations is a new model for social service/justice work that does not require organizations to hire full-time staff, which encourages a "careerist" path where only a few people are paid to work full time; social justice work needs to be carried out by millions of people (Hawk

102; A. Smith 10). Another possibility is to do grassroots fundraising, which Stephanie Guilloud and William Cordery—respectively, program director and development director with Atlanta's Project South—argue functions as "a strategy to maintain a firm connection to [their] base and to initiate community-based economic structures. [They] define *organizing* as building relationships and institutions to sustain community power, and it follows that fundraising *is* organizing" (Guilloud and Cordery 108, emphasis original). Perhaps this is what Pirzada was practicing when she solicited donations for her organizations on Twitter—using social media to do grassroots funding as a form of organizing and building a community base.[5]

In terms of the organization where Pirzada works and for which she solicits donations, HEART is funded through multiple sources, including government grants[6] (such as the Office on Violence Against Women at the US Department of Justice), foundations, corporate sponsorship, and individual donations (including NoVo Foundation, AAUW, the Afzal Family Foundation, and the Brown Family Foundation), among others. I am thus pointing out here the dilemma of how Pirzada calls out the problematic structure of donation, yet, at the same time, is invested in the system—in the nonprofit works. Nonetheless, as a whole, Pirzada's activism and social media postings allow me to theorize the practice that I call vigilant eco-love.

Vigilant Eco-Love

Vigilant eco-love is envisioned here as a practice, a mode of performing and posting on social media that would move us beyond the neoliberal self(ie). A neoliberal self(ie), no matter how empowering, entertaining, and appealing, will not move us toward social justice. As humanities and social science professor Ankica Čakardić writes:

> If we are interested in the social meaning of feminist emancipatory potential, and if we are to deal with feminism as a collectively-oriented move-

ment and political theory, then it becomes clear that feminism is not and cannot be a collection of different, scattered, individual positions. . . . The problem we are tackling here is the scope of individualism: if we stick with the descriptive approach to individual experiences and the motto "Choose to do whatever you like—it's empowering!," then we lose from sight the systemic sources of oppression and the power of articulating socially-responsible collective practices as the vehicle for emancipatory potential. After all, we need to remember that in the capitalist mode of production one person's freedom often comes at the expense of another's. (34)

The framework of scattered (even if empowered) "individual positions" such as those of the neoliberal self(ies) must be resisted. The key to transforming neoliberalism is "the feminist insistence that spheres are interlinked, and humans are interconnected and need each other's support" (Keren 123). Feminist activism, on social media or other platforms, must therefore continue to be collectively oriented, be socially responsible, be interconnected and mutually supportive, and work toward ending the systemic sources of oppression.

That Pirzada practices vigilant eco-love that is collectively oriented, socially responsible, interconnected and mutually supportive, and works to end oppression can be seen through her tweets. For example:

In order to dispel fear we must get to know one another #islamophobia101 #GetSMART16

Great piece by @—! It is so important to change the narratives about our communities and tell our own stories. Shedding light on the rise in hate directed at South Asians and making the links to white supremacy and islamophobia is part of it!

#MuslimWomensDay means making space for all the Muslim women of our diverse community—Black, Brown, immigrant, indigenous, trans, queer, young and for our resilient elders—all who

experience #genderedislamophobia. S/o to my beautiful community of reSisters!

Love this reflection of our bridging communities iftar. The work we
do at Vigilant Love is meant to heal in powerful ways. Community
gatherings like our iftar—one example of many! #VigilantLove

In these tweets Pirzada emphasizes collective and collaborative efforts
toward ending oppression. Her tweets show that she aims to make visible how oppression of one community is often linked to oppression in
other communities. She also stresses the importance of getting to know
each other and building bridges across different communities in carrying out activism. These interconnections among diverse communities,
Pirzada points out, are what make a *powerful* community: a community
relies not so much on commonality, but rather on conscious connections. It is this insistence that we build and bridge communities (rather
than focusing on individuals) that will allow us to think outside the neoliberal box. When neoliberalism erases our commitment to each other
and to the collective by overemphasizing investment in one's self, we
must choose to focus on and invest in the ecology (and the self as inseparable from ecology).

To further clarify the concept of "vigilant eco-love," throughout this
chapter I will discuss in more depth the three core social media practices
of vigilant eco-love:

(1) be "vigilant" in our love;
(2) be mindful of the well-being of the ecology and the self as part of
the ecology; and
(3) work toward an end to systemic oppression.

(1) Be Vigilant in Our Love

The term "vigilant eco-love" is inspired, of course, by the name and
healing activism practice of Vigilant Love, the organization that Pirzada

co-founded. To frame love as a form of vigilance is to call upon another property of love—not as soothing, caring, or nurturing, the "soft" properties of love, but as having to remain alert for another. In reframing love in this way, I am drawing from African American and gender and sexuality studies professor Jennifer Nash, who repositions love as "a space of vulnerability, nonsovereignty, and radical relationality . . . bring[ing] about potentially radical openness—even an openness to pain" (116–117); and English professor Lauren Berlant, who considers that "love always means non-sovereignty" ("No One"). In other words, to reimagine love as a form of vigilance is to evoke love as doing work for social justice and opening up new spaces of being and relating to others.

I find "vigilance" an intriguing and insightful trope, for it holds out the possibility of a practice that honors pain and trauma in one's body. Vigilance, according to social researcher Margaret T. Hicken, sociologist Hedwig Lee, and community health science professor Anna K. Hing, is one of the coping mechanisms for people who have experienced racism and discrimination in their lives—in their case, for "Blacks who carry the stigma burden of the racial group" (157). To remain vigilant is to carry the history of harm in one's body (both physiologically and psychologically). It is to be in a "state of participatory attention" and to be "alert and attentive" (DeLuca 19, 156). It is to embody the history, discursivity, and materiality of trauma and pain, incorporating it as part of our practice. In doing so, the subject remains vigilant in their loving, living, and interrelating with all others within their ecology. It does not mean remaining invested in the wound as such, but rather bearing witness (the body as the witness) to the violence that has been done and the structure that has allowed it to happen (and therefore the need to continue to be vigilant against power and those in power to prevent future violence). Vigilance thus becomes a site where the impact of the structure and the structural is affectively lodged in the individual (body).

I evoke the trope of vigilance here to follow in the footsteps of Vigilant Love, which reclaims the word "vigilant" in strategic and subversive ways. George W. Bush, then the president of the United States, in a speech delivered in Atlanta in November 2001, stated:

> A terrorism alert is not a signal to stop your life. It is a call to be *vigilant*, to know that your government is on high alert and to add your eyes and ears to our efforts to find and stop those who want to do us harm.
>
> . . .
>
> Our citizens have new responsibilities. We must be *vigilant*. . . .
>   We will not give in to exaggerated fears or passing rumors. We will rely on good judgment and good old common sense. . . .
>   We will not judge fellow Americans by appearance, ethnic background or religious faith. ("Text: President Bush," emphasis mine)

In his speech, Bush calls *specifically* for vigilance and asks citizens to be the eyes and ears for the state in their effort to stop the terrorists. The state encourages the use of vigilance toward the suspicious other (often racialized and marginalized) members of the community. (Although Bush explicitly states that "we" should not discriminate against other people based on their ethnic background or religious faith, his speech actually exposes the assumption about whom vigilance should be directed toward. His speech functions as a rhetorical response to increased reporting—citizens calling the police—against people speaking Arabic or who appear to be Arabs or Muslims.)

According to Bush's speech, in the post-9/11 era to be vigilant is the "new responsibilit[y]" of citizens. And it should be carried out *for* the state. However, Vigilant Love reoccupies the meanings and practices of what it means to be vigilant. Vigilant Love insists that we practice vigilance, not toward the racialized and oppressed other, but rather toward the ones in power or those who are violent against other members in the community. The trademarked slogan "If you see something, say something" that was employed in the task of Islamophobia is turned on its head: it is now used by Vigilant Love *against* Islamophobia. Vigilant Love calls for people to be vigilant and say or tweet something when they see social injustice in their communities, so that collectively they can end systemic oppression. In this chapter, I propose the term "vigilant eco-love" to name a practice in which we are vigilant in our love and in the name of love (eco-love), instead of in the name of the state.

To be vigilant is thus to refuse to play the neoliberal game of feeling the need to fix the pain. This position is in tune with that which cultural studies scholar Hoang Tan Nguyen describes in his book, *A View from the Bottom: Asian American Masculinity and Sexual Representation*: "subjects do not seek to overcome injury but those that have learned to live with past and present damage, in particular, everyday injuries marked by gender, race, and sexuality, that cannot find relief or make amends through legitimate social or political means" (25). A vigilant eco-love subject does not aim to "overcome injury" as such, but rather to consider pain simply, as Gloria Anzaldúa courageously writes, as "the way of life" (50).

To carry, rather than avoid, dismiss, or "fix" pain and trauma in one's body is to practice vigilant eco-love and subvert neoliberalism. If neoliberalism frames "survivors/victims" as "damaged," "unregulated," and "emotionally unstable" people who are "in need of fixing," to refuse to see oneself as damaged and in need of fixing is to move beyond a neoliberal way of dealing with pain (Dang 2). Indeed, as mentioned in chapter 2, when people see themselves as needing to be healed and purchase commodities and services to that end, it sustains the neoliberal economy.

Rather than seeing a person as damaged, the vigilant eco-love standpoint sees the *entire ecosystem* as not working and therefore in need of transformation because everything is interconnected. Unless individual therapy is done within a community that is supportive and has itself been transformed, healing cannot truly happen (Saul 4). Efforts to simply transform the individual out of the trauma of racism/hetero/sexism/capitalism/neoliberalism/nationalism without aiming to change the ecology that creates these problems in the first place do not go far enough.

Being immersed in their ecology, a person who practices vigilant eco-love considers being vigilant and speaking out as forms of care and love for the community. For instance, to practice vigilance in our love means to call out people when they are not aware of their behaviors that harm others. Pirzada tweets:

Another important step: stop tweeting about believing survivors unless you yourself practice that. It's a scary time for survivors. We are mapping what our safe spaces are. Don't say you support survivors when and if you normalize sexual predators in community spaces. Do better.

Why are some people so comfortable around sexual predators?! God forbid they support the folks who are trying to protect community. Fear God y'all. Not the loss of your social capital and proximity to power. #muslimsurvivors #BelieveSurvivors

I'm so disappointed by those who in the name of fighting islamophobia still cannot hold space for the complex reality that somebody can experience islamophobia while still being a sexual predator. We can and should be able to understand that. And not disregard survivors' truths.

I'm so sick of Muslim men protecting other Muslim men and erasing the lived experiences of survivors in our community.

To all the survivors in our community triggered by our Muslim male scholars equating your experiences to zina, I am sorry our community sucks. I believe you. Your experience is yours to share. We will hold space for you to speak your truth always. #believesurvivors

Rape is not zina. Rape is not zina. Rape is not zina. Rape is not zina. Rape is not zina. Rape is not zina. Rape is not zina. Rape is not zina. Rape is not zina. RAPE IS NOT ZINA #RapeIsNotZina

First of all, it is important to notice the difference in how Pirzada frames the issue of sexual harassment as an issue for vigilant eco-love practice, versus its framing from the neoliberal self(ie) gaze that we saw in previous chapters. Those earlier tweets and postings are consistent with the neoliberal logic that often focuses on the self and how the individual has either overcome a traumatic event against all systemic odds or is not ready to share their story, for example. Pirzada's tweets focus on the ecology, the structure, and the systemic oppression, rather than on individuals per se. She focuses on how power works and how people's reaction to someone else's sexual harassment story is often dangerously entangled in their own desire to preserve their "social capital and proximity to power." She also points out that there are damaging ramifications when people tweet that they support survivors but continue to protect and normalize sexual predators. Pirzada thus calls out the male leaders in her Muslim community for their sexist behaviors and asks them, as well as others who defend sexual predators, to "do better." This request to do better can be seen as a form of care and love—vigilant eco-love—for the community so that the entire ecology can do better, grow, and eventually transform. What is important in the practice of calling out each other is to remember that we are intersectional beings who are always implicated in multiple systemic hierarchies of race, gender, sexuality, spirituality, and nationality. These social locations produce conditions where other people may oppress us; simultaneously, we may occupy a position where we oppress others.

Vigilance functions as a form of awareness of one's relationality and intersectionality vis-à-vis other beloved members of the community (but not in the name of, or for, the state). Being vigilant is a condition of always being "alert and attentive" to how people may perform in ways that are triggering to others and to hold them accountable for their behaviors. The social media practice of vigilant eco-love thus involves constantly being vigilant of other people's (and, of course, one's own) postings and to call each other out, in the name of love for the community, when postings trigger and oppress others. For instance, in the tweets quoted above, because Pirzada vigilantly loves and is committed to her Muslim community, she asks her Muslim leaders to do better, to not protect Muslim men who are sexual harassers, and to not equate rape with *zina* (the sinful act of adultery). Rather than simply surrendering to love, she remains vigilant in her love. A subject who practices vigilant eco-love knows that *to love unconditionally is an obstacle to social justice.* Unconditional love may work for romantic cards and movies, but not for conscious relationships or social justice work. Vigilant eco-love is therefore never unconditional. Unconditional love leads to power imbalances and social injustice.

The spirit of vigilant eco-love is what sparked the creation of this book. As I have pointed out, perhaps rather redundantly, this book is *not* a criticism of the specific women whom I truly admire. rupi kaur's Instagram account, for example, is one that I follow and love. I find her poems powerful and use them as a pedagogical tool in my own classrooms. Margaret Cho remains *the* female comedian I consider as one of the best, funniest, and most critical in articulating insightful commentaries about various social issues. As a feminist, Cho skillfully deploys humor as a vehicle for activism and social change. Hence, I hope it is clear that my intention here is not to criticize their work or undermine their commendable feminist activism. Rather, this is my way of practicing vigilant eco-love: emphasizing that we remain vigilant in our love for others so that we may be able to see when and how hegemonic ideologies operate through us all, and that we call out and help each other to do better when that does happen.

Lastly, the trope of "vigilance" is evoked in this chapter as it paves the way for thinking about what it means to be a "vigilante." Feminist American studies scholar Laura Mattoon D'Amore offers the concept of "vigilante feminism," defining it as "the performance of vigilantism by girls and women who have undertaken their own protection, and the protection of others, against violence—such as sexual assault, abduction, abuse, and trauma—because they have been otherwise failed in that manner" (387). To a certain extent, the women I discuss in this book do practice vigilante feminism, particularly as it is framed as "a response to violence against women" that "uses patriarchal means to undergird its own takeover" (rather than dismantle patriarchy) (390). However, the women I examine in this book do not, as the vigilante feminist characters in the novels and movies D'Amore analyzes, use "the tools of historically 'male violence'—wielding hatchets and knives . . .—and make them work for their own needs" (402).[7] Instead, the women in this book use social media to fight back and take back their power.

(2) Be Mindful of the Well-Being of the Ecology and the Self as Part of the Ecology

Because a person who practices vigilant eco-love is collectively oriented and socially responsible, their social media practice consequently prioritizes the well-being of the ecology and the self as part of the ecology, rather than merely focusing on their own neoliberal self(ie). They do not simply put themselves first, which is often the case with the neoliberal self(ie). Rather, their action is driven by their desire to achieve the "common good" (Ginwright 24).

A shift of focus from individual to ecology must indeed take place if we are to move beyond the neoliberal articulation of the self(ie) on social media. What counts as ecology will also need to be challenged and broadened. I am therefore intentional in my use of the word "ecology" rather than "structure," as I hope to emphasize the *interconnections* among different elements and environments within an ecology.

Ecology, from the Greek word "oikos, meaning an inhabited house or household—describes the *web of relationships and interconnections* among organisms and their 'homes' (their communities and biophysical environments)" (Di Chiro 200, emphasis mine). Ecology can also be understood as "the study of connection, of the *interrelationships among all forms of life* and the *physical environment*" (Conn 532, emphasis mine). Drawing from existing scholarships, I understand ecology to be an imagined system that encompasses ongoing interrelationships between people, as well as among people, their environment, and other nonhuman entities (spiritual, technological, digital, etc.), where these forms of interconnectedness are constructed through institutions, discourses, politics, and ethics and are embedded in the power hierarchy, and where people's different relationships and access to resources and power are nonetheless regulated (Chen 89; Middleton 2; Mortimer-Sandilands and Erickson 5).

Ecology emerges as an important concept in this chapter because it allows us to understand how the individual self functions as "an abstraction of the interactive relationship between a person and the environment" (Filippi 236). The self does not exist in or as itself. It is the web of relationships and the interconnections and interrelationships between the self, others, nonhuman others (including the spiritual, animal, machine), and their environments (e.g., digital and physical) that I am interested in exploring. Ecology is central to the practice of vigilant eco-love.

Indeed, I purposefully insert the term "eco" in vigilant *eco*-love to emphasize the significance of ecology. Eco-love is offered as an *antidote* to the neoliberal articulation of self-love. Vigilant eco-love practice is therefore not interested in self-love or self-care, at least not in the ways they are articulated within the neoliberal discourse. Both concepts in the neoliberal discourse have been translated into the promotion of the consumption of commodities as an investment in the self. The self is positioned not only as worthy of these commodities but also as the number one priority, above anyone or anything else, in one's life.

The "eco" in eco-love specifically refers to the articulation of love *in* and *as* ecology. I propose the term "eco-love" to highlight the ways in which the individual *and* the collective ecology are woven in and through each other, together, and simultaneously. This does not mean that vigilant eco-love practice is oblivious to the notion of caring for the self. Rather, the self is always framed as part of the ecology: the "I" in context.[8] Care for the self is an articulation of care for the ecology, and vice versa. One does not come at the expense of the other. When Pirzada tweets, "We are one American family—hurt for one is hurt for all #BmoreTogether," she highlights this very interconnectedness and embeddedness of one's self in one's ecology.

In employing and providing specific meanings for the concept "ecology," I follow in the footsteps of gender studies scholar Mel Chen, who defines ecology as "an *imagined* system, not an actual, self-regulating one" (89, emphasis mine). To further unpack the word "imagined," I would like to return here to political scientist Benedict Anderson's well-known concept of imagined community. Although Anderson uses the term "imagined community" in the context of a nation, I employ it here to refer to an ecology that is not bounded by the nation-state or by communities with set geographical and political boundaries. Rather, I use it in the sense of performative, collaborative, and collective, however broadly defined, communities.

If I frame ecology as "imagined," it is not to juxtapose it with the notion of the real or to question its "realness"—I do not subscribe to this binary notion of the virtual versus the real.[9] Rather, I employ it here the way Anderson theorizes it. First, a community (of a nation) is considered imagined because no matter how small it is, each one of its members will never be able to meet and know every single member of the community; "yet in the minds of each lives the image of their communion" (Anderson 6). Indeed, on social media, members of a digital community may never meet or know everyone. Yet, through different technological features of social media, they may feel that they belong to the same community, or what technology and social media scholar danah boyd calls "networked publics."[10]

Second, a community is imagined in the sense that it is constructed and that it matters *how* it is constructed. Anderson clarifies it thus: "communities are to be distinguished, not by their falsity/genuineness, but by the style in which they are imagined" (6). For instance, on social media, users can curate and construct their community by first identifying *who counts as part of their community: who they follow, who follows them, and who they allow to follow them.* To be able to remove or block certain people who do not contribute to one's overall well-being or whose views become increasingly hostile or to amplify specific voices that one endorses can be quite empowering. It can even function as a way to subvert the limitation imposed by the neoliberal social media platforms. In Pirzada's case, for example, her digital ecology consists of her activist groups: she often retweets postings from organizations that she works for, such as HEART and Vigilant Love, and from her fellow activists, for the purpose of mobilizing for social change rather than projecting a neoliberal self(ie). This practice of curation also demonstrates that what counts as part of an ecology is ideologically and discursively constructed: who we think is part of our ecology is a product of institutions, discourse, and politics (Mortimer-Sandilands and Erickson 5).[11] Religious discourse, for instance, often provides rigid boundaries for who should and can be included and excluded from an ecology.

It must be noted that this ability to curate and construct one's community may also serve to maintain the invisibility of marginalized people. People who are white and male tend to have more followers on Twitter than those of other genders and races (Messias et al. 266). They can exclude marginalized people from their ecology, thereby further widening the racial and gender gap in this space. According to information science scholars Linhong Zhu and Kristina Lerman, "the top 20% of Twitter users own more than 96% of all followers, 93% of the retweets, and 93% of the mentions" (1). In the world of social media, white male supremacy and the "rich-get-richer" formula still reign: white and male users tend to have the most followers, and users who have more followers have an easier time gaining still *more* followers because they are more likely to be mentioned and retweeted (Zhu and Lerman 1; Sangeet 2).

The rich-get-richer formula also holds true for the women examined in this book. As of May 3, 2019, Pirzada had the fewest number of followers of the four accounts I have analyzed: 629. By the same date, Mia Matsumiya had 51,500 followers on her Instagram; Margaret Cho had

489,000 followers on her Twitter; and rupi kaur had 3.7 million followers on her Instagram. First, the rich-get-richer formula explains why
Cho has more followers than Matsumiya and Pirzada: Cho is already a
well-known celebrity who tweets quite frequently and is therefore more
likely to have more followers. However, it does not explain why kaur has
more followers than Cho. This leads us to the next point.

Second, to gain currency and purchase in this digital space, a person/
persona must project the standpoint of a neoliberal self(ie). The more
entertaining, spectacular, and affectively evocative one's social media account is, the more famous (and viral) their postings may be. Compared
to the others examined in this book, kaur's Instagram postings project
the most elaborate and entertaining level of phantasmagoria production
and the neoliberal self(ie) gaze, with her affectively influential poems
and illustrations, staged photographs and videos, and thoughtfully se-
quenced images and poems. Pirzada's postings that practice vigilant
eco-love, from a Pakistani American Muslim woman, are collectively
oriented, and concerned about social change, may thus have less currency and be less appealing to the social media world and the neoliberal
logic that governs it. This may explain her low number of followers. As
I mentioned previously, to practice vigilant eco-love may mean to be
deemed a "failure" by the social media standard that measures success
by the number of one's followers, retweets, and mentions.

It is therefore important to amplify voices like that of Pirzada, who
performs an alternative practice that goes beyond the neoliberal self(ie),
and to make such a subversive practice more common if we are to challenge the hegemonic neoliberal self(ie) gaze. In other words, knowing
that platforms are designed to structure our online participation in ways
that serve those platforms' interests, we need to think of ways to ma-
nipulate (or "trick") the platforms to create a loving feminist ecology
that works for us. We need to seek out every crevice in the social media
world that can be claimed as a safe space for our feminist digital ecology. As such, I do not romanticize ecology as a space where all members are inherently equal, although that is certainly the goal. I recognize

that power hierarchies exist and regulate differential access to resources (Middleton 2).[12]

To be mindful of the ecology is therefore to be aware of the digital inequality[13] that permeates this space.[14] Technology companies are still making the most money; only a tiny fragment of it trickles down to content creators (Taylor 15). Another example of digital inequality can be seen in the form of "digital footprints." Communication scholars Marina Micheli, Christoph Lutz, and Moritz Büchi define digital footprints as "the aggregate of data derived from the *digitally traceable behavior and online presence associated with an individual,*" that include "liking, favoriting, following or commenting" and "browsing histories, search queries, purchase histories and geolocation information" (243, 245, emphasis original). Digital footprints can be generated by the self through active participation (e.g., posting, commenting), by others through passive participation (e.g., being tagged, rated, searched by others), and by algorithms (244). This means that people such as Pirzada, who do not post as often as Cho or do not have as many followers as kaur, may remain unknown in the big scheme of digital things. Social media in this way reinforces rather than challenges existing inequality (Yoo and Zúñiga 33). Knowing this, when we practice vigilant eco-love on social media, we need to be conscious about posting contents and amplifying voices (by retweeting) of people who could contribute to the transformation of the ecology as a whole.

When answering a call from a hashtag that is framed to evoke personal narratives, people who practice vigilant eco-love would thus insist on providing ecological explanations. For instance, in responding to the hashtag "#WhyIDidntReport," Pirzada's tweets assert that the answers to why "I" didn't report sexual violence/abuse cannot be found in individual stories. The problem is not with the individual, but rather in the context, in the ecology, that makes reporting difficult:

> #WhyIDidntReport because of "Log Kya Kehenge?"—what will people say? Can I still get married? Will people think bad of me and my family? The social consequences of disclosure in societ-

ies where we don't understand sexual violence as crimes that are not the victims fault.

#WhyIDidntReport because of the stereotypes that Muslim women are oppressed and Islam is an inherently violent religion. Instead of spending the energy it takes to fight stereotypes while getting help, we stay silent instead. #genderedislamophobia

#WhyIDidntReport because we don't trust law enforcement. How can we report to the very entities that profile us and promote islamophobic policies

In these examples, the "I" of why I didn't report is not necessarily about the "I" per se, but rather where the "I" is situated/located. It is about the "I" in the context: of a family that revictimizes rather than supports the victim, of a society that is Islamophobic and sexist and makes it harder for Muslim women to report, and of laws and policies that still harm women and Muslims. Indeed, in the ecological healing approach, it is important to be able to "contextualize the pain" that people experience (Ginwright 97). First, when pain is contextualized, victims/survivors feel humanized throughout the entire process. Second, to focus on the context means that we demand that the change needs to happen not only at the individual but also at the ecological level. As community organizers Nicole Burrowes, Morgan Cousins, Paula X. Rojas, and Ije Ude point out, "personal healing in isolation from a larger community cannot transform the world; neither can social action without personal and emotional development" (228). In other words, when practicing vigilant eco-love, we would demand that transformation happen to the *entire* ecology and the self as part of (not separate from) that ecology.

To practice vigilant eco-love is to be invested in our ecology. We are therefore deeply embedded in our locale. People who practice vigilant eco-love have "a sense of responsibility for home, community, town, and country" (Filippi 238). For Pirzada, it is her designating Los Angeles as "fields of care" that furthers her activism (Filippi 238). In one of her interviews, Pirzada shares, "when it comes to effecting change through creating safe spaces . . . there is no better place than Los Angeles." She says, "I need to be where my community is, and that's here. . . . This is the place where I've found people who align with those values the most. We're dedicated to honoring the work of people before us who struggled, and Los Angeles really creates a space where we can all honor that shared struggle and shared history." Here, she grounds and roots herself in a particular place, the city of Los Angeles, deeming it important in her work of "effecting change through creating safe spaces." It is this deep and meaningful attachment (a sense of responsibility) to one's locale that provides people who practice vigilant eco-love with a sense of self that is deeply embedded within an ecology.

People who practice vigilant eco-love recognize that, for some people, spirituality is an important part of an ecology, and one that needs to be transformed as well. Spirituality is indeed crucial for Pirzada, as she tweets:

The struggle is real. To maintain my spiritual health when I see how survivors are disposable in so many community spaces, I remind myself of how much Allah (swt) loves me- and that people will always be flawed. Still, we deserve better. #survivorloveletter @hearttogrow

Dear Muslim survivor, it is not our fault. We are not to be blamed for the harm that was brought upon us. We seek justice however feels right—whether on this earth or in the hereafter. I believe Allah (swt) is just and They believe us. #SurvivorLoveLetter @ hearttogrow

My body craves the prayer, the Duaa that prays for my safety-physical, emotional, spiritual. The Duaa that demands an end to toxic masculinity. The Duaa that calls on our Protector to send our survivors some love, some time for healing, some strength.

May we envision the world we want to live in. With spiritual nourishment from imams that affirm your existence. May the doors of the masjid always be open for you, through the doors that are genderless. #survivorloveletter

My #SurvivorLoveLetter is a dua for my trans, non-binary and gender non-conforming survivors today. I love you. May Allah (swt) send protection against erasure of your being in all the spaces you are in. May safety, healing and resources be in abundance.

Religion has healing potential, but it's also conflictual
-@— #niswa #DVAM

First, I would like to note here that hashtags function as a mode of curating and imagining one's community. In this case, when a person participates in the hashtag #survivorloveletter, they may feel that they are part of that conversation and community. Hashtags and hyperlinks could also function as devices to contextualize one's posting within its ecology. Second, the ability to imagine is part of activist/activism work. It therefore matters who one imagines with and for, and with which/ whose tools one imagines. In this case, Pirzada imagines *with* and *for* her Muslim community of *all genders* and with the tools found outside the hegemonic neoliberal discourse. Through her tweets, she teaches people "to create the type of communities in which they want to live"—that is, to be able to envision "the otherwise"[15] is an essential part of not only a "healing" process but also of activist work (Ginwright 12). Her vision of a transformed ecology includes changes that happen in spiritual spaces, such as having masjids/mosques and spiritual communities be "genderless" and accept "trans, non-binary and gender non-conforming survivors" whose existence has been erased in the spiritual community. This concept of the "genderless" and accepting people of all genders is quite subversive when contextualized within a space that often segregates and allocates resources based on one's gender. In focusing on the well-being of her ecology, Pirzada demands that the cultural and gendered practices of how Islam is interpreted in her community be changed. Her Twitter articulation of Islam and its relationship to women, gender, and sexual violence is nuanced and progressive, validating the experiences of being a Muslim woman of color in the toxic masculinity culture of the United States. Although she relies on Allah swt (*subhanahu wa ta'ala*—the most glorified) as the "just" force, she ultimately recognizes that religion has "healing potential, but it's also conflictual." In other words, she does not romanticize religion to be the absolute elixir for all ailments in the world.

Third, Pirzada's tweets highlight the importance of spirituality in activism and healing work. As staff chaplain Linda Filippi argues, "at the core of ecological survival is reconciliation with self, with others, with nonhuman nature, and with the holy" (234). In this view, connection to the divine, to the holy, is important if transformation of the *entire* ecology is to happen. In many cultures, trauma is often addressed through narratives of spirituality. This is especially helpful when the trauma itself comes from being disconnected from ancestral and spiritual practices that have helped one and one's forbears to know who they are and how to navigate their lives (Ramírez 31). Pirzada's tweets acknowledge that spirituality and maintaining her spiritual health are crucial in the activist work that she does. When she was ready to quit, for instance, it was Allah who gave her the strength to persist. She tweets: "I think about the many times I wanted to quit. The work, the community, the faith. Something pulled me back—always believing that I can't find healing for my trauma without You. Yah Allah, bring me strength to persist as so many others have. #survivorloveletter @hearttogrow." The connection that she feels with Allah recommits her to all that she's ready to abandon. Even her healing is impossible, she asserts, without Allah. As a whole, then, her tweets suggest that transformation in the spiritual sphere is needed as part of the entire ecological transformation if we are to work toward social justice and an end to systemic oppression. It is important that people who do not practice spirituality of any kind, in however way it is defined, are aware that spirituality may still be a part of the *entire* ecology that may also need to be transformed as well—and therefore for them to respect, have conversations, create connections, and work with each other to achieve the *collective* goal of ecological transformation.

It is also worth noting that in her tweets Pirzada at times attaches emotions to spirituality and trauma/healing/activist work. For instance, she tweets:

I'm ready for a masjid where *I don't have* to *worry* about if the imam will recognize me as a human being who can consent. Who understands that consent is ongoing, and is not a given when I signed the nikkah contract. That #consentisfard (emphasis mine)

Where and when can we find some spiritual healing? *I'm so drained*. Give me a spiritual leader who is going to affirm my survivorhood, tell me they believe me, and stand firmly for justice against their kin, their bros and themselves. #believesurvivors #rapeisnotzina (emphasis mine)

In such tweets, she speaks against masjids where imams do not understand consent, especially during the *nikkah* or marriage contract, which contributes to her feeling worried. She also speaks against spiritual leaders who do not believe survivors or who consider rape as zina and who make her feel "drained." In showing her "againstness" toward the practice of Islam in everyday life, Pirzada uses the language of the affective ("worry," "drain," etc.). This emotional againstness is what women's studies and critical race and ethnic studies scholar Sylvia Chan-Malik calls Muslim women's "affective insurgency." Chan-Malik argues that

the encounter between Islam as lived religion and racial form in the United States . . . produces Muslim women's being as a continual process of "affective insurgency." . . . "[A]ffective insurgency" . . . refer[s] to the multiscalar, diffuse, and ever-shifting forms of againstness that . . . are the hallmark of U.S. Muslim women's lives. . . . [T]his againstness is not, nor has ever been, directed at a singular target; instead, it is a set of affective responses that emerge out of the ways Islam is consistently lived insurgently by women, responses that arise out of the ways U.S. Muslim women engage, navigate, and counter the ways Islam is imagined as an unruly and insurgent political presence at various moments in history. (15–16)

Pirzada's tweets at times highlight her emotions (or her emotional "againstness") regarding her lived experience of being a Muslim woman of color in the Unites States. Through such tweets, she affirms not only that spiritual space is a significant part of the ecology but also that spirituality and spiritual practices affect one's everyday feeling and living.

It is crucial to consider various elements of the ecology (spiritual, digital, political, etc.) if we are to achieve the well-being of the ecology and the self as part of the ecology. When people have the ability to engage in social media in ways that contextualize the self in the ecology, even the act of calling out, which I find important and necessary in our practice of vigilant eco-love, can be turned into something that is productive and useful, rather than destructive and hurtful. To date, the callout culture on social media has been expressed mostly in extravagant displays of contempt and cruelty (rather than, say, encouragements to correct one's behavior—see chapter 3). When this practice of calling out is rectified by contextualizing the behavior within its ecology (i.e., through the vigilant eco-love practice discussed in this chapter), perhaps we will be more open to correcting our course when we are at the receiving end of a callout on social media, because we will be able to see that we, too, are a product of our ecology; what we post reveals and reflects the relationships we have with others and the dominant ideologies and discourses operating within the ecology. Our efforts to transform ourselves are attempts to improve the ecology, and vice versa. Perhaps, then, when we are being called out, rather than being defensive, which is a sign of being worried about our own (neoliberal) self(ie)-image instead of the well-being of the ecology, we can simply say what poet and author Claudia Rankine, during an interview with journalist Krista Tippett, suggested we say when being called out, "Did I say anything else?" To do so is to indicate that we are listening and learning from others, are acknowledging our mistakes, and are willing to do better. Thoughtfully engaging with others in such a way moves us toward the well-being of the ecology.

(3) Work toward an End to Systemic Oppression

It follows, then, that what I am arguing here is not simply a shift from the neoliberal self(ie) to a vigilant eco-love practice, although that is certainly a major part of the change that needs to happen. I hope what has become clear thus far is that what is necessary is to transform the entire ecology—of which the self is only a part. What I aim to highlight in this section is that connections built *solely* on social media—the world of phantasmagoria—will not transform the entire ecology because phantasmagoria creates and reproduces rather than challenges affect alienation (see chapter 2); and also, digital ecology is only one part of the entire ecology.

In working toward an end to systemic oppression, people who practice vigilant eco-love use social media to call for collective action and invite others to show up at protests, marches, and other community events. As Canada Research Chair in Digital Media and Global Network Society Merlyna Lim argues, social movements will inevitably involve "hybrid human-communication-information networks that include social media," however, "the human body will always be the most essential and central instrument" (129) in this struggle. People who practice vigilant eco-love do not use social media only to build and maintain online relationships and communities, they also aim to change laws and policies and promote other forms of structural, political, and legal changes by showing up at places that matter. For example, Pirzada tweeted about the rally on September 2, 2015, at the California governor's office in support of AB 953, which aimed to restrict racial and identity profiling and make law enforcement agencies more transparent and accountable (Weber). Her tweet that day began with a picture of a sunrise over Interstate 5, with a caption that says, "Starting the day on interstate 5. Sacramento here we come! #AB953 #CAIR #getonthebus #OCCCOPico." The Twitter thread that came after this first tweet focused on the event. A few of these tweets were:

> In the Capitol building. #nojusticenopeace #AB953 #ShutItDown [Tweeted with a picture of the rally]

> Doing a die-in for 4.5 min in the hallway #AB953 #wearenottargets

> Closing song and prayer #AB953 #BlackLivesMatter #WeAreNotTargets [Tweeted with a video of the protesters singing a song]

These tweets exemplify how Pirzada uses social media to report protests (or community events) and invite and engage others to take part in collectively oriented actions that demand social change for the betterment of the community. When it comes to organizing and working toward social change, it is important to do collective action over time. People need to *continually* show up if change is to finally occur. For that to happen, people who perform vigilant eco-love must therefore be consistent in their social media practice of mobilizing for change.

I would like to digress for a moment to acknowledge that being physically present at social protest events may not be possible for some people who may have limitations. For example, it is often assumed that people are sufficiently healthy, able-bodied, and middle class (or have the time and financial and childcare resources) to take a bus or drive to the protests. In other words, social justice places and community organizing events are not always inclusive.

To make a strategy work, when people who practice vigilant eco-love invite others (especially women or other marginalized groups of people) to show up for protests or community events (or to share their stories of pain/trauma/violence online), they must make sure that these places are accessible, inclusive, safe, nurturing, and nontoxic. Because of people's physical and psychological limitations (or other limitations such as one's immigration status), we need to rethink face-to-face activism and further incorporate digital or other forms of technology and social media so that people who are homebound or have other restrictions can still participate in social justice work, even when they cannot physically attend. We need to put in place structural supports to enable people to effortlessly show up for community gatherings and protests. In an ecology that truly values the power of the collective, these community-building meetings should be considered basic necessities. Attending protests and community events should not be a luxury.

Moreover, although the social media practice of vigilant eco-love does not always involve inviting people to show up in public spaces, it nonetheless aims to raise awareness about social issues in their communities in an effort to end systemic oppression. People who practice vigilant eco-love often incorporate critical, engaged, and feminist pedagogy in their social media practice. Their postings often revolve around helping other people understand social issues better. They take the time to unpack how certain things happen and what people can do to challenge and overcome various social problems. On her Twitter, Pirzada frequently raises awareness about social issues and social change:

In case you didn't know, Los Angeles is scheduled to receive half a mill from DHS and we barely know anything about the CVE grant—what indicators they're going to use, what the MOU's look like, what has DHS asked of them. This money does not make us safe. #StopCVE

We need trainings for our imams on how to direct women's health questions to professionals re:mental and sexual health #girlgetcovered

Drafted a menu outline for a comprehensive sex Ed programme
for Muslim girls aged 13 and up! #muslimsexed

As a Muslim Sex Educator, I encourage my students to critically
analyze the messages they receive from the media about sex.
#MuslimSexEd

These tweets exemplify how Pirzada uses social media to educate others about social issues, rather than simply to project a neoliberal self(ie).
She alerts people about a CVE grant that the city of Los Angeles is about
to receive and why it may pose problems for their communities. Her
tweets also explain what she does as a sex educator, such as drafting a
menu for comprehensive sex education or teaching her students to critically decode media representations of sex.

Teaching or consciousness raising is indeed important and can be
framed as an antidote for the neoliberal self(ie) as it shifts the focus to
sharing (knowledge) with others and the transformation of the entire
ecology. Social media is used here not as a means to create a phantasmagoria, but rather as a tool for consciousness raising and mobilization
for social change, which is crucial in ending systemic oppression. People
who practice vigilant eco-love understand that transformation needs to
happen to the entire ecology and that it is thus important that everyone
within that ecology learn (or unlearn) the what, why, and how of social
change and its creation.

Conclusion: The Politics of Otherwise

This book subscribes to the notion that "technology affected the social
imaginary" (Buck-Morss 29), and this particular chapter aims to do the
work of the imaginary: to theoretically and politically imagine "what else
might be possible" in eluding the neoliberal imperative of social media if
we are to continue using it to address the racial/political/structural/gendered pain of sexual violence and demand that the ecology that enables

and encourages such pain to happen in the first place be transformed. Through an examination of Sahar Pirzada's social media activism, this chapter builds an argument for an alternative practice, "vigilant eco-love," that emerges as one possibility for feminist social media practice that attempts to subvert the limits of the neoliberal self(ie) gaze in the phantasmagoric world of social media.

As a theoretical concept, vigilant eco-love cannot escape the short-comings of its imagined presence, as with any other theory. Whatever limitations that this concept bears, they reveal my own lack of creativity and curiosity, that is, my inability to assemble tools outside existing dis-courses with which I can otherwise do the work of imagining.

To imagine is to yearn for the "otherwise," the elsewhere, or the something-other-than. It is to come into cognitive contact with the limi-tations of the present and to then have the desire for the otherwise. In other words, the "politics of otherwise" is crucial for it names the how, where, what, and who of the current system that is not working. It *is* a way of seeing. It makes visible the problems with what is and propels us to move toward something else. Because once one sees what is, one can-not unsee it. One then seeks the otherwise. The politics of otherwise is therefore always subversive in nature, as it seeks to bring down and go beyond the status quo.

To be engaged in the politics of otherwise is therefore a political act. It does the work of taking back power and making the claim that not only people in power can imagine, but that the community can as well, that the people who are part of the ecology at large can collectively imagine a better ecology. As such, the politics of otherwise is integral to and a form of vigilant eco-love. The love for the ecology—for it to "do better"—demands that we remain vigilant toward what is and perpetually seek those places where the otherwise exists.

In the spirit of being vigilant toward what is, I would like to propose here three sets of practical questions, revolving around content, con-text, and the collective, that we can ask ourselves before posting any-thing on social media so that we can be more aware of our own practice.

First, in terms of the content of our social media posting: *Is the content about ourselves, our personal stories, or our community/collective/system/ ecology? Does the content invite others to do collective action, broadcast community events and programs, or simply project oneself as a successful neoliberal self(ie)? What stories does our posting tell?* In other words, as Pirzada tweets, "If data were going to win us policy, we would have won already. We need storytelling." Her tweet reminds us that how we frame our story matters. If we want to move toward social justice, we need to craft stories that reflect our community, our interconnectedness, our social responsibility, our support for each other, and our goal to end systemic oppression.

The second set of practical questions that we should ask ourselves before posting on social media revolves around context: *When we tell a story about ourselves or anything at all, do we contextualize our posting within a larger context? Does the context we provide allow other people to understand how the ecology/structure/ideology works and therefore possibly evoke social change?* In the world of social media, where context becomes increasingly obsolete, to insist that we provide context (by way of Bitly, hyperlinks, or hashtags, etc.), to take more space than the 280 characters that they allot us, is to subvert the very limitation of the platform.

The third and final set of practical questions that we need to be mindful about if we want to subvert the neoliberal gaze and practice a vigilant eco-love social media presence focuses on the collective: *Does this posting prioritize the collective? Is it "collectively oriented"? Does it aim to harness the power of the collective? Is it "socially responsible"? Does it work to connect with and support each other? Does it work toward ending systemic oppression?* These questions, in their insistence on the power of the collective, would allow us to escape the social media imperative of focusing on ourselves as individuals, turning ourselves into successful neoliberal self(ies) and our social media into phantasmagorias.

To ask these practical questions before we post anything on social media is to practice self-reflexivity, that is, to be "vigilant" about our own social media practice. It is also in the spirit of self-reflexivity that we can ask ourselves, if at any moment we find ourselves projecting a neoliberal self(ie) on social media: what is my own investment in this way of representing myself? What is the *dividend* that neoliberalism and capitalism give me when I project myself from the standpoint of the neoliberal self(ie)? To understand our own investment in the system is to see how the system works to absorb *us* in its machine and keep it running for *them*.

This exercise of locating ourselves within the maintenance of the system is key, as these practical questions should not be read as being concerned with ourselves per se. In other words, when someone asks, "What should I do? How can I change my behavior so that I don't become a racist or a neoliberal feminist?" the first thing we need to do is to shift the questions. This is not about you, me, or any individual no longer being a racist or a neoliberal feminist. Rather, it is about how we can work together toward ending racism and neoliberalism. It is about the practices that we engage in to take down systemic oppression, instead of worrying about whether or not we are racists or neoliberal feminists. I am not at all saying that individuals should not change. However, changes that happen *only* at the individual level because a person is concerned with their own self-image, instead of the system as a whole, is not going to take us far in making systemic changes.

In posing these practical questions, I certainly am not arguing that we use social media *solely* for feminist advocacy work. By all means, if we feel so inclined, we may continue to post food pictures (something that I personally find contain all the pleasures and none of the guilt), cat pictures, or family pictures. We can continue to create and celebrate various relationships and accomplishments in this digital space. My invitation here is simply that when we carry out our feminist activism on social media that we be mindful about its ecology, ideology (how dominant ideologies structure our posting/activism), mode of performing and interconnecting, and ramifications.

Finally, this chapter has pointed out that subjects who practice vigilant eco-love situate their practice within an ecology—they do not prioritize the self above other people (rejecting the neoliberal slogan of "put yourself first"). Practicing vigilant eco-love means that we are not interested in projecting a successful and appealing neoliberal self(ie). Rather, we insist on representing the "I" in context and aim to transform the entire ecology by, among other things, enacting collective action and encouraging others to do the same. I hope that the imaginary work of theorizing vigilant eco-love practice may provide us with a glimpse of how the digital road to social justice may not always have to be paved with neoliberal intentions.

Coda

It may be odd to end a book with a story of how it all began. And yet, a closing that explains and meets its beginning is the note that this book will end on.

It may be odd to end a theoretical book with a short personal note. And yet, what is theoretical is always political, is always personal, is always political, is always theoretical.

And so I end, or begin here.

* * *

I could not quite put my finger on it. The bombardment of social media postings that catalog endless accomplishments, extravagant successes, and performed celebrations of the self, all of which turned everything into an opportunity, a positive emotion, and a cause for personal transformation. Failing to perform such a presentation of the self, one is doomed to be ostracized, trolled, controlled. At first, I found them to be amusing, then, annoying, and eventually, deeply troubling. But these postings were easier to stomach or ignore when they were posted by subjects who label themselves "influencers" or "life coaches" and clearly stand on the neoliberal side of the political economy. When I saw these postings being posted by activists, feminists, or those who embrace the more radical side of history, including my own communities of practice, albeit in different forms and formats, I began to hold my breath. I was waiting for Something to emerge and reveal itself, as I could feel Its shiny presence but had yet to meet It. I didn't even know *how* to talk about it.

This book is thus an attempt to put into words Something that I wasn't able to put my finger on. It is my struggling to come up with a language to access that which can approximate its existence and effects. It is to then underscore what is at stake here: when we are not aware of our social media practice, the neoliberal logic that governs this space can shapeshift us into neoliberal self(ies). Our feminist work will continue to be co-opted by the neoliberal machine and used for its gain unless we are conscious about our social media practice and work *collectively* against the neoliberal machine of social media.

If neoliberalism empties feminism "of its elements of collective struggle" (Prügl 626), then, to refuel feminism, we must return to the power of the collective. I agree with law professor Hila Keren, who affirms that "other forms of feminism that work outside of the market and are structural and collective in nature must not only be maintained but also further developed to resist neoliberalism's 'divide and conquer' techniques" (118). If we are to still embrace the slogan "the personal is political" that has outlived the second-wave feminist movement, we must not let it be resignified to highlight the politics of the personal that is articulated through the neoliberal language of "personal responsibility," personal choice, and freedom that often comes at the expense of others (the "say 'no' to others, and take care of yourself first" attitude). We must insist on collective politics that emphasizes the personal in a way that refers to our daily, intimate, mundane lives as a site for organizing political and ecological changes.

To this end, and as an antidote to the neoliberal self(ie) gaze, I offer in this book a theorization of the "vigilant eco-love" practice, which is a practice that frames the self as part of an ecology, performs eco-love (instead of the neoliberal version of self-love) with vigilance, and works toward ecological rather than individual transformation. Certainly, I do not theorize this practice as *the only* subversive practice on social media; it is merely offered as one option among many possible alternatives out there. Nonetheless, I insist that, in whatever way such a subversive practice is reimagined, being collectively oriented and performing collective action that aims to change the structure of and transform the entire ecology remain central to feminist social media practice.

My naming this practice "vigilant eco-love" is indeed an invitation to return to love. But love is resignified here as an epistemic device, a tool in the contentious process of knowledge production. In this book, I ask love to do the work of unmasking the power structure. I stick with the texts (i.e., social media campaigns and accounts) that I love, by feminists whom I genuinely admire. By sticking with them, yet being vigilant about them and aiming to care for the ecology, I arrive at my analysis. Love takes me to these epistemic spaces. Love defines which texts to examine; (vigilant) love directs how to encounter and engage with the texts; and love determines what purposes my readings of these texts serve. Love makes me ponder what it means to theorize about the *limits* of feminist activism on social media by focusing on social media campaigns that are the most "successful," loved, and celebrated—such as rupi kaur's, Mia Matsumiya's, Margaret Cho's, and Sahar Pirzada's, which may represent different forms of feminism—instead of those that are actually "limited" by social media. I am not interested in claiming which feminism is more authentic (e.g., is celebrity feminism less political?). Rather, I am invested in dismantling the neoliberal ideology in any and all forms of feminist activism on social media. In the name, work, and practice of love, this book theorizes the forms that social media addiction and attachment (as properties of love) take and perform as, and what they do to our feminist fight for social justice.

Behind the grand guise of my love for the movements, however, I shall not hide another pretext of this book: I must admit that I wrote it because I dare not confront (nor do I find any use in online confrontation with) the beloved people in my communities of practice who project neoliberal self(ie)s on their social media. This book thus serves as a way for me to offer an unhurried objection to the way we (myself included) practice activism on social media. Certainly, my criticisms do not hinge on the practice of these feminists as *individual* actions; rather, they focus on the *structures* that shape their practices. To criticize the individual is to perform a neoliberal mode of reading that sees individuals as the site of the problem. In this book, by contrast, I contend that what individuals share on social media is revealing of the dominant ideologies operating within their tweets and conversations. It is these ideologies and how they work that I am making visible and criticizing, reflecting back on historian Joan Scott's argument: "It is not individuals who have experience, but subjects who are constituted through experience" (25). Thus, instead of being intended as criticisms of these feminists, my vigilant eco-love readings of their feminist social media campaigns aim to expose the collision and collusion between feminism and neoliberalism on social media, the troubles that are brewing underneath feminist activism on social media and its limits, and the limits of social media itself in bringing about significant social change.

I also wrote this book to shine a bright, yet troubling light on the pressure to speak up to prove oneself as a feminist/activist on social media. On these digital platforms, silence is too easily stigmatized and equated with complicity in the power structure. Speaking up on social media becomes compulsory for those who need to perform their feminist subjectivity. For instance, during the #MeToo campaign, some other women and I were not ready to share our stories on social media. Yet we felt the pressures to do so and were even stigmatized for being silent. I therefore dedicate chapter 4 to interrogating the currency of silence on social media and articulating the need to insist on maintaining our spaces of silence, especially when the pressures to speak can generate more pain and become another site where the reenactment of violence is performed.

Beyond the multifaceted issues and theories that this book has struggled through, it has a rather modest goal: to reveal the underlying neoliberal structure of social media that limits our feminist activism in this space, so that we will no longer be controlled by it or be used for its (or our own) neoliberal gain. To return to the ghost figure of phantasmagoria, I hope this book can haunt its readers as they participate on social media, so they can perpetually self-reflect on their practice and avert and subvert the neoliberal self(ie) gaze.

In the end, I hope this book has carved a path and can serve as an open invitation for its readers to remain critical of the social media practices of feminist activists whom we love deeply and vigilantly and of our own practices as well—an inevitably difficult endeavor that is also necessary. It remains important to continue imagining alternative modes of doing feminist activism on social media so that we can eventually transform the *entire* ecology, including the digital environment within which our lives are increasingly immersed. I am genuinely eager to see what other conversations and social media practices become visible and possible, in part, because of this book.

ACKNOWLEDGMENTS

This is my favorite part of the book: where I get to pour out all my love to the special people who have made it possible for me to sculpt this book into being.

Claire Moses has been there, always, receiving emails each time I *thought* I had found a new angle for my book. She never dismissed any of them, no matter how random or absurd. Instead, she would say, "Tell me more." With that, I would feel the courage to explore the unsettling ground of the fresh, unfertilized soil of my thoughts. Not all drafts were worthy of her reading, yet she read them with her meticulous eyes, intelligent mind, and generous heart all the same. I admire her wholeheartedly and thank her infinitely. I also would like to thank her book club for reading the first draft of this book: Deborah Rosenfelt and Debra Bergoffen.

Heather Rellihan has been a dear friend, whose kindness I still aim to emulate in my own life. My gratitude runs deep for her reading of this book with her exquisite and inquisitive mind. She has helped sharpen all of the dull edges of this book. Kimberly Williams shared not only her thought-provoking (and funny!) feedback with me but also my passion for ice cream. This adventure of writing is that much sweeter and more enjoyable because of her. I am grateful for their presence in my life. The marvelous and magical time spent in Tuscany, Italy, writing, giving each other feedback, and laughing with both of these souls will forever be in my heart, and to almost quote Jordin Sparks, like a tattoo.

The editors and staff members at NYU Press have been generously supportive in shepherding this project until the end. I am immensely grateful to Eric Zinner, whose astute insight helped me reimagine this book to be better than it could ever be. For advocating my book and teaching me patience and persistence when these words were so foreign to me, I thank him deeply and dearly. Lisha Nadkarni was the first editor to show interest in my book and I thank her for seeing the potential of this book even at its early stage. I also would like to thank the anonymous readers whose encouraging and brilliant suggestions helped me revamp this entire book. Any crystal-clear aura emitting from this book is indebted to them. Dolma Ombadykow and Furqan Sayeed, whose awesomeness made the publishing process less daunting and more wonderful—I thank them sincerely.

If my journey in academia is filled with vagabond joy, it is because every year I get to take a heart-nourishing trip to some rejuvenating corner of the world to spend some splendid time with brave, bodacious, and brilliant women at the Creative Connections Writing Retreat. They truly are my role models for how to be a powerful and compassionate woman in academia. Special thanks to Tanya Golash-Boza for her friendship and inspiring presence. I strive to be a better scholar and person because of her.

My dear friends and write-on-site fellows in Honolulu have shared with me not only a slice of paradise called Hawai'i (and some fresh colorful drinks over gorgeous sunsets!) but also a stimulating writing space where I feel lovingly supported: Christine Beaule, Jan Brunson, Michelle Manes, Anna Stirr, and Younga Park. I am grateful for their friendship. I also cherish my Indonesian community in Honolulu, who have shared with me much laughter and delicious homemade Indonesian food. Their friendship is essential to my sanity.

The writing fellowship at Faber Residency in Olot, Catalonia, gifted me the quiet time to really think and type and the opportunity to connect with other feminist writers from around the world. It was truly a writer's dream to be a part of their exceptional program. I am tremendously grateful for their support. This book is also shaped by the critical feedback from amazing audiences at the Faber Residency lecture series, Universitat de Barcelona, and Escola Oficial d'Idiomes at Olot. What a privilege to be able to share my work in these gorgeous spaces and with marvelous people! I also would like to thank the students at NYU Shanghai, whose brilliant questions became the seed of chapter 5, without which this book would never have been complete.

Special thanks also goes to Margaret Carnegie, whose research assistance has been crucial for my book. Collecting data from the vast virtual world is a tedious job. Yet she manages to do so with much care and diligence. I am sincerely grateful for her help, especially for chapters 2 and 3. I also would like to thank Wendy Bolton, who has been a magical editor who makes my writing sparkle, and Meghan Drury, whose sharp reading of the final version of this book seals it with a thundering clasp of delight.

Agung Nugrahaeni and Ibnu Magda are pretty much dream siblings. Although I don't share my academic world with them, I share with them my love of delicious and decadent food and, of course, of traveling. These are what nourish me from the inside out, what makes my heart glow, and my tummy sing songs of joy! I love them to chocolate biscuit with caramel pieces.

There will always be a special kind of love for Diza. Her charming beauty, sophisticated thinking, thoughtful heart, and fashionable style make this world a more dazzling place to be in. In the most depressing of times, I would simply need to think of her (or talk to her!), and the way she sprinkles sweetness and hope on any situation would make me feel like this life is still worth living and this book, still worth writing. I love her to the glowing moon and back.

I also would like to thank you, the readers of this book, for your willingness to entertain whatever ideas I am brave enough to put forth and engage with them in ways that will advance our field. You are my communities of practice. I appreciate you and look forward to reading your books, too! Salam.

A small portion of chapter 2 has been accepted for publication in *Diogènes* as "The Performativity of Pain: Affective Excess and Asian Women's Sexuality in Cyberspace," doi: 10.1177/0392192120970412.

NOTES

1. THE NEOLIBERAL SELF(IE)

1 I retain any errors, typos, misspellings, etc., to preserve the original expression.

2 Throughout this book, I use the terms "neoliberal self(ie) gaze" and "neoliberal self(ie)" interchangeably as I intend for the term to refer not only to the function of the gaze but also to the technology of the self(ie) on social media.

3 I use the identifier "Muslim" for Pirzada as I yield to Pirzada's self-description: she uses "Muslim" to label herself—and to assert that her feminist activism is rooted in Islamic values and the Muslim community.

4 It is worth noting that neoliberal feminism first grew out of media and mainstream representations of feminism (rather than being developed by a feminist theorist or presented as an academic manifesto—in other words, no one claims themselves to be a neoliberal feminist).

5 I theorize "the neoliberal self(ie)" not as a mere visual construction, the way "selfie" has often been understood.

6 rupi kaur, whose Instagram account I analyze in chapter 2, perhaps hinted at this point when she posted a caption to accompany an image of herself wrapped in black fabric, on October 2, 2019, "many tried/but failed to catch me/i am the ghost of ghosts/everywhere and nowhere/i am magic tricks/within magic within magic/none have figured out/i am a world wrapped in worlds/folded in suns and moons/you can try but/you won't get those hands on me." That is, as the neoliberal self(ie) of the twenty-first-century digital phantasmagoria, she is "the ghost of ghosts," who embodies, performs, and becomes the "magic tricks" itself, which in the digital world lives inside infinite, never-ending magic, "a world wrapped in worlds," existing within layers of simulated reality, a point that I will discuss further in chapter 2. As a side note, throughout the book, when making references to the date of a social media post, I use the local Hawai'i time as it appears on my social media feed.

7 As legal and new media scholar Michael Beurskens argues, "researchers must use best efforts to remove any personal references from the data sets. They have to remove user names or replace them with pseudonyms (including those used in the tweet's contents) and anonymize location data. Cleaning up personal data (like pet names, food eaten, and others) is infeasible (but would probably be required under the current legal regime)" (132).

8 The first hashtag to popularize the feature was #sandiegofire, which web developer Nate Ritter used to live-tweet forest fires sweeping through the San Diego area in the fall of 2007 (Guha 155). When the hashtag was first proposed by blogger Chris Messina earlier that year, it was rejected by Twitter, which at the time preferred the "trending topic algorithm" (Brock, "From the Blackhand" 538).

2. "MAKING GOLD OUT OF IT"

1 On her official website, kaur says that her choice to not use any capitalization in her poems is a way to honor her mother tongue, Punjabi, and its Gurmukhi script, which does not have any uppercase or lowercase letters. For her, this also represents visual equality between the letters.

2 For this chapter, I discursively analyzed all her postings from May 18, 2013 (her first posting), to May 3, 2019—a total of 834 postings.

3 For more on the definition of phantasmagoria and how social media functions as phantasmagoria, please see chapter 1.

4 I emphasize the word "also" here to clarify that I am not arguing that we should focus only on the structural. However, as long as we focus only on individuals and their personal responsibility, social justice will never be achieved.

3. MASKING PAIN, UNMASKING RACE

1 As of May 3, 2019, Matsumiya had posted 102 images and was followed by 52,600 people. For this chapter, I discursively analyzed all 102 postings on her Instagram account.

2 Mainstream U.S. media began to use the term "sexual harassment" for "unwanted sexual attention" around 1975 when the *New York Times* published an article titled, "Women Begin to Speak Out against Sexual Harassment at Work" (Thomas and Kitzinger 2). That sexual harassment gradually became widely known as an important women's issue was due to feminism and feminist theorists, especially feminist legal theorists. In the present day, the #MeToo movement further invigorates and makes mainstream the fight against sexual harassment at a more global scale than ever before.

Sexual harassment often happens when women's visibility in public spaces threatens the patriarchal public/private divide, and it therefore serves to regulate women's presence and mobility in public spaces (Megarry 52–53). Matsumiya recognizes this as she points out, "the overall reason we get these messages is because we're all women with some degree of visibility on the internet, whether very low or high. ANY degree of visibility as a woman is all you need to be harassed."

Online sexual harassment, according to Megarry, is "a political term [as] it identifies the abuse of women online as a manifestation of male dominance which functions to perpetuate male social control in cyberspace" (52). An example of online harassment is a comment that a man made on one of Matsumiya's selfies:

"Ugly! no make up." Telling her that she is ugly without makeup can be seen as an attempt to discourage Matsumiya from posting more selfies, unless she wears makeup and turns herself into a sexual object for male desire. This comment polices women's bodies and is uttered to regulate women's online and public presence, with the aim of exerting male dominance in online spaces.

3 See chapter 1 for a definition of phantasmagoria and the framing of social media as phantasmagoria.

4 Matsumiya mentions the person's Instagram handle or name in the screenshot caption, such as, "my best friend, @---, received this" or "submitted by---" when she posts images that are not hers.

5 See chapter 2 for a discussion of social media as a space of affective simulation.

6 Indeed, as lawyer and legal scholar James Whitman points out, shaming is one of the five basic forms of punishment: "deprivations of life (execution); of liberty (imprisonment); of bodily safety and integrity (corporal violence); of property (fines); and of . . . 'dignity' (shaming)" (1060).

7 I would like to thank Heather Rellihan for her astute analysis on this issue.

8 I counted only once in cases where a person was included more than one time; two of the images in this analysis are photos of women.

9 Because online shaming has devastating effects, some scholars argue against it. They argue that shaming as punishment encourages "citizens to resort to dehumanizing and brutalizing behavior towards the offender or the social delinquent," and it turns the shamed individual into a "plaything" and a "social untouchable" (A. Cheung 305). Trial by Internet mob is dangerous, as media scholar Anne Cheung argues, because it violates one's privacy and dignity. In her view, no one, not even criminals, should ever have their dignity taken away from them (302, 320). She argues that "dignity should prevail over the right of freedom of expression in the case of online shaming"—here dignity is defined as "one's innate personhood, integrity, and self-respect," couched within "the protection of privacy rights as part and parcel of one's personhood and integrity" (A. Cheung 306).

10 Although Matsumiya's strategy can certainly be categorized as online shaming and may inflict pain on the harassers, her activity should not be perceived as cyber-bullying. Cyber-bullying, according to de Vries, is "more personal and malicious than shaming. In addition, shaming [is] focused on the actions, with the opportunity for a positive outcome, whereas bullying [is] focused on the traits of the individual, with the individual involved described as the 'victim.' Other distinctions [are] that shaming is deserved (not least because it can be supported with 'evidence') and a one-off activity, whereas bullying is sustained and intentionally harmful" (2057). Matsumiya's postings indeed have the goal of eradicating sexual harassment, rather than merely belittling the harassers.

11 Matsumiya acknowledged during an interview on nbcnews.com that she would "delete or blur" personal information of the harassers who have apologized

(Guillermo). This follows the general rule of online shaming, at least according to the young people whom de Vries interviewed, who explained to her that shaming is not appropriate when people who have performed bad behavior apologize (2057). An apology becomes the retributive justice that Matsumiya seeks and accepts from the harassers.

12 Although online shaming has become more common, it remains a contentious issue. There are some scholars who see virtue in shaming. Legal scholar Daniel Solove, for example, argues that shaming is necessary to "*maintain its norms of civility and etiquette*," especially "in a *world of increasingly rude and uncivil behaviour*" (quoted in de Vries 2056, emphasis original). Legal scholar Dan Kahan also argues that humiliation sanctions are not necessarily worse than prison (Whitman 1057–1058, 1062). Some offenders might even choose shame over prison (Whitman 1062). Scholars who are pro-shaming see it as having the potential to be more effective than prison, especially for sexual or commercial offenses (Whitman 1058, 1062).

Some people believe, however, that in the modern era shaming no longer works, considering it to be effective only when there are face-to-face interactions. In the modern Western world, where it is relatively easy for people to physically relocate, public, face-to-face shaming may not have the intended effect—after being shamed, people can simply move and start over somewhere else (Whitman 1063; de Vries 2054).

13 An example of how the neoliberal ideology informs Matsumiya's campaign can be seen in this posting:

To the women, I'm so, so sorry that you've been subjected to this sort of thing. I completely understand and empathize how demeaning and frightening it can be. It's important for us to speak out about it and let everyone know that we don't condone this behavior and I hope you'll join me. To the men who send messages like this to a woman, this behavior needs to stop. Please consider that there's a real human being on the other side and we don't like being sent these types of lewd messages. They scare and disgust us.

Here, by way of addressing women and men as *individuals*, rather than focusing on sexual harassment as a structural and systemic violence issue, Matsumiya once again frames the issue of and the solution to sexual harassment at the individual level: men need to change their behavior.

14 I find it interesting that Matsumiya's Instagram handle (and the hashtag that she uses) is called perv_magnet. Asked in her nbcnews.com interview why she chose that name for the account, she responded:

I think it's a variety of factors. My race attracts fetishists and leads some people to objectify me and believe I'm submissive. I'm also 4′9″, which attracts another type of fetishist, and I probably appear physically vulnerable. Just these two physical factors alone, to some, make me look very defenseless, which is what a predator is always looking for. I know this happens to other Asian women in general. I've talked to so many about it, both offline and online. It's a terrible mix of misogyny, fetishism, and racism. Throw in that I'm also a musical performer and I become the recipient of so much disgusting, unacceptable, predatory behavior.

Matsumiya is eloquent here in making visible the working of "misogyny, fetishism, and racism." However, her perv_magnet handle emphasizes *her* as a "magnet" for perverts (albeit sarcastically and jokingly), rather than the problematic structure that she fluently names: hetero/sexism and racism. Her Instagram handle absorbs the neoliberal aura of social media by focusing on and framing sexual harassment in individual terms: herself as a magnet and the sexual harassers as "perverts." Even the choice of word, "magnet," hints that the magnet creates the situation, "attracts" things—that's what it does, that's its nature.

15 I need to clarify here that I am not arguing that the kawaii aesthetic always operates within a neoliberal logic. It is the particular ways in which Matsumiya uses it that are constrained by the neoliberal logic.

4. SILENCE AS TESTIMONY IN MARGARET CHO'S #12DAYSOFRAGE

1 This was Cho's answer when asked on the television show *The View* why she launched the campaign.

2 That some of Cho's followers have thought of agency in the collective, although in a negative sense, can be seen when they talk about how their mothers didn't do anything: the mothers' failure becomes *their* failure to heal. As a tweet goes, "@margaretcho I'm angry with my parent for not protecting me. She could have saved me. Knew abt it and did nothing. #12daysofrage." This narrative of mother-blaming is not unique to #12daysofrage. As psychologist Janice Haaken argues, "For many survivors, the absent mother, her failure to protect her daughter from abuse, emerges as a dominant motif" (26). Of course, this issue begs for a deeper discussion that is beyond the scope of this chapter. Suffice it to say here that, in this tweet, the agency of daughters is articulated through the agency (or the lack thereof) of mothers. The agency is thought of in the collective.

3 This notion of the self as the collective self can also be seen in Korean American literature from 1920 to 1950, in which the self is often depicted as a "collective self." In much of this literature, authors use the singular pronoun "I" to signify a Korean national identity—the homeland, or the "collective consciousness of the Korean people" (J. Lee 79). For Korean American writers of the time, "I" became a function of the "collective whole" (80). Similarly, in the Confucian tradition, the self "was to be expressed through 'dyadic' relationships, an awareness of man's [*sic*] ties to his society" (Wei-Ming 233; J. Lee 78). In such instances, the self is not articulated in individual terms. My conceptualization of the collective self differs

in that I do not intend to frame the collective self within a national identity as such, but rather, as a collective that is performed on social media.

5. WHAT ELSE MIGHT BE POSSIBLE?

1 See https://twitter.com/hearttogrow?lang=en and https://hearttogrow.org.

2 As of May 3, 2019, Pirzada had 629 followers, was following 449 people, had 1,015 tweets, and 2,174 likes. I analyze all 1,015 of her tweets.

3 He defines NPIC as "the set of symbiotic relationships that link together political and financial technologies of state and owning-class proctorship and surveillance over public political intercourse, including and especially emergent progressive and leftist social movements, since about the mid-1970s" (Rodríguez 22).

4 Nonprofit organizations have been considered problematic because they are often focused on getting funding and hence "niche marketing the work of [their] organizations," instead of organizing (A. Smith 10).

5 It must be noted that, at times, the model that nonprofit organizations use as they aim to do community outreach on the Internet follows that of for-profit corporations, such as sending e-newsletters, "junk" or random self-promotion mail, or selling their "products" and soliciting donations.

6 A full list of HEART's supporters and partners can be retrieved from its website, at https://hearttogrow.org/our-supporters.

7 Vigilante feminism suggests a position outside the boundaries of feminism's antiviolence stance (D'Amore 391).

8 If in chapter 4 the "I" or the agency is located in the collective, in this chapter, such a subjectivity is taken to the next level: it is located not only in the collective (community/with-other-ness) but also in the entire ecology.

9 Please revisit chapter 2 for my discussion of challenging the binary of the real versus the virtual, particularly as it pertains to the notion of the digital space as a space of affective simulation.

10 boyd defines "networked publics" as "publics that are restructured by networked technologies. As such, they are simultaneously (1) the space constructed through networked technologies and (2) the imagined community that emerges as a result of the intersection of people, technology, and practice" (8). Networked publics allow people to spend and enjoy time together (9). boyd also specifies that the qualities of the connections that are formed through networked technologies may differ from those developed through old ways of connecting (such as hanging out at the mall) because "networked technologies alter the social ecosystem and thus affect the social dynamics that unfold" (10). In other words, the specificity of the digital environment lends itself to new ways of relating to and imagining this ecology.

11 Environmental humanities scholar Catriona Mortimer-Sandilands and environmental history scholar Bruce Erickson define "queer ecology" as "an ongoing relationship between sex and nature that exists *institutionally, discursively, scientifically, spatially, politically, poetically, and ethically*" (5, emphasis mine).

12 Native American studies scholar Elisabeth Middleton offers the concept "political ecology" to describe the ways in which "communities negotiate resource claims within a globalized political-economic context, linking grounded understanding of community, place, and political economy to larger cultural processes facing historically colonized communities" (2).

13 Technology scholar Ramesh Srinivasan observes: "digital technologies are not neutral. They are socially constructed—created by people within organizations, who in turn approach the design process based on a set of values and presumptions" (2).

14 For instance, technology consultant Sara Wachter-Boettcher, in her book *Technically Wrong*, shows that Apple, for instance, in 2016 still had "68 percent male [employees] globally, and 77 percent male in technical roles" (20). In terms of race, only 9 percent of the company's staff was Black (20). For Google, the numbers were "81 percent male in 2016"; "1 percent were Black, and 3 percent were Hispanic" (20). At Airbnb, "10 percent of staff came from 'underrepresented groups'" (20). Gender and racial composition matter because they shape the culture of the companies and therefore the design and function of their products and services; biases at the staffing level are inevitably reflected in the digital ecology as well (19).

15 Kandice Chuh popularizes the notion "imagine otherwise" in her book, *Imagine Otherwise: On Asian Americanist Critique*, which invites us to envision productive and provocative ways of employing the Asian Americanist critique lens in the face of its limitations.

WORKS CITED

Ahmed, Sara. "The Contingency of Pain." *Parallax*, vol. 8, no. 1, 2002, pp. 17–34.

———. *The Cultural Politics of Emotion*. Edinburgh University Press, 2014.

———. "Not in the Mood." *New Formations*, no. 82, 2014, pp. 13–28.

———. "Speaking Out." *Feminist Killjoys* (blog), June 2, 2016, www.feministkilljoys.com.

Akyel, Esma. "#Direnkahkaha (Resist Laughter): 'Laughter Is a Revolutionary Action.'" *Feminist Media Studies*, vol. 14, no. 6, 2014, pp. 1093–1094.

Albinsson, Pia, et al., editors. *The Rise of the Sharing Economy: Exploring the Challenges and Opportunities of Collaborative Consumption*. Praeger, 2018.

Anderson, Benedict. *Imagined Communities: Reflections on the Origin and Spread of Nationalism*. 1983. Verso, 1991.

Andreotti, Libero, and Nadi Lahiji. *The Architecture of Phantasmagoria: Specters of the City*. Routledge, 2016.

Anzaldúa, Gloria. *Borderlands/La Frontera: The New Mestiza*. Aunt Lute Books, 1987.

Atkey, Ronald. "Canadian Immigration Law and Policy: A Study in Politics, Demographics and Economics." *Canada-United States Law Journal*, vol. 16, 1990, pp. 59–78.

Bahadur, Nina. "How One Woman Is Using Instagram to Call Out Gross, Creepy Men." *Huffington Post*, October 9, 2015, www.huffpost.com.

Baudrillard, Jean. *Simulacra and Simulation*. Translated by Sheila Glasser, University of Michigan Press, 1994.

Bay-Cheng, Laina. "The Agency Line: A Neoliberal Metric for Appraising Young Women's Sexuality." *Sex Roles*, vol. 73, no. 7, 2015, pp. 279–291.

Benjamin, Walter. *The Arcades Project*. Translated by Howard Eiland and Kevin McLaughlin, edited by Rolf Riedemann, Belknap Press, 1999.

Berlant, Lauren, and Michael Hardt. "No One Is Sovereign in Love." *No More Pot Lucks*, 2011, http://nomorepotlucks.org.

Beurskens, Michael. "Legal Questions of Twitter Research." *Twitter and Society*, edited by Katrin Weller et al., Peter Lang, 2014, pp. 123–136.

Bivens, Kristin Marie, and Kirsti Cole. "The Grotesque Protest in Social Media as Embodied, Political Rhetoric." *Journal of Communication Inquiry*, vol. 42, no. 1, 2018, pp. 5–25.

Bonilla, Yarimar, and Jonathan Rosa. "#Ferguson: Digital Protest, Hashtag Ethnography, and the Racial Politics of Social Media in the United States." *American Ethnologist*, vol. 42, no. 1, 2015, pp. 4–17.

Borges-Rey, Eddy. "News Images on Instagram." *Digital Journalism*, vol. 3, no. 4, 2015, pp. 571–593.

Bost, Suzanne. "Gloria Anzaldúa's Mestiza Pain: Mexican Sacrifice, Chicana Embodiment, and Feminist Politics." *Aztlán*, vol. 30, no. 2, 2005, pp. 5–34.

Botoman, Eleonor. "'What Happens When Your Home, When Your Body, Is Attacked?'" *Bust*, September 1, 2016, www.bust.com.

Bow, Leslie. *Partly Colored: Asian Americans and Racial Anomaly in the Segregated South*. New York University Press, 2010.

boyd, dannah. *It's Complicated: The Social Lives of Networked Teens*. Yale University Press, 2014.

Brock, André. "Critical Technocultural Discourse Analysis." *New Media & Society*, vol. 20, no. 3, 2018, pp. 1012–1030.

———. "From the Blackhand Side: Twitter as a Cultural Conversation." *Journal of Broadcasting & Electronic Media*, vol. 56, no. 4, 2012, pp. 529–549.

Brown, Wendy. *Edgework: Critical Essays on Knowledge and Politics*. Princeton University Press, 2005.

———. "Neo-liberalism and the End of Liberal Democracy." *Theory & Event*, vol. 7, no. 1, 2003. *Project MUSE*, doi:10.1353/tae.2003.0020.

———. *States of Injury*. Princeton University Press, 1995.

———. "Wounded Attachments." *Political Theory*, vol. 21, no. 3, 1993, pp. 390–410.

Brownmiller, Susan. *Against Our Will: Men, Women, and Rape*. Simon & Schuster, 1975.

Buck-Morss, Susan. "Aesthetics and Anaesthetics: Walter Benjamin's Artwork Essay Reconsidered." *October*, vol. 62, Autumn, 1992, pp. 3–41.

Budgeon, Shelley. "Individualized Femininity and Feminist Politics of Choice." *European Journal of Women's Studies*, vol. 22, no. 3, 2015, pp. 303–318.

Burrowes, Nicole, et al. "On Our Own Terms: Ten Years of Radical Community Building with Sista II Sista." *The Revolution Will Not Be Funded: Beyond the Non-profit Industrial Complex*, edited by INCITE! Women of Color Against Violence, South End Press, 2007, pp. 227–234.

Čakardić, Ankica. "Down the Neoliberal Path: The Rise of Free Choice Feminism." *AM Journal of Art and Media Studies*, vol. 14, 2017, pp. 33–44.

Chan-Malik, Sylvia. *Being Muslim: A Cultural History of Women of Color in American Islam*. New York University Press, 2018.

Chasteen, Amy. "Constructing Rape: Feminism, Change, and Women's Everyday Understandings of Sexual Assault." *Sociological Spectrum*, vol. 21, no. 2, 2001, pp. 101–139.

Chen, Guan-Rong. *Recollecting Memory, Reviewing History: Trauma in Asian North American Literature*. 2008. University of Texas, PhD dissertation.

Chen, Mel. *Animacies: Biopolitics, Racial Mattering, and Queer Affect*. Duke University Press, 2012.

Chen, Tina. *Double Agency: Acts of Impersonation in Asian American Literature and Culture*. Stanford University Press, 2005.

Cheng, Anne Anlin. *The Melancholy of Race*. Oxford University Press, 2001.

Cheung, Anne. "Revisiting Privacy and Dignity: Online Shaming in the Global E-village." *Laws*, vol. 3, 2014, pp. 301–326.

Cheung, King-Kok. *Articulate Silences: Hisaye Yamamoto, Maxine Hong Kingston, Joy Kagawa*. Cornell University Press, 1993.

Chou, Rosalind. *Asian American Sexual Politics: The Construction of Race, Gender, and Sexuality*. Rowman & Littlefield, 2012.

Chow, Kat, and Elise Hu. "Odds Favor White Men, Asian Women on Dating App." *Code Switch* (blog), November 30, 2013, www.npr.org.

Christian, Aymar Jean. "Video Stars: Marketing Queer Performance in Networked Television." *The Intersectional Internet: Race, Sex, Class, and Culture Online*, edited by Safiya Umoja Noble and Brendesha M. Tynes, Peter Lang, 2016, pp. 95–113.

Chuh, Kandice. *Imagine Otherwise: On Asian Americanist Critique*. Duke University Press, 2003.

Clair, Robin. "*Imposed Silence* and the Story of the Warramunga Woman: Alternative Interpretations and Possibilities." *Silence, Feminism, Power: Reflections at the Edges of Sound*, edited by Sheena Malhotra and Aimee Carrillo Rowe, Palgrave, 2013, pp. 85–94.

Clark, Rosemary. "'Hope in a Hashtag': The Discursive Activism of #WhyIStayed." *Feminist Media Studies*, vol. 16, no. 5, 2016, pp. 788–804.

Cohen, Margaret. "Walter Benjamin's Phantasmagoria." *New German Critique*, no. 48, 1989, pp. 87–107.

Conn, Sarah. "Living in the Earth: Ecopsychology, Health, and Psychotherapy." *Consciousness and Healing: Integral Approaches to Mind-Body Medicine*, edited by Marilyn Schlitz et al., Elsevier Churchill Livingstone, 2004, pp. 530–541.

Cruz, Edgar Gómez, and Helen Thornham. "Selfies beyond Self Representation: The (Theoretical) F(r)ictions of a Practice." *Journal of Aesthetics & Culture*, vol. 7, 2015, http://dx.doi.org/10.3402/jac.v7.28073.

D'Amore, Laura Mattoon. "Vigilante Feminism: Revising Trauma, Abduction, and Assault in American Fairy-Tale Revisions." *Marvels & Tales*, vol. 31, no. 2, 2017, pp. 386–405.

Dang, Michelle. "Creating Ripples: Fostering Collective Healing from and Resistance to Sexual Violence through Friendships." *The International Journal of Narrative Therapy and Community Work*, vol. 1, 2018, pp. 1–9.

Danico, Mary Yu, editor. *Asian American Society: An Encyclopedia*. Sage, 2014.

Daniels, Jessie. "Race and Racism in Internet Studies: A Review and Critique." *New Media & Society*, vol. 15, no. 5, 2012, pp. 695–719.

Dellarocas, Chrysanthos. "The Digitization of Word of Mouth: Promise and Challenges of Online Feedback Mechanisms." *Management Science*, vol. 49, no. 10, 2003, pp. 1407–1424.

DeLuca, Sandra. *Finding Meaning Places for Healing: Toward a Vigilant Subjectivity in the Practice of a Nurse Educator.* 2000. University of Toronto, PhD dissertation.

D'Enbeau, Suzy. "Feminine and Feminist Transformation in Popular Culture: An Application of Mary Daly's Radical Philosophies to Bust Magazine." *Feminist Media Studies*, vol. 9, no. 1, 2009, pp. 17–36.

Detel, Hanne. "Disclosure and Public Shaming in the Age of New Visibility." *Media and Public Shaming: Drawing the Boundaries of Disclosure*, edited by Julian Petley, Tauris, 2013, pp. 77–96.

de Vries, Amy. "The Use of Social Media for Shaming Strangers: Young People's Views." 48th Hawaii International Conference on System Sciences, 2015, pp. 2053–2062.

Dewey, Caitlin. "Can Online Shaming Shut Down the Internet's Most Skin-Crawly Creeps?" *Washington Post*, September 16, 2015, www.washingtonpost.com.

Di Chiro, Giovanna. "Polluted Politics? Confronting Toxic Discourse, Sex Panic, and Eco-Normativity." *Queer Ecologies: Sex, Nature, Politics, Desire*, edited by Catriona Mortimer-Sandilands and Bruce Erickson, Indiana University Press, 2010, pp. 199–230.

Douglas, Mary. *Implicit Meanings: Essays in Anthropology*. Routledge & Kegan Paul, 1975.

Dua, Enakshi. "Exclusion through Inclusion: Female Asian Migration in the Making of Canada as a White Settler Nation." *Gender, Place & Culture*, vol. 14, no. 4, 2007, pp. 445–466.

Duncan, Patti. *Tell This Silence: Asian American Women Writers and the Politics of Speech*. University of Iowa Press, 2004.

Edwin, Steve. *Cultural Healing: Gender, Race, and Trauma in Literature of the Americas*. 2004. Stony Brook University, PhD dissertation.

Evans, Brad, and Henry Giroux. *Disposable Futures: The Seduction of Violence in the Age of the Spectacle*. City Lights, 2015.

Ewens, Hanah. "Woman Documents Ten Years of Online Harassment on Instagram." *Dazed*, October 16, 2015, www.dazeddigital.com.

Ferguson, Michaele L. "Neoliberal Feminism as Political Ideology: Revitalizing the Study of Feminist Political Ideologies." *Journal of Political Ideologies*, vol. 22, no. 3, 2017, pp. 221–235.

Fidyk, Alexandra. "Attuned to Silence: A Pedagogy of Presence." *Silence, Feminism, Power: Reflections at the Edges of Sound*, edited by Sheena Malhotra and Aimee Carrillo Rowe, Palgrave, 2013, pp. 114–128.

Filippi, Linda. "Place, Feminism, and Healing: An Ecology of Pastoral Counseling." *The Journal of Pastoral Care*, vol. XLV, no. 3, 1991, pp, 231–242.

Flores, Pamela, et al. "Reviving Feminism through Social Media: From the Classroom to Online and Offline Public Spaces." *Gender and Education*, doi: 10.1080/09540253.2018.1513454.

Forte, Jeanie. "Focus on the Body: Pain, Praxis, and Pleasure in Feminist Performance." *Critical Theory and Performance*, edited by Janelle Reinelt and Joseph Roach, University of Michigan Press, 1992, pp. 248–262.

Foucault, Michel. *Discipline and Punish: The Birth of the Prison*. Translated by Alan Sheridan, 2nd ed., Vintage Books, 1995.

Friedman, Megan. "This Woman Has Been Collecting Disgusting Online Messages from Guys for More than 10 Years." *Cosmopolitan* (blog), October 20, 2015, www.cosmopolitan.com.

Fries, Christopher, and Paul Gingrich. "A 'Great' Large Family: Understandings of Multiculturalism among Newcomers to Canada." *Refuge*, vol. 27, no. 1, 2010, pp. 36–49.

Fung, Richard. "The Trouble with 'Asians.'" *Negotiating Lesbian and Gay Subjects*, edited by Monica Dorenkamp and Richard Henke, Routledge, 1995, pp. 123–130.

Gardner, Mia. "Poem Collections That Will Delicately Heal Your Soul and Mend Your Heart." *Coture Social*, February 28, 2018, www.coturesocial.com.

Gerbaz, Alex. "The Ethical Screen: Funny Games and the Spectacle of Pain." *The Cinema of Michael Haneke: Europe Utopia*, edited by Ben McCann and David Sorfa, Wallflower Press, 2012, pp. 163–171.

Gill, Rosalind, and Akane Kanai. "Mediating Neoliberal Capitalism: Affect Subjectivity and Inequality." *Journal of Communication*, vol. 68, 2018, pp. 318–326.

Gillespie, Tarleton. *Custodians of the Internet: Platforms, Content Moderation, and the Hidden Decisions That Shape Social Media*. Yale University Press, 2018.

Ginwright, Shawn. *Hope and Healing in Urban Education: How Urban Activists and Teachers Are Reclaiming Matters of Heart*. Routledge, 2016.

Giovanni, Chiara. "The Problem with Rupi Kaur's Poetry." *BuzzFeed*, August 4, 2017, www.buzzfeednews.com.

Glenn, Evelyn Nakano. *Issei, Nisei, War Bride: Three Generations of Japanese American Women in Domestic Service*. Temple University Press, 1986.

Gotham, Kevin Fox. "Make It Right?: Brad Pitt, Post-Katrina Rebuilding, and the Spectacularization of Disaster." *Commodity Activism: Cultural Resistance in Neoliberal Times*, edited by Roopali Mukherjee and Sarah Banet-Weiser, New York University Press, 2012, pp. 97–113.

Gredel, Eva. "Digital Discourse Analysis and Wikipedia: Bridging the Gap between Foucauldian Discourse Analysis and Digital Conversation Analysis." *Journal of Pragmatics*, vol. 115, 2017, pp. 99–114.

Guha, Pallavi. "Hash Tagging but Not Trending: The Success and Failure of the News Media to Engage with Online Feminist Activism in India." *Feminist Media Studies*, vol. 15, no. 1, 2015, pp. 155–157.

Guillermo, Emil. "Meet the Woman behind 'Perv Magnet,' a Project Documenting Online Harassment." *NBC News*, November 4, 2015, www.nbcnews.com.

Guilloud, Stephanie, and William Cordery. "Fundraising Is Not a Dirty Word: Community-Based Economic Strategies for the Long Haul." *The Revolution Will Not Be Funded: Beyond the Non-profit Industrial Complex*, edited by INCITE! Women of Color Against Violence, South End Press, 2007, pp. 107–111.

Gunne, Sorcha. "Questioning Truth and Reconciliation: Writing Rape in Achmat Dangor's *Bitter Fruit* and Kagiso Lesego Molope's *Dancing in the Dust*." *Feminism,*

Literature and Rape Narratives: Violence and Violation, edited by Sorcha Gunne and Zoë Brigley Thompson, Routledge, 2010, pp. 164–180.

Haaken, Janice. "Heretical Texts: *The Courage to Heal* and the Incest Survivor Movement." *New Versions of Victims: Feminists Struggle with the Concept*, edited by Sharon Lamb, New York University Press, 1999, pp. 13–41.

Haiman, John. *Talk Is Cheap*. Oxford University Press, 2001.

Halberstam, Judith. *The Queer Art of Failure*. Duke University Press, 2011.

Harvey, David. "Neo-liberalism as Creative Destruction." *Geografiska Annaler*, series B, vol. 88, no. 2, 2006, pp. 145–158.

Hedges, Elaine, and Shelley Fisher Fishkin. *Listening to Silences: New Essays in Feminist Criticism*. Oxford University Press, 1994.

Hermansen, Marcia, and Mahruq Khan. "South Asian Muslim American Girl Power: Structures and Symbols of Control and Self-Expression." *Journal of International Women's Studies*, vol. 11, no. 1, 2009, pp. 86–105.

Hicken, Margaret, et al. "The Weight of Racism: Vigilance and Racial Inequalities in Weight-Related Measures." *Social Science & Medicine*, vol. 199, 2018, pp. 157–166.

hooks, bell. *Feminist Theory: From Margin to Center*. 2nd ed., South End Press, 2000.

———. *Talking Back: Thinking Feminist, Thinking Black*. South End Press, 1989.

"How Poet Rupi Kaur Became a Hero to Millions of Young Women." *PBS NewsHour*, January 2, 2018, www.pbs.org.

Huang, Josie. "Even Before #MeToo, Muslim Educators Worked to Demystify Sex and Battle Abuse." *SCPR*, May 22, 2018, www.scpr.org.

Huang, Li, et al. "The Highest Form of Intelligence: Sarcasm Increases Creativity for Both Expressers and Recipients." *Organizational Behavior and Human Decision Processes*, vol. 131, 2015, pp. 162–177.

Ibrahimhakkioglu, Fulden. *The Politics of Paranoia: Affect, Temporality, and the Epistemology of Securitization*. 2016. University of Oregon, PhD dissertation.

Jones, Amelia. "Performing the Wounded Body: Pain, Affect and the Radical Relationality of Meaning." *Parallax*, vol. 15, no. 4, 2009, pp. 45–67.

Juschka, Darlene. "Pain, Gender, and Systems of Belief and Practice." *Religion Compass*, vol. 5, no. 1, 2011, pp. 708–719.

Kabir, Ananya Jahanara. "Double Violation? (Not) Talking about Sexual Violence in Contemporary South Asia." *Feminism, Literature and Rape Narratives: Violence and Violation*, edited by Sorcha Gunne and Zoë Brigley Thompson, Routledge, 2010, pp. 146–163.

Kane, Gerald, and Alexandra Pear. "The Rise of Visual Content Online: Image Really Is Everything to the Digital Economy." *MIT Sloan Management Review*, vol. 4, Jan. 2016, https://sloanreview.mit.edu.

Kang, Jaeho. *Walter Benjamin and the Media: The Spectacle of Modernity*. Wiley, 2014.

Kapoor, Ilan. *Celebrity Humanitarianism: The Ideology of Global Charity*. Routledge, 2012.

Karavanta, Assimina. "The Gendered Subaltern's Cartography of Pain: A Figuration of Homo Sacer in a Global World." *Reconstructing Pain and Joy: Linguistic, Literary and Cultural Perspectives*, edited by Anna Despotopoulou et al., Cambridge Scholars Publishing, 2008, pp. 209–227.

Kassam, Ashifa. "Rupi Kaur: 'There Was No Market for Poetry about Trauma, Abuse, and Healing.'" *The Guardian*, August 26, 2016, www.theguardian.com.

Kayi-Aydar, Hayriye. "Multiple Identities, Negotiations, and Agency across Time and Space: A Narrative Inquiry of a Foreign Language Teacher Candidate." *Critical Inquiry in Language Studies*, vol. 12, no. 2, 2015, pp. 137–160.

Keren, Hila. "Women in the Shark Tank: Entrepreneurship and Feminism in a Neoliberal Age." *Columbia Journal of Gender and Law*, vol. 34, no. 1, 2016, pp. 75–123.

Kim, Claire J. "The Racial Triangulation of Asian Americans." *Politics & Society*, vol. 27, no. 1, 1999, pp. 105–138.

Kim, Elaine. "Home Is Where the Han Is: A Korean American Perspective on the Los Angeles Upheavals." *Asian American Studies: A Reader*, edited by Jean Yu-wen Shen Wu and Min Song, Rutgers University Press, 2000, pp. 270–289.

Kim, Ju Yon. *The Racial Mundane: Asian American Performance and the Embodied Everyday*. New York University Press, 2015.

Kim, Yongseok, and Darlene Grant. "Immigration Patterns, Social Support, and Adaptation among Korean Immigrant Women and Korean American Women." *Cultural Diversity and Mental Health*, vol. 3, no. 4, 1997, pp. 235–245.

Kivel, Paul. "Social Service or Social Change?" *The Revolution Will Not Be Funded: Beyond the Non-profit Industrial Complex*, edited by INCITE! Women of Color Against Violence, South End Press, 2007, pp. 129–149.

Kudhail, Priya. "Rupi Kaur, Giving the Voice Back to the Voiceless." *Seen and Heard: Literary Cultures*, vol. 1, no. 2, April 2018, https://journals.ntu.ac.uk/index.php/litc/article/view/97.

Lamb, Sharon. "Constructing the Victim: Popular Images and Lasting Labels." *New Versions of Victims: Feminists Struggle with the Concept*, edited by Sharon Lamb, New York University Press, 1999, pp. 108–138.

Latina Feminist Group. *Telling to Live: Latina Feminist Testimonios*. Duke University Press, 2001.

Lee, Erika. *The Making of Asian America: A History*. Simon & Schuster, 2015.

Lee, John Kyhan. *The Notion of "Self" in Korean-American Literature: A Sociohistorical Perspective*. 1990. University of Connecticut, PhD dissertation.

Lee, Mary Paik. *Quiet Odyssey: A Pioneer Korean Woman in America*. Edited by Sucheng Chan, University of Washington Press, 1990.

Lee, Rachel. *The Exquisite Corpse of Asian America: Biopolitics, Biosociality, and Posthuman Ecologies*. New York University Press, 2014.

———. "Where's My Parade: Margaret Cho and the Asian American Body in Space." *The Drama Review*, vol. 48, no. 2, 2004, pp. 108–132.

Lee, Shelley Sang-Hee. *A New History of Asian America*. Routledge, 2014.

Lehner, Sharon. "My Womb, the Mosh Pit." *The Feminism and Visual Culture Reader*, edited by Amelia Jones, Routledge, 2010, pp. 656–660.

Lerum, Kari, and Shari L. Dworkin. "Sexual Agency Is Not a Problem of Neoliberalism: Feminism, Sexual Justice, & the Carceral Turn." *Sex Roles*, vol. 73, 2015, pp. 319–331.

Leve, Michelle. "Reproductive Bodies and Bits: Exploring Dilemmas of Egg Donation under Neoliberalism." *Studies in Gender and Sexuality*, vol. 14, no. 4, 2013, pp. 277–288.

Lim, Merlyna. "Roots, Routes, and Routers: Communications and Media of Contemporary Social Movements." *Journalism and Communication Monographs*, vol. 20, no. 2, 2018, pp. 92–136.

Lo, Kwai-Cheung. *Excess and Masculinity in Asian Cultural Productions*. State University of New York Press, 2010.

Lorde, Audre. *Sister Outsider: Essays and Speeches*. 1984. Crossing Press, 2007.

Lowe, Lisa. "The International within the National: American Studies and Asian American Critique." *Cultural Critique*, no. 40, 1998, pp. 29–47.

Macherey, Pierre. *A Theory of Literary Production*. Routledge, 1978.

Magasic, Michelangelo. "The 'Selfie Gaze' and 'Social Media Pilgrimage': Two Frames for Conceptualising the Experience of Social Media Using Tourists." *Information and Communication Technologies in Tourism*, edited by Alessandro Inversini and Roland Schegg, Springer, 2016, pp. 173–182.

Maira, Sunaina. "Youth Culture, Citizenship, and Globalization: Muslim Youth in the United States after September 11th." *Asian American Studies Now: A Critical Reader*, edited by Jean Yu-wen Shen Wu and Thomas Chen, Rutgers University Press, 2010, pp. 333–353.

Malhotra, Sheena. "The Silence in My Belly." *Silence, Feminism, Power: Reflections at the Edges of Sound*, edited by Sheena Malhotra and Aimee Carrillo Rowe, Palgrave, 2013, pp. 219–229.

Markham, Annette. *Life Online: Researching Real Experience in Virtual Space*. AltaMira Press, 1998.

Marwick, Alice. "Ethnographic and Qualitative Research on Twitter." *Twitter and Society*, edited by Katrin Weller et al., Peter Lang, 2014, pp. 109–121.

McCormack, Donna. *Queer Postcolonial Narratives and the Ethics of Witnessing*. Bloomsbury, 2014.

Megarry, Jessica. "Online Incivility or Sexual Harassment? Conceptualising Women's Experiences in the Digital Age." *Women's Studies International Forum*, vol. 47, 2014, pp. 46–55.

Messias, Johnnatan, et al. "White, Man, and Highly Followed: Gender and Race Inequalities in Twitter." *Proceedings of WI '17*, Leipzig, Germany, 2017, pp. 266–274.

Micheli, Marina, et al. "Digital Footprints: An Emerging Dimension of Digital Inequality." *Journal of Information, Communication and Ethics in Society*, vol. 16, no. 3, 2018, pp. 242–251.

Middleton, Elisabeth. "A Political Ecology of Healing." *Journal of Political Ecology*, vol. 17, 2010, pp. 1–28.

Min, Pyong Gap, and Young I. Song. "Demographic Characteristics and Trends of Post-1965 Korean Immigrant Women and Men." *Korean American Women from Tradition to Modern Feminism*, edited by Young I. Song and Ailee Moon, Praeger, 1998, pp. 45–63.

Minh-ha, Trinh T. "Not You/Like You: Post-colonial Women and the Interlocking Questions of Identity and Difference." *Making Face, Making Soul/Haciendo Caras: Creative and Critical Perspectives by Women of Color*, edited by Gloria Anzaldúa, Aunt Lute Books, 1990, pp. 371–375.

———. *Woman, Native, Other: Writing Postcoloniality and Feminism*. Indiana University Press, 1989.

Minocha, Urmil. "South Asian Immigrants: Trends and Impacts on the Sending and Receiving Societies." *Center for Migration Studies Special Issue: Pacific Bridges*, vol. 5, no. 3, 1987, pp. 347–373.

Moraga, Cherríe, and Gloria Anzaldúa, editors. *This Bridge Called My Back: Writings by Radical Women of Color*. 4th ed., State University of New York Press, 2015.

Morales, Aurora Levins. "Radical Pleasure: Sex and the End of Victimhood." *Women's Lives: Multicultural Perspectives*, edited by Gwyn Kirk and Margo Okazawa-Rey, McGraw-Hill Education, 2012, pp. 283–284.

Morris, David B. *The Culture of Pain*. University of California Press, 1991.

Mortimer-Sandilands, Catriona, and Bruce Erickson. "Introduction: A Genealogy of Queer Ecologies." *Queer Ecologies: Sex, Nature, Politics, Desire*, edited by Catriona Mortimer-Sandilands and Bruce Erickson, Indiana University Press, 2010, pp. 1–47.

Nakamura, Lisa. "Cybertyping and the Work of Race in the Age of Digital Reproduction." *The New Media and Cybercultures Anthology*, edited by Pramod K. Nayar, Wiley-Blackwell, 2010, pp. 132–150.

Nakano, Mei T. *Japanese American Women: Three Generations, 1890–1990*. Mina Press Publishing, 1990.

Nash, Jennifer. *Black Feminism Reimagined: After Intersectionality*. Duke University Press, 2019.

Newman, Melissa. "Image and Identity: Media Literacy for Young Adult Instagram Users." *Visual Inquiry: Learning and Teaching Art*, vol. 4, no. 3, 2015, pp. 221–227.

Nguyen, Tan Hoang. *A View from the Bottom: Asian American Masculinity and Sexual Representation*. Duke University Press, 2014.

Niiya, Brian, editor. *Japanese American History: An A to Z Reference from 1868 to the Present*. Facts on File, 1993.

Noble, Safiya Umoja. *Algorithms of Oppression: How Search Engines Reinforce Racism*. New York University Press, 2018.

Noble, Safiya Umoja, and Brendesha M. Tynes. "Introduction." *The Intersectional Internet: Race, Sex, Class, and Culture Online*, edited by Safiya Umoja Noble and Brendesha M. Tynes, Peter Lang, 2016, pp. 1–18.

Okihiro, Gary Y. *American History Unbound: Asians and Pacific Islanders.* University of California Press, 2015.

Oksala, Johanna. "The Neoliberal Subject of Feminism." *Journal of the British Society for Phenomenology,* vol. 42, no. 1, 2011, pp. 104–120.

Olsen, Tillie. *Tell Me a Riddle.* Edited by Deborah Rosenfelt, Rutgers University Press, 1995.

Park, Sungjin, et al. "The Network of Celebrity Politics: Political Implications of Celebrity Following on Twitter." *Annals, AAPSS,* vol. 659, May 2015, doi: 10.1177/0002716215569226.

Parsons, Josephine. "Advice on Art, Poetry and Protest with Rupi Kaur." *Junkee,* May 25, 2017, www.junkee.com.

Pascucci, Margherita. *Capital and the Imaginary: A Study on the Commodity as a Poetical Object.* 2003. New York University, PhD dissertation.

Pelle, Susan. "The 'Grotesque Pussy': 'Transformational Shame' in Margaret Cho's Stand-Up Performances." *Text and Performance Quarterly,* vol. 30, no. 1, pp. 21–37.

Peng, Rong, et al. "Success Factors in Mobile Social Networking Application Development: Case Study of Instagram." Proceedings of the 29th Annual ACM Symposium on Applied Computing, Gyeongju, Republic of Korea, 2014, ACM New York, pp. 1072–1079.

Pérez, Kimberlee. "My Monster and My Muse: Re-writing the Colonial Hangover." *Silence, Feminism, Power: Reflections at the Edges of Sound,* edited by Sheena Malhotra and Aimee Carrillo Rowe, Palgrave, 2013, pp. 200–216.

Pfaelzer, Jean. "Tillie Olsen's 'Tell Me a Riddle': The Dialectics of Silence." *Frontiers: A Journal of Women Studies,* vol. 15, no. 2, 1994, pp. 1–22.

Pham, Minh-Ha T. *Asians Wear Clothes on the Internet: Race, Gender, and the Work of Personal Style Blogging.* Duke University Press, 2015.

Philipose, Liz. "The Politics of Pain and the End of Empire." *International Feminist Journal of Politics,* vol. 9, no. 1, 2007, pp. 60–81.

Polloc, Della. "Keeping Quiet: Performing Pain." *Silence, Feminism, Power: Reflections at the Edges of Sound,* edited by Sheena Malhotra and Aimee Carrillo Rowe, Palgrave, 2013, pp. 159–175.

Poolakasingham, Gauthamie, et al. "'Fresh Off the Boat?' Racial Microaggressions That Target South Asian Canadian Students." *Journal of Diversity in Higher Education,* vol. 7, no. 3, 2014, pp. 194–210.

Pour-Khorshid, Farima Patricia. *H.E.L.L.A: A Bay Area Critical Racial Affinity Group Committed to Healing, Empowerment, Love, Liberation, and Action.* 2018. University of California, Santa Cruz, PhD dissertation.

Prügl, Elisabeth. "Neoliberalising Feminism." *New Political Economy,* vol. 20, 2015, pp. 614–631.

Puschmann, Cornelius, et al. "Epilogue: Why Study Twitter?" *Twitter and Society,* edited by Katrin Weller et al., Peter Lang, 2014, pp. 425–432.

A Question of Silence. Directed by Marleen Gorris, Quartet Films, 1982.

Radway, Janice. *Reading the Romance: Women, Patriarchy, and Popular Culture.* University of North Carolina Press, 1984.

Rahman, Tabassum. *The Experiences of South Asian American Muslim Women: A Postmodern Approach.* 2002. Alliant International University San Diego, PsyD clinical dissertation.

Rajiva, Mythili. "'Better Lives': The Transgenerational Positioning of Social Mobility in the South Asian Canadian Diaspora." *Women's Studies International Forum*, vol. 36, 2013, pp. 16–26.

Ralston, Helen. "Canadian Immigration Policy in the Twentieth Century: Its Impact on South Asian Women." *Canadian Woman Studies*, vol. 19, no. 3, 1999, pp. 33–37.

Ramírez, Sara Alicia. *Subjects of Trauma: The Decolonial Tactics of Self-Making and Self-Healing by Queer Xicana Feminist Teatristas.* 2016. University of California, Berkeley, PhD dissertation.

Rayside, David. "Muslim American Communities' Response to Queer Visibility." *Contemporary Islam*, vol. 5, 2011, pp. 109–134.

Reed, Jennifer. "Sexual Outlaws: Queer in a Funny Way." *Women's Studies*, vol. 40, 2011, pp. 762–777.

Ridgway, Jessica, and Russell Clayton. "Instagram Unfiltered: Exploring Associations of Body Image Satisfaction, Instagram #Selfie Posting, and Negative Romantic Relationship Outcomes." *Cyberpsychology, Behavior, and Social Networking*, vol. 19, no. 1, 2016, pp. 2–7.

Rightler-McDaniels, Jodi, and Elizabeth Hendrickson. "Hoes and Hashtags: Constructions of Gender and Race in Trending Topics." *Social Semiotics*, vol. 24, no. 2, 2014, pp. 175–190.

Rockwell, Patricia, and Evelyn Theriot. "Culture, Gender, and Gender Mix in Encoders of Sarcasm: A Self-Assessment Analysis." *Communication Research Reports*, vol. 18, no. 1, 2001, pp. 44–52.

Rodríguez, Dylan. "The Political Logic of the Non-profit Industrial Complex." *The Revolution Will Not Be Funded: Beyond the Non-profit Industrial Complex*, edited by INCITE! Women of Color Against Violence, South End Press, 2007, pp. 21–40.

Rosenfelt, Deborah, editor. *Tell Me a Riddle.* Rutgers University Press, 1995.

Rottenberg, Catherine. *The Rise of Neoliberal Feminism.* Oxford University Press, 2018.

Rowe, Aimee Carrillo, and Sheena Malhotra. "Still the Silence: Feminist Reflections at the Edges of Sound." *Silence, Feminism, Power: Reflections at the Edges of Sound*, edited by Sheena Malhotra and Aimee Carrillo Rowe, Palgrave, 2013, pp. 1–22.

Russo, Ann. "Between Speech and Silence: Reflections on Accountability." *Silence, Feminism, Power: Reflections at the Edges of Sound*, edited by Sheena Malhotra and Aimee Carrillo Rowe, Palgrave, 2013, pp. 34–49.

Sandoval, Chela. *Methodology of the Oppressed.* University of Minnesota Press, 2000.

Sandoval, Jorge. "The RuPaul Effect: The Exploration of the Costuming Rituals of Drag Culture in Social Media and the Theatrical Performativity of the Male Body in the Ambit of the Everyday." *Theatre Symposium*, vol. 26, 2018, pp. 100–117.

Saraswati, L. Ayu. "La douleur mise en scène: excès affectif et sexualité des femmes asiatiques dans le cyberspace." Translated by Nicole G. Albert. *Diogène*, vol. 2, no. 254/255, 2016, pp. 204–228.

———. "Why Non-story Matters: A Feminist Autoethnography of Embodied Meditation Technique in Processing Emotional Pain." *Women's Studies International Forum*, vol. 73, 2019, pp. 1–7.

———. "Wikisexuality: Rethinking Sexuality in Cyberspace." *Sexualities*, vol. 16, no. 5/6, 2013, pp. 587–603.

Saul, Jack. *Collective Trauma, Collective Healing: Promoting Community Resilience in the Aftermath of Disaster*. Routledge, 2014.

Scott, Joan W. "'Experience.'" *Feminists Theorize the Political*, edited by Judith Butler and Joan W. Scott, Routledge, 1992, pp. 22–40.

Shade, Leslie. "Hop to It in the Gig Economy: The Sharing Economy and Neo-liberal Feminism." *International Journal of Media & Cultural Politics*, vol. 14, no. 1, 2018, pp. 35–54.

Shah, Nishant. "Subject to Technology: Internet Pornography, Cyber-terrorism and the Indian State." *Inter-Asia Cultural Studies*, vol. 8, no. 3, 2007, pp. 349–366.

Shariff, Farha. *Straddling the Cultural Divide: Second-Generation South Asian Canadian Secondary Students Negotiate Cultural Identity through Contemporary Postcolonial Fiction*. 2012. University of Alberta, PhD dissertation.

Shimizu, Celine. *The Hypersexuality of Race: Performing Asian/American Women on Screen and Scene*. Duke University Press, 2007.

Sinopoli, Dana L. *The Post-rape Sexual Healing Process: A Women's Story Project through Feminist Epistemology*. 2009. Chicago School of Professional Psychology, PhD dissertation.

Smith, Andrea. "Introduction: The Revolution Will Not Be Funded." *The Revolution Will Not Be Funded: Beyond the Non-profit Industrial Complex*, edited by INCITE! Women of Color Against Violence, South End Press, 2007, pp. 1–18.

Smith, Erica. "Poet Rupi Kaur: 'In Moments of Tragedy, Art Is the Core'—BUST Interview." *Bust*, August 8, 2016, www.bust.com.

Sobchack, Vivian. "The Scene of the Screen: Envisioning Cinematic and Electronic 'Presence.'" *Electronic Media and Technoculture*, edited by John Thornton Caldwell, Rutgers University Press, 2000, pp. 137–155.

Somaini, Antonio. "Walter Benjamin's Media Theory: The Medium and the Apparat." *Grey Room*, vol. 62, 2016, pp. 6–41.

Sorapure, Madeleine. "Screening Moments, Scrolling Lives: Diary Writing on the Web." *The New Media and Cybercultures Anthology*, edited by Pramod K. Nayar, Wiley-Blackwell, 2010, pp. 499–514.

Sperb, Jason. "Removing the Experience: Simulacrum as an Autobiographical Act in American Splendor." *Biography*, vol. 29, no. 1, 2006, pp. 123–139.

Spivak, Gayatri. "Can the Subaltern Speak." *Marxism and the Interpretation of Culture*, edited by Cary Nelson and Lawrence Grossberg, University of Illinois Press, 1988, pp. 271–313.

Steele, Catherine Knight. "Signifyin', Bitching, and Blogging: Black Women and Resistance Discourse Online." *The Intersectional Internet: Race, Sex, Class, and Culture Online*, edited by Safiya Umoja Noble and Brendesha M. Tynes, Peter Lang, 2016, pp. 73–93.

Sthanki, Maunica. "The Aftermath of September 11: An Anti–Domestic Violence Perspective." *Body Evidence: Intimate Violence against South Asian Women in America*, edited by Shamita Das Dasgupta, Rutgers University Press, 2007, pp. 68–78.

Stringer, Rebecca. *Knowing Victims: Feminism, Agency and Victim Politics in Neoliberal Times*. Routledge, 2014.

Stuart, Avelie, and Ngaire Donaghue. "Choosing to Conform: The Discursive Complexities of Choice in Relation to Feminine Beauty Practices." *Feminism & Psychology*, vol. 22, 2012, pp. 98–121.

Sturken, Marita. "Advertising and the Rise of Amateur Photography: From Kodak and Polaroid to the Digital Image." *Advertising & Society Quarterly*, vol. 18, no. 3, 2017. *Project MUSE*, doi:10.1353/asr.2017.0021.

Sturken, Marita, and Douglas Thomas. "Introduction: Technological Visions and the Rhetoric of the New." *Technological Visions: The Hopes and Fears That Shape New Technologies*, edited by Marita Sturken et al., Temple University Press, 2004, pp. 1–18.

Takaki, Ronald T. *Strangers from a Different Shore: A History of Asian Americans*. Little, Brown, 1989.

Tambe, Ashwini. "Reckoning with the Silences of #MeToo." *Feminist Studies*, vol. 44, no. 1, 2018, pp. 197–203.

Tarnopolsky, Christina H. *Prudes, Perverts, and Tyrants: Plato's Gorgias and the Politics of Shame*. Princeton University Press, 2010.

Taylor, Astra. *The People's Platform: Taking Back Power and Culture in the Digital Age*. Picador, 2014.

"Text: President Bush on Homeland Security." *Washington Post*, November 8, 2001, www.washingtonpost.com.

Thomas, Alison, and Celia Kitzinger. "Sexual Harassment: Reviewing the Field." *Sexual Harassment: Contemporary Feminist Perspectives*, edited by Alison Thomas and Celia Kitzinger, Open University Press, 1997, pp. 1–18.

Thorpe, Holly, et al. "Sportswomen and Social Media: Bringing Third-Wave Feminism, Postfeminism, and Neoliberal Feminism into Conversation." *Journal of Sport and Social Issues*, vol. 41, no. 5, 2017, pp. 359–383.

Tran, Sharon. "Kawaii Asian Girls Save the Day! Animating a Minor Politics of Care." *MELUS: Multi-ethnic Literature of the U.S.*, vol. 43, no. 3, 2018, pp. 19–41.

Tremblay, Mark. *Flânerie: From the Streets to the Screen.* 2015. Dartmouth College, master's thesis.

Turkle, Sherry. "'Spinning' Technology: What We Are Not Thinking about When We Are Thinking about Computers." *Technological Visions: The Hopes and Fears That Shape New Technologies,* edited by Marita Sturken et al., Temple University Press, 2004, pp. 19–33.

Ty, Eleanor. "Teaching Literatures in the Age of Digital Media." *Canadian Review of Comparative Literature/Revue Canadienne de Littérature Comparée,* vol. 45, no. 2, 2018, pp. 213–221.

Tynes, Brendesha, et al. "Digital Intersectionality Theory and the #Blacklivesmatter Movement." *The Intersectional Internet: Race, Sex, Class, and Culture Online,* edited by Safiya Umoja Noble and Brendesha M. Tynes, Peter Lang, 2016, pp. 21–40.

Vanderbeeken, Robrecht. "The Screen as an In-Between." *Foundations of Science,* vol. 16, no. 2–3, 2011, pp. 245–257.

Wachter-Boettcher, Sara. *Technically Wrong: Sexist Apps, Biased Algorithms, and Other Threats of Toxic Tech.* W.W. Norton, 2017.

Walker, Nancy. *A Very Serious Thing: Women's Humor and American Culture.* University of Minnesota Press, 1988.

Wallis, Lauren. "#selfiesinthestacks: Sharing the Library with Instagram." *Internet Reference Services Quarterly,* vol. 19, no. 3–4, 2014, pp. 181–206.

Walton, S. Courtney, and Ronald E. Rice. "Mediated Disclosure on Twitter: The Roles of Gender and Identity in Boundary Impermeability, Valence, Disclosure, and Stage." *Computers in Human Behavior,* vol. 29, 2013, pp. 1465–1474.

Washington, Myra. "Asian/American Masculinity: The Politics of Virility, Virality, and Visibility." *The Intersectional Internet: Race, Sex, Class, and Culture Online,* edited by Safiya Umoja Noble and Brendesha M. Tynes, Peter Lang, 2016, pp. 61–71.

Watson, Cate. "Notes on the Variety and Uses of Satire, Sarcasm and Irony in Social Research, with Some Observations on Vices and Follies in the Academy." *Power and Education,* vol. 3, no. 2, 2011, pp. 139–149.

Weber, Shirley. "Bills to Curb Racial Bias in Policing (AB 953 and AB 619)." *ACLU Northern California* (blog), www.aclunc.org.

Wei-Ming, Tu. "Selfhood and Otherness in Confucian Thought." *Culture and Self: Asian and Western Perspectives,* edited by Anthony J. Marsella et al., Tavistock Publications, 1985, pp. 231–251.

Wendorf, Jessica, and Fan Yang. "Benefits of a Negative Post: Effects of Computer-Mediated Venting on Relationship Maintenance." *Computers in Human Behavior,* vol. 52, 2015, pp. 271–277.

Whitman, James. "What Is Wrong with Inflicting Shame Sanctions?" Faculty Scholarship Series, Paper 655, 1998, https://digitalcommons.law.yale.edu/fss_papers/655.

Williams, Kimberly A. "Women@Web: Cyber Sexual Violence in Canada." *Introduction to Women's, Gender and Sexuality Studies: Interdisciplinary and Intersectional*

Approaches, edited by L. Ayu Saraswati et al., Oxford University Press, 2017, pp. 496–500.

Windle, Joe. "'Anyone Can Make It, but There Can Only Be One Winner': Modelling Neoliberal Learning and Work on Reality Television." *Critical Studies in Education*, vol. 51, no. 3, 2010, pp. 251–263.

Yamamoto, Traise. *Masking Selves, Making Subjects: Japanese American Women, Identity, and the Body*. University of California Press, 1999.

Yoo, Sung Woo, and Homero Gil de Zúñiga. "Connecting Blog, Twitter and Facebook Use with Gaps in Knowledge and Participation." *Communication & Society*, vol. 27, no. 4, 2014, pp. 33–48.

Zhu, Linhong, and Kristina Lerman. "Attention Inequality in Social Media." Proceedings of the ASE/IEEE Conference on Social Computing, 2015.

Žižek, Slavoj. *How to Read Lacan*. Granta Books, 2006.

———. *On Violence: Six Sideways Reflections*. Picador, 2008.

———, screenplay and presenter. *The Pervert's Guide to Cinema*. Directed by Sophie Fiennes, Mischief Films/Amoeba Film, 2006.

INDEX

AAUW, 143

activism: celebrity activism, 115–16; community activism, 141; consciousness-raising activism, 84, 117; face-to-face activism, 166; social media activism, 9, 27, 31, 102, 115, 137. *See also* feminist activism

Adorno, Theodor, 60

adultery (*zina*), 151, 162

affect alienation, 33; defined, 52; digital politics of anesthetics and, 52–67; kaur soothing, 59–60; phantasmagoria and, 52–53, 78, 164

affect aliens, 52

affective atmosphere, 12, 34–36, 38, 58

affective insurgency, 162–63

affective simulation, 53–54, 58, 62, 131–32

Afzal Family Foundation, 143

Against Our Will (Brownmiller), 126–27

agency: agency line, 127; as carrying pain, 133–34; as collective articulation, 129–32; leaking self as, 132–33; performing silence as, 128–29

Ahmed, Sara, 33, 52, 134

Airbnb, 72, 76, 189n14

Akhtar, Ayesha, 137

algorithms: algorithmic oppression of Internet, 19; algorithm system of curation, 57, 66; digital footprints and, 157; in social media, 56–57

All-American Girl, 105

Ancheta, Angelo, 15

Anderson, Benedict, 154

Andreotti, Libero, 63, 66

Anzaldúa, Gloria, 51, 118, 148

Apple, 189n14

Arab Americans, 138–39

The Arcades Project (Benjamin), 10

Asian Americans: being marginalized, without being at margin, 18–19; digital media and, 18–19; as double agents, 15; as epistemological object, 14; as place-holder of ideology, 13; racial oscillation and, 12–19; responding to, 13; sexual harassment of, 14, 87; as subjective discourse, 14. *See also* Japanese Americans; Korean Americans; South Asian Americans

audience: affective response of, 35–36; alienation of, 33; as fan base, 6; for neo-liberal self(ie), 8; perceived desire of, 7–8; reaction of, 132; sharing economy of emotions and, 79; taste of, 26, 52; tricking of, 11–12

awareness-raising, 166–67. *See also* consciousness-raising activism

Baudrillard, Jean, 54

Bay-Cheng, Laina, 127

Benjamin, Walter, 9–10, 61

Berlant, Lauren, 146

Beurskens, Michael, 183n7

Black abjection, 14–15

Bow, Leslie, 14

boyd, dannah, 154, 188n10

Brock, André, 19

Brown, Wendy, 32

Brown Family Foundation, 143

ABOUT THE AUTHOR

L. Ayu Saraswati is an award-winning author and associate professor in Women's Studies at the University of Hawai'i, Mānoa. Her book *Seeing Beauty, Sensing Race in Transnational Indonesia* won the NWSA Gloria E. Anzaldúa Book Prize. She is the co-editor of *Feminist and Queer Theory* and *Introduction to Women's, Gender & Sexuality Studies.* Her articles have appeared in *Feminist Studies, Women's Studies International Forum, Meridians* (also included in its "best of" special twentieth-anniversary issue), and *Gender, Work & Organization* (noted as one of the journal's most downloaded articles in 2017/2018).